### Praise for *War on Virtue*

"Bill Donohue has crafted a devastating diagnosis of the Left's war on the 'vital virtues' underlying the achievement of the American dream: self-discipline, personal responsibility, and perseverance. Donohue persuasively contends that the ruling elites are robbing a generation of Americans of their deepest aspirations by rewarding irresponsible behavior and ridiculing the 'bourgeois virtues' necessary for success. Jam-packed with essential data and rigorously argued, *War on Virtue* both identifies what ails us and maps the surest road to recovery."

—Thomas D. Williams, Ph.D.
**Rome Bureau Chief for Breitbart News**

"*War on Virtue* is an insightful, informed, wise analysis of the current American crisis—and its solution. It should be read by every American, and especially our moral leaders."

—**David Horowitz, Author,** *Dark Agenda:*
*The War to Destroy Christian America*

"Bill Donohue has long been a fearless fighter for the Catholic Faith. In this lively book, he applies that same spirit to exposing the war on virtue by America's new elite class of cultural revolutionaries. Driven by vice, this secular, progressive ruling class is hellbent on redefining America as we've long known it. Bill Donohue, unafraid as always, engaging as always, is courageously committed to exposing them."

—**Paul Kengor, Ph.D., Senior Editor,** *American Spectator*

"Like the American Founders, Bill Donohue knows that virtue matters most. Without it, the American dream dies. Donohue takes the gloves off in limning the 'ruling class' for undercutting the virtues necessary for a free and prosperous America. But he does more. This urgent book doesn't waste a word in concisely diagnosing the moral corruption that is taking us down, as well as assigning responsibility for it. It offers a sweeping analysis, larded with ample evidence and compelling examples, of how every aspect of life is affected—education, family, demographics, race, sex, gender, media, manners, politics, and culture. This is an angry book because there is a lot to be angry about. But it also gives hope by recalling the moral foundations of virtue and happiness. It turns out that the way back is the way forward. Let Donohue be your guide back to virtue."

—**Robert Reilly, Director, Westminster Institute**

"The sad news about this book is that it had to be written; the good news is that Bill Donohue knew how to address the War on Virtue. Millennia of common sense, deeply reflective philosophy, and religious commitment are under attack by the elites of Western society. Bill exposes their superficial theories, which, in effect, harm everyone, especially the poor and the vulnerable. He turns a spotlight on their hypocritical failure to live what they recommend for the poor and the vulnerable, as well as their obvious goal of maintaining their own status, privilege, and wealth while they attack everyone else's. This is a must-read for anyone who wants to understand the madness that would destroy our society. It is an antidote in its presentation of the key virtues and the multiracial and multicultural exemplars of success."

—**Fr. Mitch Pacwa, S.J., Founder, Ignatius Productions**

# War on Virtue

Also by Bill Donohue
from Sophia Institute Press:

*Unmasking Mother Teresa's Critics*

Bill Donohue

# War on Virtue
## How the Ruling Class
## Is Killing the American Dream

CRISIS
PUBLICATIONS

Manchester, New Hampshire

Crisis Publications
Box 5284, Manchester, NH 03108
1-800-888-9344

www.CrisisMagazine.com

Sophia Institute Press® is a registered trademark of Sophia Institute.

paperback ISBN 978-1-64413-884-7
ebook ISBN 978-1-64413-885-4
Library of Congress Control Number: 2023932053

First printing

*For my sons-in-law*
*Paul and Jay*

# Contents

# War on Virtue

# Introduction

In 1931, in the depths of the Depression, historian James Truslow Adams coined the term "the American dream." His blockbuster book, *The Epic of America*, described "a land in which life should be better and richer and fuller for every man, with opportunity for each according to his ability or achievement."[1] Indeed, the American dream is what has inspired immigrants from all over the world to come to the United States—and they continue to come, some legally and some illegally, at great risk to themselves.

To be sure, many have achieved the American dream, and most still aspire to it. But the policies of the Left are making it increasingly difficult for millions of Americans to realize their dreams. In fact, so-called progressivism has proven to be one of the most regressive forces in the country. As members of the ruling class—the elites in government, law, business, education, the media, the entertainment industry, the arts, and many of the big foundations—adopt progressive politics, they are pounding nails into the coffin of the American dream.

[1]   James Truslow Adams, *The Epic of America* (Boston: Little, Brown, 1931), 363.

The making of the American dream and the attempts being made to thwart it are the subjects of this book. The American dream cannot be realized without the exercise of core virtues—virtues that the ruling class is committed to subverting.

But no matter: the dream is not dead. Indeed, the conclusion that Samuel J. Abrams reached in 2019, after a major study on the American dream was published by the American Enterprise Institute (AEI) and the National Opinion Research Center (NORC, affiliated with the University of Chicago) was that "the American dream is alive and well for an overwhelming majority of Americans."[2]

The purpose of this book is to describe the virtues required to achieve the American dream and to highlight the threats to those virtues—and the ongoing assault on those virtues—by our ruling class.

The AEI-NORC survey found that 40 percent of respondents said their families were living the American dream; another 40 percent said they were on their way to achieving it; only 18 percent reported that it was out of reach. As might be expected, older Americans are more likely to say that they have achieved the American dream, and most young people say they are on their way to doing so.

When respondents were asked what "the American dream" means to them, the top two answers would have put a smile on Adams's face: "to have freedom of choice in how to live one's life" was chosen by 85 percent; 83 percent selected "to have a good

---

[2]  Jeremy Engle, "Do You Think the American Dream Is Real?", *New York Times*, February 12, 2019, https://www.nytimes.com/2019/02/12/learning/do-you-think-the-american-dream-is-real.html.

family life." And whereas only 16 percent said that "to become wealthy" was their idea of the American dream, 71 percent wanted "to retire comfortably" and 59 percent desired "to own a home."

Though money alone does not secure the American dream, it certainly makes achieving it that much easier. The survey found that 58 percent of those with household incomes of $75,000 or more said their families were living the American dream; only a third (34 percent) of those making $30,000 to 74,999 came to this conclusion; and the figure drops to 27 percent for those making less than $30,000. Education is positively correlated with income, so it is not surprising that a majority (54 percent) of the best educated (those with college degrees or above) said their families were living the American dream, whereas only 27 percent of those with no high school diploma felt this way.[3]

Importantly, the survey research discloses that most Americans think that "working hard" is the best way to secure the American dream. This explains why 70 percent of Americans believe that the American dream is personally achievable—and only a minority (29 percent) believe it is unattainable.[4]

This kind of optimism is quintessentially American. As Adams explained more than a hundred years ago, "optimism became so general throughout all classes." He noted that "however badly off a

[3]  Samuel J. Abrams, Karlyn Bowman, Eleanor O'Neil, and Ryan Streeter, "AEI Survey on Community and Society: Social Capital, Civic Health, and Quality of Life in the United States," American Enterprise Institute, February 5, 2019, 29–30, https://www.aei.org/wp-content/uploads/2019/02/AEI-Survey-on-Community-and-Society-Social-Capital-Civic-Health-and-Quality-of-Life-in-the-United-States.pdf?x91208.

[4]  Mohamed Younis, "Most Americans See American Dream as Achievable," Gallup, July 17, 2019, https://news.gallup.com/poll/260741/americans-american-dream-achieveable.aspx.

large multitude of the new immigrants might be at the lower rung of the American economic ladder, they were used to a low standard of living, and in almost every respect ... they found themselves far better off than they had been in the countries from which they came."[5] Speaking of the English, the Irish, the Scottish, and the Germans, he said "they all had glimpsed the American dream."[6]

What was true of the early immigrants to America is also true today of African Americans and Hispanics. Almost half, in both communities, believe they are on their way to achieving the American dream; and fewer than 20 percent of them believe the dream is out of their reach.[7] It is also encouraging to note that more than three-quarters (77 percent) of Hispanics—a higher share than among the public (62 percent)—believe that most people can get ahead with hard work.[8] Muslims are also believers in the American dream: 70 percent say most people who want to get ahead can make it in America if they are willing to work hard.[9]

But if hard work is essential to achieving the American dream, at least in its material sense, we need to know what factors facilitate work. It is the thesis of this book that the American dream, at least as far as upward mobility is concerned, cannot be realized without three individual virtues: self-discipline, personal responsibility,

---

[5]   Truslow Adams, *The Epic of America*, 184.

[6]   Ibid., 68.

[7]   Abrams et al., "AEI Survey on Community and Society," 29.

[8]   Mark Hugo Lopez, Ana Gonzalez-Barrera, and Jens Manuel Krogstad, "Latinos Are More Likely to Believe in the American Dream, but Most Say It Is Hard to Achieve," Pew Research Center, September 11, 2018, https://www.pewresearch.org/fact-tank/2018/09/11/latinos-are-more-likely-to-believe-in-the-american-dream-but-most-say-it-is-hard-to-achieve/

[9]   Timothy P. Carney, *Alienated America: Why Some Places Thrive While Others Collapse* (New York: Harper, 2019), 128.

and perseverance. These three virtues—these vital virtues—may not guarantee success, but their absence guarantees failure. As we shall see, those who are at the top of the economic ladder embody these virtues to a large degree.

Of course, economic success has never been the full measure of the American dream. Even for Adams, the American dream was not "a dream of merely material plenty, though that has doubtless counted heavily. It has been much more than that. It has been a dream of being able to grow to the fullest development as man and woman." To accomplish this goal, Adams recognized "the need for a scale of values" that recognized "our communal spiritual and intellectual life."[10] Our scale of values was bequeathed to us by our Judeo-Christian heritage. Preeminent among these values—and, indeed, among the values described by the Catholic Church—is the dignity of every human being. Regardless of our ascribed characteristics or our stations in life, we are all equal in the eyes of God. In fact, this tenet is sacrosanct, so it can never be compromised without sinning.

Virtue is a critical component of the "scale of values." From the ancient world to the latest surveys of the American people, happiness has always been tied to virtue—and Catholicism has long taught that virtue builds character and is indispensable to the well-being of individuals and society.

The cardinal virtues of prudence, justice, fortitude, and temperance were described by Plato and Cicero and then given a Catholic understanding by Sts. Augustine, Gregory the Great, and Thomas Aquinas. But in addition to these foundational virtues, there is another virtue that is most important to the realization of the American dream: patriotism. It may not ensure economic success

---

[10]  Adams, *The Epic of America*, 405, 410, 411.

the way the vital virtues do, but it is a necessary component of the American dream. As Tocqueville noted, love of country is a great binding force, and it preserves the America that vouchsafes the American dream. To put it differently, if Americans become convinced that their country is fatally flawed, why will they bother to defend it?

This book contends that all of these virtues are under serious attack by the ruling class. Sadly, and ironically, it is those who are living the American dream to its fullest who are killing others' prospects of succeeding, especially the most vulnerable among us. The fact is, large segments of the ruling class no longer champion self-discipline, personal responsibility, and perseverance for those trying to climb the economic ladder; indeed, some seek to destroy these virtues. Similarly, patriotism is under attack, and the ones leading the charge often occupy elite positions of power.

America has always been a land of hope and opportunity. I am hopeful that this book, by showing how the ruling class is killing the American dream, will help to save, restore, and preserve that dream.

# 1

# Why Virtue Matters

## The Vital Virtues

We all know people who have excelled in school and in the workplace. We've all heard about athletes, actors, dancers, and musicians who have performed spectacularly. Some may have been blessed with exceptional natural abilities. But few could have risen to the top without a lot of hard work. Indeed, many people who were not endowed with God-given talents nevertheless manage to find their way to the top because of their exceptional determination.

In short, success is not a function of luck. It is the result of self-discipline, personal responsibility, and perseverance: the vital virtues.

There are many other virtues, of course—and all are worthy of emulation. Many virtues lead to inner peace and even sanctification. But the vital virtues are the keys to worldly success and to the measure of happiness that worldly success provides.

Let's start at the very beginning. Thousands of years ago, the Greek philosopher Aristotle—who was the pupil of Plato and the teacher of Alexander the Great—contemplated virtue. In his *Nicomachean Ethics*, he said that virtue is achieved by doing self-controlled acts. Moreover, according to Aristotle, moral virtue is necessary if people are to reach their potential. If we do not control our passions, we are destined for failure.

This is true not just in ages gone by, but right here, right now—today. Before we begin our examination of why the vital virtues are critical, let's briefly look at a few individuals who lived by them.

Ken Sylvester is the author of a book on leadership, and he cites Jackie Robinson as a model citizen who personified self-discipline. Robinson was the first African American to play professional baseball. He played for the Brooklyn Dodgers—but he had to endure cruel comments on and off the field. Sylvester writes:

> Underlying Robinson's numerous awards was a world class demonstration of self-control and emotional maturity. When he crossed the color lines at the ballpark, Robinson tried to relax and focus on the game, not on the constant catcalls. Off the field, the former UCLA four-sport star would also deal with bigotry, anonymous death threats, racial slurs, sitting in the back of the bus, "no colored" served or housed here signs, and opponents were out to injure him.[11]

President Harry Truman was famous for the words "the buck stops here." It was not just a throwaway line: those words were mounted on a walnut base and sat prominently on his desk in the White House. He meant what he said: he took personal responsibility for his decision to use the atomic bomb against Japan in World War II. "It is an awful responsibility that has come to us," he said in August 1945.[12] Most historians realize he was in

[11] Quoted in J. D. Meier, "Jackie Robinson: A Story in Self-Control," Sources of Insight, https: sourcesofinsight.com/jackie-robinson -story-of-self-control/.
[12] "Harry Truman's Decision to Use the Atomic Bomb," National Park Service, https:nps.gov/articles/trumanatomicbomb.htm.

a very difficult position and acknowledge that he shouldered the responsibility for what he did.

In his influential work *The Book of Virtues*, Bill Bennett cites the Rev. Martin Luther King Jr. as representative of the virtue of perseverance. King never gave up the fight for civil rights, knowing full well that the American dream could be realized by calling upon Americans of all races to make good on the promise of the Declaration of Independence and the Constitution. They were the basis of a "promissory note to which every American was to fall heir."[13] King saw it as his job to inspire his fellow African Americans to persevere in their struggle for freedom.

These examples are just highlights. We could pick many others. But if we are to understand the vital virtues, we need to stop and think deeply about them — as a sage or a philosopher would. Gertrude Himmelfarb, the distinguished American historian, understood as well as anyone the powerful role that virtue has played in Western civilization. The great philosophers, she contends, "insisted upon the importance of virtues not only for the good life of individuals but for the well-being of society and the state."[14] Similarly, the *Catechism of the Catholic Church* (CCC) teaches that the exercise of human virtues leads to "a morally good life" (1804). Indeed, the good society can never be achieved without the widespread prevalence of virtue. But if virtue is to prevail, those in positions of authority must themselves live virtuous lives — or, at the very least, must recognize and respect virtue.

Virtue does not come easy; vice does. People are naturally inclined to satisfy their own interests, appetites, and passions.

---

[13]   Martin Luther King Jr., "I Have a Dream" speech, Washington, D.C., August 28, 1963.

[14]   Gertrude Himmelfarb, *The Demoralization of Society: From Victorian Virtues to Modern Values* (New York: Vintage Books, 1994), 9.

Unfortunately, these impulses tend to result in self-destruction and damage to society. The only way to protect individuals from themselves and to protect society from individuals is to teach virtue, beginning at a very young age. Aristotle said that virtue is primarily learned not through abstract reasoning but through repetition and habit. The *Catechism* cites the virtue of perseverance, and repetition, as necessary to the acquisition of other virtues. "Human virtues acquired by education, by deliberate acts and by a perseverance ever-renewed in repeated efforts are purified and elevated by divine grace" (1810).

Self-discipline, personal responsibility, and perseverance must be practiced to be learned—and the more frequent and intense the demands placed on us, the better and faster we learn. Parents and teachers must demand that children practice the vital virtues. Employers must also demand excellence from their employees. Community leaders, coaches, and the clergy must do their part. If virtuous demands are not made, vice will win—and everyone will lose.

### Bourgeois and Victorian Values

The modern world, to a large degree, is the fruit of bourgeois, or "middle class," values. How so? Listen to Tom Wolfe, one of the most perceptive students of American culture. He gave the commencement address to the Boston University class of 2000, and his theme was the indispensable nature of bourgeois values to the modern world.

Those who are imbued with these values, he told the graduates, are found all over the world, from Bombay to Barcelona. Wherever you find "the wheel, the shoe, and the toothbrush," he said, you find the same things. "And what are those things? Peace, order, education, hard work, initiative, enterprise, creativity, cooperation, looking out for one another, looking out for the future of children, patriotism, fair play, and honesty."[15]

Wolfe bemoaned the extent to which intellectuals now disparage bourgeois values. He noted with characteristic sarcasm their stunning ignorance, especially their failure to appreciate how bourgeois values made America the land of dreams come true. "This is the first country on earth in which the ordinary working man has the political freedom, the personal freedom, the free time, the money, the wherewithal to express himself in any way that he may want."[16] Perhaps the snobbishness—the deadly vice of pride—that afflicts many thinkers makes them unable to appreciate the freedoms and standard of living that surprise and delight many first-generation immigrants.

Howard Husock is another writer who fully grasps the importance of bourgeois values. Bourgeois norms, he contends, are apparent in everything from education to temperance. They constitute "the ethical soil in which individuals and their communities can thrive."[17] In the nineteenth century, they were made manifest by the work of moral reformers; in the twentieth century, their presence undergirded the burgeoning affluent society. Those who sneer at bourgeois values, notes historian Deirdre Nansen McCloskey, fail to understand their *ethical* centrality to the creation of the modern world.[18]

---

[15]  Tom Wolfe, Commencement address to the Boston University Class of 2000, May 21, 2000, https://101bananas.com/library2/wolfe.html.

[16]  Ibid.

[17]  Howard A. Husock, "*Who Killed Civil Society? The Rise of Big Government and Decline of Bourgeois Norms* (New York: Encounter Books, 2019), 142.

[18]  Deirdre Nansen McCloskey, *Why Liberalism Works: How True Liberal Values Produce a Freer, More Equal, Prosperous World for All* (New Haven: Yale University Press, 2019), 199.

The English idea of Victorian values, says Himmelfarb, is more comprehensive than bourgeois values: Victorian values include respect for "the family as well as hard work, thrift, cleanliness, self-reliance, self-respect, neighborliness, patriotism."[19] Nonetheless, there is considerable overlap. She prefers to speak of virtues, not values, and credits Bennett for celebrating such Victorian virtues as "self-discipline, work, responsibility, perseverance, and honesty."[20]

One of the great achievements of the Victorians was their success in teaching the common man to honor and practice Victorian virtues. In fact, by the end of the nineteenth century, "the working classes became more puritanical and moralistic as the middle classes became more relaxed and permissive."[21] They had developed the "self-control, self-discipline, [and] self-respect" that made liberal society thrive.[22]

One proof that Victorian virtues succeeded can be found in Victorian crime statistics. During the heyday of the Victorian period in England, 1857 to 1901, crime dropped precipitously. Not only did serious offenses decline, but a wide range of morally destitute acts declined as well. That this took place at a time when the population was growing rapidly makes the progress all the more impressive.

One reason for this success was the stability of the family. One-parent families—which are notorious seedbeds of crime and delinquency—were unusual in Victorian England. The rate of illegitimacy declined by almost half between the mid-nineteenth

---

[19]   Himmelfarb, *The Demoralization of Society*, 5.
[20]   Ibid., 17.
[21]   Ibid., 30–31.
[22]   Ibid., 51.

century and the beginning of the twentieth. Not everyone lived a perfectly virtuous life. It was fairly common, for instance, for girls to get pregnant before marrying—but then they got married. And the men did not abandon their responsibility—which was a tribute to a moral code that placed a premium on family unity. Another sign of family stability was the very low divorce rate; it remained low even after divorce laws were relaxed.

Standards of living, especially for the working class, also rose dramatically during this period. Improvements in technology certainly played a large role in providing this increase. But it was the vital virtues that powered the work ethic that developed the technology.

Even vulnerable members of society, whose living standards were still low, benefitted from the virtuous social atmosphere. New organizations were established to assist the poor and the infirm, the elderly, abandoned children, widows, and the handicapped; even penitent prostitutes were offered services. Orphanages and hospitals were founded, with religious entities playing a major role. Children, including the children of the poor, were more universally educated, and many achieved a high degree of literacy, even before public education was established in 1870. Finally, moral reforms on institutional violence, ranging from bans on flogging in the armed services to combating the slave trade, were successfully implemented.

### Self-Discipline

The religious roots of self-discipline are deeply embedded in Western civilization. From the time of the early rabbinic teachings, self-discipline was regarded as the most important virtue one could possess. Xenophon, a disciple of Socrates, insisted that self-control was not merely another virtue but was the "foundation of all the virtues."[23] Moses appealed to the Jews to practice self-control in every aspect of their lives. Indeed, self-discipline is central to Mosaic law: the Ten Commandments' injunctions "Thou shalt not ..." would be unnecessary if virtue came naturally to us. The apostle Peter instructs us to "make every effort to supplement [our] faith with virtue, and virtue with knowledge, and knowledge with self-control." (2 Pet. 1:5–6). Paul observed that "Every athlete exercises self-control in all things," noting the necessity to "discipline [our] body and keep it under control" (see 1 Cor. 9:25, 27).

In our society, however, it is not the exercise of self-discipline that is most noted—it is its absence. From road rage and overexcited sports fans to drug addiction and violent crime, our all-too-frequent inability to control our impulses has become a national disgrace.

Benjamin Franklin urged parents to instill this virtue at an early age, stressing that "temperance" and "order" were two of the most critical behavioral traits they needed to inculcate.[24] Calvin Coolidge was just as confident that self-discipline is the key to individual success. "The worst evil that could be inflicted upon the youth of the land would be to leave them without restraint and completely at the mercy of their own uncontrolled inclinations," he said. "Under such conditions education would be impossible, and all orderly development intellectually or morally would be hopeless."[25]

---

[23] Jason Barney, "Educating for Self-Control, Part 1: A Lost Christian Virtue," Educational Renaissance, January 3, 2109, https://educationalrenaissance.com/2019/01/03/educating-for-self-control-a-lost-christian-virtue/.

[24] Shai Afsai, "Benjamin Franklin's Virtues and Jewish Practice," January 10, 2021, https://jewishboston.com/read/benjamin-franklins-virtues-and-jewish-practice/.

[25] Edward Short, "Coolidge and the Catholics," *Human Life Review* (Summer 2021): 75.

It bodes ill for our society that such commonsense observations are now more likely to be greeted with scorn than with applause. Instead of insisting on self-discipline in the home and in the classroom, too many parents, even in affluent neighborhoods, indulge their children — or other people's: the elites who command the education establishment routinely allow unruly students to disrupt classes with impunity.

Andy Andrews, Stephen R. Covey, and Brian Tracy are three of the most famous students of self-development. These best-selling authors and motivational speakers have identified seven habits that highly successful people possess. Self-discipline is listed by all of them. Tracy considers it to be "the one habit that guarantees all the others." Indeed, the ability to "discipline yourself, master yourself, to control yourself, is the most important single quality that you can develop as a person. The habit of self-discipline goes hand in hand with success in every area of life."[26]

Researchers at the University of Chicago found that self-control was among "humankind's most valuable assets." In fact, they found that "the more self-control people reported having, the more satisfied they reported being with their lives."[27] They are happy not only in the short-term but in the long-term as well.

Young people have often found it hard to exercise impulse control, but today's youth find it even harder. "If the complaints

[26] Brian Tracy, "7 Habits of Successful People That Will Make You Feel Unstoppable in 2020," Brian Tracy International, https://briantracy.com/blog/personal-success/seven-good-habits-of-highly-successful-people-goal-oriented/.

[27] Lindsay Abrams, "Study: People with a Lot of Self-Control Are Happier," *Atlantic*, July 1, 2013, https://www.theatlantic.com/health/archive/2013/07/study-people-with-a-lot-of-self-control-are-happier/277349/.

of American educators are to be believed," writes Kay S. Hymow-itz, "today's schoolchildren are C students at best when it comes to self-control" and related habits. Employers, she says, complain about millennials who "have trouble getting to work on time" and "dealing with workplace discipline."[28]

As an employer, I have observed what Hymowitz describes, in particular with respect to workplace discipline. Many young people consider a dress code to be not only antiquarian and unnecessary but an infringement on their liberty; many find the expectation that work be delivered on time as burdensome—not all young people but too many of them.

One of the reasons young people find it difficult to practice self-discipline is their heavy dependence on social media. In a study published by two Turkish researchers, heavy social media users tend to be impulsive, and this has negative behavioral consequences, such as "failing to spend time effectively, failing to plan, and developing an addiction to social media." Impulsivity, moreover, is a risk factor tied to "obesity, sex addiction, alcohol and drug addiction, internet addiction, pathologic game playing, and risky behaviors." It also increases loneliness.[29]

In a major survey of the state of American life, researchers at the American Enterprise Institute found that young people were, sadly, the most likely group to experience loneliness. In fact, 34 percent of eighteen- to twenty-nine-year-olds said they "rarely or

[28] Kay S. Hymowitz, "The Cultural Contradictions of American Education," in Michael J. Petrilli and Chester E. Finn Jr., eds., *How to Educate an American: The Conservative Vision for Tomorrow's Schools* (West Conshohocken, PA: Templeton Press, 2020), 184.

[29] Mustafa Savci and Ferda Aysan, "Relationship between Impulsivity, Social Media Usage and Loneliness," *Educational Process: International Journal* 5, no. 2 (Summer 2016): 106–115.

never feel part of a group of friends" — much higher than any other age group. Older adults, and those who are religious, experience the lowest degree of loneliness.[30]

No segment of the population spends more time on social media than young girls. According to psychology professor Jean Twenge, "we've known from academic research for many years that the longer a teen girl spends on social media, the more likely she is to be depressed and to engage in behaviors like self-harm [such as] cutting." In fact, the suicide rate has doubled for ten- to fourteen-year-olds since 2007.[31]

It is clear that self-control is vitally important to achieving the American dream. Worldly success is an elusive goal for those unable to practice self-control; and impulsive behavior can make it impossible to achieve.

## Perseverance

Researcher Andy Andrews lists persistence, or perseverance, as one of the seven attributes necessary for success. Perseverance is casually known in psychology circles as "grit," the ability to pursue goals through thick and thin. An Indonesian study published in 2021 found that successful athletes showed a high rate of grit and that they believed that "success is obtained through effort and hard work."[32]

No one knew this truth better than Vince Lombardi, the legendary Green Bay Packers coach (the Super Bowl trophy, officially

---

30   Abrams et al., "AEI Survey on Community and Society," 24–26.
31   Interview with Jean Twenge on *Tucker Carlson Tonight*, September 29, 2021.
32   Surahman, Iswinarti, "How to Cultivate Perseverance and Passion for Long-term Goals? Review of Grit Predictors," *American Research Journal of Humanities Social Sciences* 3, no. 1 (2021): 73, https://www.arjhss.com/wp-content/uploads/2021/01/K417176.pdf.

the Lombardi Trophy, is named after him): "The price of success is hard work, dedication to the job at hand, and the determination that whether we win or lose, we have applied the best of ourselves to the task at hand."[33]

Basketball superstar Michael Jordan was a model of grit. "If you're trying to achieve, there will be roadblocks. I've had them; everybody has had them. But obstacles don't have to stop you. If you run into a wall, don't turn around and give up. Figure out how to climb it, go through it, or work around it."[34]

Hall of Fame Mets baseball player Tom Seaver showed his grit by centering his life on pitching. Pitching, he said, determined "what I eat, when I go to bed, what I do when I'm awake. It determines how I spend my life when I'm not pitching."[35]

Super Bowl champion quarterback Tom Brady credits his ability to persevere in the face of adversity as one of the primary reasons he is such a success. He recalls that in high school and college, he struggled to excel in football—and that his struggle continued even at the beginning of his pro career. So what made him the most storied quarterback in history? "Discipline, determination, work ethic, leadership—those are all very sustainable and endearing traits."[36]

Business managers know what it takes to succeed. David DeSteno, writing in the *Harvard Business Review*, noted that "a

[33] "Perseverance and Hard Work Inspirational Quotes," Be Inspired, July 12, 2017, https://beinspiredchannel.com/perseverance -hard-work-inspirational/.

[34] Ibid.

[35] Angela Duckworth, *Grit: The Power of Passion and Perseverance* (New York: Scribner, 2016), 63.

[36] Rick Stroud, "Tom Brady Has Message of Perseverance for 2020 Senior Class," *Tampa Bay Times*, May 18, 2020, https://tampabay.com/sports/bucs/2020/05/18/tom-brady-has-message -of-perseverance-for-2020-senior-class/.

willingness to accept sacrifices in the moment—to work, practice, or otherwise persevere in the face of difficulties—is what drives productivity, innovation, and thereby, prosperity. It's a trait any manager should value among members of their team."[37]

No author is better known for understanding the value of grit than psychologist Angela Duckworth. What makes high achievers a success? A combination of passion and perseverance, she says, giving a nod to the latter as the more important. Duckworth also found that "grittier" persons are happier than their less determined peers.

In fact, Duckworth developed a Grit Scale to measure the importance of perseverance. In one study, involving more than twelve hundred West Point cadets, grit proved a more reliable predictor of accomplishment than sheer talent. In fact, grit "not only predicts academic grades, but military and physical fitness marks as well."[38]

Consider those who work in sales, where rejection is commonplace and switching jobs is routine: those who scored high on the Grit Scale were the most likely to stay on the job and succeed. No other personality trait was better at explaining job retention.[39]

Ivy League students who did well on the Grit Scale received the highest grades. Surprisingly, SAT scores and grit were inversely correlated, meaning that those who scored above average on the college entrance exam tended to be less gritty than those who did not do as well.[40] But perhaps this should not surprise us: in my

---

[37] David DeSteno, "The Connection between Pride and Persistence," *Harvard Business Review*, August 22, 2016, https://hbr.org/2016/08/the-connection-between-pride-and-persistence.

[38] Duckworth, *Grit*, 10.

[39] Ibid., 10–11.

[40] Ibid., 14.

years of teaching both elementary school students and graduate students, I found that those who were not as talented as others but who applied themselves often did better than their more gifted classmates. I have also found this as an employer. I would much rather hire, and work with, someone of average abilities who works hard than a less determined individual with greater abilities.

Freud understood that people are prone to yield to their id, or what he referred to as "the pleasure principle." But if we are to become productive members of society, we must check our appetites and our passions; our desire for instant gratification must be controlled. Our digital culture makes it hard. In 2000, Microsoft published a study showing that the average attention span was twelve seconds; by 2013 it had shrunk to eight seconds.[41] This is one reason students have a hard time paying attention in class. It also explains why we channel surf and tune out speakers who don't entertain us.

But much worse: without perseverance, we will struggle in vain to achieve the American dream.

### Personal Responsibility

There are lots of people who have been dealt a bad hand in life, such as having a deadbeat dad or an alcoholic mother. Indeed, many people carry heavy crosses. But the hard truth is that, with respect to achieving personal success, it doesn't really matter. Moving forward requires personal responsibility. In fact, the harder your circumstances, the more you have to be responsible for yourself because nobody else will do things for you. That's just the way it is.

---

[41]  Consumer Insights, Microsoft Canada, *Attention Spans*, Spring 2015, http://pausethinkconsider.com/wp-content/uploads/2016/09/microsoft-attention-spans-research-report.pdf.

But it's much better to recognize reality—even if it is a hard reality—because then you can start to change it.

The same truth applies to groups. We all know that there are racial and ethnic groups whom history has placed in a disadvantaged spot. Such groups have every right to advocate for the removal of any remaining barriers to their success. But in the end, their future still lies within themselves.

Accountability is a key component of personal responsibility. Those who hold themselves accountable for their actions, rather than those who look for excuses, are the ones on their way to achieving the American dream. But accountability—and this is important—must apply not just to ourselves but also to those in our charge. For example, parents who do not hold their children accountable for their behavior are doing them a disservice. This is likewise true of teachers, coaches, employers, community leaders, the clergy—all have a duty to hold those under them responsible for their decisions.

We should be creating a culture in which personal responsibility is encouraged and developed. Instead, all too often we reward irresponsible behavior. For example, illegal aliens who crash our southern border are offered free lawyers to defend them against the authorities who want to deport them.

Young people, in particular, have to be told about the dangers that accompany risky behavior. Alcohol and drugs are killing record numbers of young men and women—and too often there are adults in their lives who might have warned them about the dangers and helped them before it was too late. Young people are not ready for sex. Yet our society is highly sexualized and glorifies sexual experimentation. If teenagers were made aware of the real-life consequences of sex, they would tend to be more responsible and avoid much life-changing heartache and pain.

Public policy must also play a role in encouraging personal responsibility. For example, a decent society will provide for those unable to provide for themselves. But for the able-bodied and mentally competent who seek assistance, policies have to be carefully written to avoid moral hazard.

Exercising the vital virtues is the most reliable way to achieve success in school and in the workplace. But the ruling class has failed to promote this reality. It acts as though self-discipline, personal responsibility, and perseverance are somehow unrelated to achievement. The net effect is innumerable lost opportunities for developing these characteristics.

## Virtuous Groups

At the beginning of the chapter, I mentioned examples of individuals who exhibited particular virtues. Here I would like to show groups that manifest certain virtues to an unusual degree. We will look at Jews, Mormons, Asians, and Nigerians and discover what has made some ethnic and religious groups more successful than others.

### Vital Virtues Exercised by Jews

Jews make up less than one-half of 1 percent of the world's population. But the percentage of Nobel Prize winners they compose is astonishingly high. In the first half of the twentieth century, Jews won 14 percent of the Nobel Prizes in literature, chemistry, physics, and medicine/physiology. In the second half of the last century, the figure rose to 29 percent; it has since risen to about a third.[42] No other religious or ethnic group comes even close to

---

[42]  Charles Murray, "Jewish Genius," *Commentary*, April 2007, https://www.commentary.org/articles/charles-murray/jewish -genius/.

the record of the Jews; this is especially true of Nobel Prize winners in economics, medicine, and science. Jewish success in the entertainment industry is also remarkable: Hollywood studios are disproportionately run or owned by Jews. "As a small but hugely influential group defined by a combination of religious, ethnic, and cultural characteristics," writes George Washington University political scientist Samuel Goldman, "American Jews can be seen as successors to the WASPs of the 20th century."[43]

Of the four arguably most influential people in the modern era—Darwin, Marx, Freud, and Einstein—only Darwin was not Jewish. "From 1870 to 1950," writes social scientist Charles Murray, "Jewish representation in literature was four times the number one would expect. In music, five times. In the visual arts, five times. In biology, eight times. In chemistry, five times. In physics, nine times. In mathematics, twelve times. In philosophy, fourteen times."[44]

In the corporate world, Jews have done incredibly well. Many of the most prestigious CEOs in the United States are Jewish. Moreover, no demographic group rivals their representation on the Forbes 400 list of the richest persons. Their contributions to education, the arts, medicine, law, and architecture are also extraordinary. The number of Jewish intellectuals, in almost every field, outpaces all competitors.

What explains Jewish success? Murray sees a genetic component. He does not dismiss cultural factors. But he maintains that "intelligence has to be at the center of the answer. Jews have been

---

[43] Samuel Goldman, "How American Jews Lost by Winning," *Week*, August 6, 2021, https://theweek.com/feature/opinion/1003383/how-american-jews-lost-by-winning.

[44] Murray, "Jewish Genius."

found to have an unusually high mean intelligence as measured by IQ tests since the first Jewish sample were tested."[45]

Thomas Sowell notes that when Jewish immigrants made their way from Eastern Europe to America in the late nineteenth century—almost three million did so—they were not highly educated. Indeed, many were illiterate. Nevertheless, "their affinity for education was extremely high."[46]

Where did that "affinity" come from? Judaism.

Some historians draw attention to the year AD 64, when the Palestinian sage Joshua ben Gamla mandated that all Jewish males had to attend school, starting at age six. Within a century, the literacy rate for Jewish males was effectively 100 percent.

Six years later, in 70, the destruction of the second Temple forced Jews to concentrate on prayer and mastery of the Torah, because Temple worship could no longer be performed. "To study the Talmud and its commentaries with any understanding requires considerable intellectual capacity," notes Murray. "In short, during the centuries after Rome's destruction of the Temple, Judaism evolved in such a way that to be a good Jew meant that a man had to be smart."[47]

Rabbi Levi Brackman agrees. "Inherent within Jewish religious teachings and Torah stories are ideas that relate directly to behaviors and attitudes that lead directly to successful outcomes."[48]

As important as education is in accounting for Jewish success, Jewish upward mobility in the United States preceded Jewish

[45]   Ibid.

[46]   Thomas Sowell, *Ethnic America: A History* (New York: Basic Books, 1981), 73.

[47]   Murray, "Jewish Genius."

[48]   Rabbi Levi Brackman, "Why Jews are Disproportionately Successful, September 5, 2008, https://www.ynetnews.com/articles /0,7340,L-3592566,00.html.

educational achievement. It was hard work, not advanced schooling, that allowed Jews to improve their economic status. Jewish women worked the "sweatshops," and although working conditions were harsh, this allowed mothers to be with their children, who also worked in the sweatshops. Jewish families saved whatever they could, and when they could afford it, they spent it on education.[49] It was the vital virtues that proved to be the lever of mobility. Indeed, Murray cites perseverance as one of a cluster of traits (including ambition, imagination, and curiosity) that proved to be determinative.[50]

Self-discipline and personal responsibility are also Jewish characteristics. Parental discipline is noted in the book of Deuteronomy, making it quite clear that parents have a duty to discipline their children, holding them responsible for their behavior. In fact, parents are authorized to punish their child for wrongdoing, so adamant is the biblical injunction on discipline. Discipline is seen as a means of education and a source of authority.

Moreover, those who have studied why some religious and ethnic groups have succeeded more than others are quick to mention that impulse control is a key variable. There is nothing new about nurturing self-control in the Jewish tradition. The need to defer self-satisfaction has ancient roots, and although most Jews today are not observant, they have not abandoned this precept.

The husband-and-wife team of Amy Chua and Jed Rubenfeld, two outstanding Yale scholars, have detailed the importance of impulse control as a lever to success, citing Jews and Mormons as exemplifying this virtue.[51] So let's turn to Mormons.

---

[49] Sowell, *Ethnic America*, 84–85, 91, 178.
[50] Murray, "Jewish Genius."
[51] Amy Chua and Jed Rubenfeld, *The Triple Package: How Three Unlikely Traits Explain the Rise and Fall of Cultural Groups in America* (New York: Penguin Press, 2014).

*Vital Virtues Exercised by Mormons*

"If there's one group in the U.S. that's hitting it out of the park with conventional success," write Chua and Rubenfeld, "it's Mormons."[52] They offer many examples. In the corporate world, Mormons have made a name for themselves in JetBlue, J. W. Marriott, Citigroup, Dell, Fisher-Price, American Express, Kodak, Black & Decker, Lufthansa, and in many of the Fortune 500 companies. In government, Mormons such as Mitt Romney, Orrin Hatch, Harry Reid, and Jon Huntsman have left their mark. Also, the Mormon Church is incredibly wealthy, relative to its small size, and its land ownership is equally impressive. By any measure, Mormons are one of the most successful groups in the country.

As with Jews, the vital virtues, nurtured in the family, account for their stunning record. Chua and Rubenfeld explain that "strict self-discipline is a fixed star of Mormon culture, manifest in their abstemiousness, their grueling two-year missions, and their sexual conservatism relative to the permissiveness more typical in America."[53]

Mormons also embody strong, intact families and communities. While intact families do not ensure that children will exercise the vital virtues, intact families provide a big leg up compared with one-parent families. The Family Home Evening is a prime example. One night a week, family members gather for prayer, singing, and religious readings. Family meals and religious rituals are commonplace, but so is fasting. These routines create strong bonds among all age groups.

The two-year mission required of Mormons is not something most American youth can relate to or even understand. At age

[52] Ibid., 30–32.
[53] Ibid., 187.

nineteen, Mormons are expected to travel to another state or country and spend their time serving the church by teaching others about their culture and their religion. Once they complete their mission, young Mormons usually return home, attend college, and get married. At a young age, they learn that volunteering is an important aspect of serving their community.

The vital virtues are officially stressed by the Church of Jesus Christ of Latter-day Saints whose website says, "Virtue is a prerequisite to entering the Lord's holy temples and to receiving the Spirit's guidance."[54] Behaviorally, this is made manifest in teaching young people to abstain from sex and alcohol, thus encouraging them to practice self-discipline. Adults are also expected to avoid caffeine (they eschew coffee and soft drinks) and not to use tobacco.

Sociologist Rodney Stark has studied why Mormons are so successful. He says that "Latter-day Saint success is rooted in theology." Like Catholics and Protestants, Mormons are expected not to sin. However, they also believe that each person is capable of sinlessness—and indeed they expect as much. Whether or not the theology is true on a metaphysical level, with respect to worldly behavior it seems to account for their "relatively strict moral standards," which include "a separate and distinctive life style or morality in personal and family life, in such areas as dress, diet, drinking, entertainment, use of time, sex, child rearing, and the like."[55]

As with Jews, education is emphasized more by Mormons than by most other religious and ethnic groups. Indeed, it is a critical

[54] "Virtue," Church of Jesus Christ of Latter-day Saints, https://www.churchofjesuschrist.org/study/manual/gospel-topics/virtue.

[55] Rodney Stark, "The Basis of Mormon Success," Religious Studies Center, https://rsc.byu.edu/latter-day-saint-social-life/basis-mormon-success.

component in their quest for divinity. Mastering the teachings of their religion is not merely a pathway to economic success; it is a road to spiritual perfection. As a result, Mormons excel in school—and their median income exceeds the national average.[56]

It takes self-discipline to abstain. Without an ingrained sense of personal responsibility, volunteering to help the community would be difficult. It takes perseverance to spend two years in service to others. Thus do Mormons excel in exercising the vital virtues.

## Vital Virtues Exercised by Asians

The remarkable educational and economic success of Asians is the latest example of the American dream coming true for millions of immigrants. But to be clear, it was not accomplished by dreaming alone. It was mostly the result of hard work.

It is not uncommon for Asian immigrant children, soon after they arrive in the United States, to excel in their command of the English language, even if their parents barely speak a word of it. As far as Asians' economic success goes, no racial, ethnic, or religious group has a higher median household income.[57]

Asians, of course, are hardly a monolithic group. They vary considerably on the basis of culture and historical experiences. The six largest Asian nationalities are Chinese, Indians, Filipinos, Vietnamese, Koreans, and Japanese. The richest are those from India, the Philippines, Japan, and Sri Lanka. Indians also have the highest level of educational attainment.

---

[56] Chua and Rubenfeld, *Triple Package*, 33–34.
[57] "Asian Women and Men Earned More Than Their White, Black, and Hispanic Counterparts in 2017," U.S. Bureau of Labor Statistics, August 29, 2018, https://www.bls.gov/opub/ted/2018/asian-women-and-men-earned-more-than-their-white-black-and-hispanic-counterparts-in-2017.htm.

But Asians as a group exhibit the vital virtues par excellence. One reason they do is their tradition of collectivism, a tradition that puts family interests ahead of individual interests. The dominant culture in America celebrates individual autonomy and focuses heavily on self-fulfillment. It relishes equality and challenges to authority. By contrast, Asians tend to stress hierarchy and obedience to authority. Why does this matter? Because it is much easier to inculcate in young people a reverence for the vital virtues when there is group support and a focus on the family. Our young selves have little interest in virtue; they must be trained for it.

Among Chinese Americans, Confucianism plays a significant cultural role, though few identify with it as their religion of choice. It teaches respect for authority and hierarchical structures in general. It stresses loyalty and correct behavior, qualities that are frequently underemphasized in most American homes. Those who are raised in an environment where human relations are understood to rely on mutual obligations get a leg up in everything from academic achievement to workplace productivity.

SAT scores reflect Asians' academic success. The College Board benchmark score for math is 530, which indicates that a college freshmen will perform satisfactorily in math. Eighty percent of Asians meet that benchmark; for whites, the figure is only 59 percent. An impressive 35 percent of all Asian SAT takers achieve top SAT scores—between 700 and 800—whereas only 9 percent of whites and 1 percent of blacks perform at this level.[58] Predictably, Asians earn a disproportionate number of PhDs in math, electrical

---

[58]   Heather Mac Donald, "The NIH's Diversity Obsession Subverts Science," *Wall Street Journal*, June 30, 2021, https://www.wsj.com/articles/the-nihs-diversity-obsession-subverts-science-11625090811.

engineering, neuroscience, biochemistry, molecular biology, and genetics. Students from India and China, in particular, excel in engineering.

Are Asians naturally gifted? Measured by IQ, they are. They outscore Europeans, Africans, and Hispanics. Furthermore, IQ scores are a good indicator of how well someone will do in school.[59] But there is more to the "Asian advantage" than mere intelligence.

Just as Jews and Mormons have a tradition of being exam-oriented, so do Indians and Chinese. In her book on Asian success, Maya Thiagarajan, who grew up mostly in India, recounts her conversations with Asian mothers. She heard things such as "Exams force the teachers to be accountable"; "How would we know how our kids are performing, and whether they have really mastered all the material, if we didn't have exams?" She also offered evidence that exams help students who come from poor families. "While the top students in America are on a par with the top students in Korea and Japan," she writes, "the bottom students in America are far behind the bottom students in Korea and Japan."[60]

Native intelligence, a strong emphasis on education, and a talent for exam taking helps explain why Asians, in general, do so well in the United States. But without citing the role that the family plays in transmitting the vital virtues, their success cannot be fully explained.

As far back as 1966, it was evident to American journalists that there was something special about Asians. *U.S. News & World*

59 Charles Murray, *Two Truths about Race in America* (New York: Encounter Books, 2021), 36, 43.
60 Maya Thiagarajan, *Beyond the Tiger Mom: East-West Parenting for the Global Age* (Tokyo: Tuttle Publishing, 2016), 91–93.

*Report* ran a lengthy story on this subject, noting that a trip to Chinatown, whether in San Francisco or New York City, left a distinct impression on the visitor. Juvenile delinquency and crime were low; people worked hard; parental authority was ubiquitous; and welfare dependency was virtually nonexistent.

Jean Ma, publisher of a Chinese newspaper in Los Angeles, understood why. "We're a big family. If someone has trouble, usually it can be solved within the family. There is no need to bother someone else. And nobody will respect any member of the family who does not work and who just plays around."[61] In other words, Asians have a built-in safety net, one based on self-reliance and voluntary assistance. They have little need for government handouts. That it works is obvious—and particularly compared with welfare programs, the difference is dramatic.

Fast-forward to today. Asians are even more successful than they were in the 1960s. "It is no secret how this happened," explains author Larry Alexander. "As a group—and obviously there are individual exceptions—Asians are committed to and exemplify the three core bourgeois values of strong families, hard work, and devotion to education."[62]

To these traits we can add personal responsibility and perseverance. These virtues, and not simply education, facilitated the Asian rise to the top. "Education was not the cause of the Japanese Americans' initial rise," writes Thomas Sowell, "just as it was not the cause of the Jews' initial rise, although both groups

---

[61] "Success Story of One Minority Group in U.S.," *U.S. News & World Report*, December 26, 1966.

[62] Larry Alexander, "The Truth about Attacks on Asians," American Thinker, April 14, 2021, https://www.americanthinker.com/blog/2021/04/the_truth_about_attacks_on_asians.html.

consolidated and further enhanced their economic positions in later generations with formal schooling."[63]

There is nothing magical about Asian success. Rather, the behavioral practices that Asians commonly enforce are stringent, at least by most American standards. For example, it is not unusual for American children, of any ethnic group, to learn how to play a musical instrument. But few can match the extent to which Asian children routinely practice the piano and the violin. Furthermore, the long hours required to master these instruments yield considerable residual benefits when it comes to education. "If they learn an instrument," says an Asian parent, "they don't have any big problems when they are learning science, mathematics. Because if you have this kind of discipline, the concentration to overcome obstacles, doing something over and over again, then you will know, 'Oh! If I put in every kind of effort, then I will win.'"[64] In other words, learning the piano or the violin nurtures impulse control, a virtue that has wide application.

Jane Kim co-authored a book with Dr. Soo Kim Abboud on the reasons why Asians succeed, and she concluded that the key is how children are raised.[65] Most American children go to school, come home, spend time with their friends—often on social media or playing video games—have dinner, do their homework, watch TV, and go to bed. Asian children are more likely to go to school, come home, do assigned chores, clean their rooms, set the table, have dinner with their family, and receive instruction from their

---

[63]  Sowell, *Ethnic America*, 177–178.

[64]  Chua and Rubenfeld, *Triple Package*, 126–127.

[65]  Dr. Soo Kim Abboud and Jane Kim, *Top of the Class: How Asian Parents Raise High Achievers—and How You Can Too* (New York: Berkley Books, 2006), 54–55.

parents on their homework. One does not have to have a PhD to figure out which students are more apt to succeed.

When I worked at the Heritage Foundation in the late 1980s, I took the Metro from Twinbrook Station in Rockville, Maryland, to Union Station in D.C. I noticed that most non-Asian young people were listening to music; their Asian peers were using their earphones to learn the English language. In the evening, while going home, I noticed Asian adults alongside the road in a lighted area selling flowers. The work ethic among Asians of all ages was striking.

Abboud and Kim give sound advice to parents on what they should demand of their children. "Adopt a strong work ethic and an attitude of perseverance and attention to detail that your child can emulate." In other words, it is the vital virtues that count. "No matter what the goal," Abboud and Kim say, "demand excellence in the end result."[66]

This kind of advice strikes many Americans as cold and unfeeling. They want to be friends with their children. They believe that it is better to treat them as near equals. Children, however, need guidance to grow, and they need to learn from their parents what is expected of them. They need to know that authority figures, such as parents, teachers, the clergy, and the police, deserve respect. Asian young people get it: they are raised to respect authority. That is why they are such high achievers.

Asian children, as a group, learn the virtue of delayed gratification better than non-Asians. "Instilling a respect for delayed gratification and its rewards starts with parents," note Abboud and Kim.[67] Diligence, perseverance, the ability to see that long-term

---

[66] Ibid., 102–103.
[67] Ibid., 37–38.

accomplishments are more satisfying than short-term ones—these are more than kernels of truth: they are the very stuff of success. That is why these authors advise parents, "Teach your children the value of delayed gratification early by using practical scenarios even they can understand."[68]

One way to instill the virtue of delayed gratification is to insist on a regular and rigorous homework schedule for those in elementary and secondary schools. Scholars from the Brookings Institution found that no racial or ethnic group spends more time doing homework than Asians. The gap between them *and everyone else* is enormous. Their research determined that Asian high school students were the most likely to do more homework, "working later into the night than other racial groups. Low-income students reported doing less homework per hour than their non-low-income peers."[69]

Educational achievement depends on more than just the student. For example, students in Asia do better on standardized tests than students in other parts of the world. That is because Asian instruction depends heavily on drill learning. It is much more rigorous than the learning provided by American schools.[70] American educators place a high value on conceptualization and analysis, which is useful if students have already mastered the basics in language, math, science, and history; but American students often have not been given a solid foundation in these fundamen-

[68] Ibid., 51.
[69] Michael Hansen and Diana Quintero, "Analyzing 'The Homework Gap' among High School Students," Brookings, August 10, 2017, https://www.brookings.edu/blog/brown-center-chalkboard/2017/08/10/analyzing-the-homework-gap-among-high-school-students/.
[70] Thiagarajan, *Beyond the Tiger Mom*, 27.

tals. Asian schools are not making a mistake when they stress memorization; rather, American schools are at fault for undervaluing this pedagogical technique.[71]

Asians have so much to teach the rest of the world that it seems logical to assume that the American ruling class would encourage educators and families to emulate them. Instead, elites appear to resent Asian success, perhaps because it violates their sense of equality and seem bent on penalizing Asians for being *too* successful: they institute quotas against Asian Americans, limiting the number of seats they can occupy in the nation's most prestigious schools.

When Bill de Blasio was mayor of New York City, he worked hard to cap the number of Asians who would be admitted to the most elite public high schools in the city. He opposed the exam-based admissions process because blacks and Hispanics did not do nearly as well on exams as whites and especially Asians did. He never explained how discrimination against Asians could be justified.

The backlash against Asian students has even inspired violence against them, on both the East Coast and the West Coast. Lee Cheng, a co-founder and director of the Asian American Legal Foundation, has condemned both the violence and the discriminatory educational policies. "The street thugs and the educrats in San Francisco share many characteristics and prejudices. Both are racist. Some are just better dressed." It got so crazy in San Francisco that Asian Americans were accused of using "white supremacist thinking to assimilate and get ahead."[72]

---

[71]   Ibid., see chap. 3.

[72]   William McGurn, "The Revolt of the Unwoke," *Wall Street Journal*, July 26, 2021, https://wsj.com/articles/asian-american-merit-testing-racism-woke-san-francisco-collins-moliga-lopez-11627329861?mod=opinion_lead_pos9.

Thomas Jefferson High School in Fairfax County, Virginia, was ranked the number-one high school in the nation by *U.S. News & World Report*. It is 70 percent Asian American. School officials decided this was outrageous—there were not enough black and Hispanic students—so they eliminated the competitive entrance exam. Asian American parents sued. This was a classic case of racism by the ruling class: instead of helping those who don't do well to improve their own test performances, they stopped testing so as to remove the Asians' competitive advantage.

Harvard and Yale are no better. Long ago, they instituted quotas to stop Asians from taking up too many seats, and that led to lawsuits. The Ivy League universities justified their discriminatory policies by citing the need for "racial balancing," a ploy that most Asians saw as insulting. Students for Fair Admissions sued Harvard and disclosed evidence detailing how the university makes admissions decisions. Harvard admits 56.1 percent of black applicants in the top academic decile, 31.3 percent of Hispanics, 15.3 percent of whites, and 12.7 percent of Asians. According to Students for Fair Admissions, which petitioned the court, a black applicant in the fourth-lowest decile "has a higher chance of admission (12.8%) than an Asian American in the *top* decile."[73]

It may be morally acceptable to consider race, as one of many variables, in admissions. But when the results are as skewed as this, it risks creating a new class of people who are victimized in the name of justice. Surely Harvard can do better than this.

---

[73] Editorial Board, "Race, Harvard and the Supreme Court," January 24, 2022, https://www.wsj.com/articles/race-harvard-and-the-supreme-court-students-for-fair-admissions-colleges-quotas-11643063228.

*Vital Virtues Exercised by Nigerians*

In 2015, Promise Amukamara was escorted onto the basketball court at Arizona State University by her four sisters, Peace, Princess, Precious, and Passionate. Their brother, Prince, who played football for the New York Giants, texted them his best wishes. Their mother proudly said, "All of them got scholarships to university." The *New York Times* wrote that "the Amukamaras are at the forefront of a growing number of Nigerian-American athletes, born in the United States, who are excelling at the top levels of high school, college and professional sports."[74]

Nigerians do not just excel in sports. They have become one of the most, if not *the* most, successful ethnic group in the United States. More than six in ten Nigerians over the age of twenty-five have a graduate degree, compared with 14 percent of Americans overall. They are overrepresented in tech companies, Wall Street investment firms, blue-chip law firms, and the health-care industry and as CEOs.

The Nigerian success story is attributable to the same cause that made Jews, Mormons, and Asians so successful: the inculcation of the vital virtues.

Nigerian culture extols family and religion, which is the font of the vital virtues. Grandparents, cousins, aunts, uncles, and in-laws all work together to form a powerful social unit. The aged are given respect; and seniority in general is given deference.

Most Nigerians who migrate to the United States are Christians from the southern part of the country; Muslims occupy the north.

---

[74] Jeré Longman, "More Nigerian-Americans Are Reaching Highest Levels of Sports," March 18, 2015, https://nytimes.com/2015/03/19/sports/more-nigerian-americans-are-reaching-highest-levels-of-sports.html.

America has been blessed to have so many well-educated Nigerian priests come to our shores. A relatively high percentage—61 percent—who come here have earned a bachelor's degree in theology, literature, or religious studies, and many have graduate degrees.[75] They are known for their hard work, and they are role models for the vital virtues.

The Nigerians who come to the United States strive to teach their children Christian virtues. Unlike so many other contemporary American ethnic groups, their young are held to high expectations, particularly with respect to schoolwork. Indeed, education is valued almost above all else. They are expected to do well in school and to consider careers that pay well, such as in law, engineering, and medicine. Mothers are known to pray out loud late at night for their children to succeed, sometimes waking them from their sleep.

In 2022, a Nigerian professor gave an important address at the annual Ramadan lecture before his hometown faculty, administrators, and students. He emphasized the importance of observing the vital virtue of perseverance. It was a "matter of principle," he said, that everyone "exercise patience, persevere and endure as the way to success," lest conditions in the country deteriorate.[76] Such an appeal was not unusual. In fact, he was tapping into a common Nigerian cultural theme that stresses the need to endure through intense periods of hardship.

[75]  Molly Fosco, "The Most Successful Ethnic Group in the U.S. May Surprise You," OZY, June 7, 2018, https://www.ozy,com/ around-the-world/the-most-successful-ethnic-group-in-the-u-s -may-surprise-you/86885/.

[76]  Yusuf Akinlotan, "ACAOSA Tasks Nigerians on Perseverance as It Commissions Mosque," Voice of Nigeria, April 19, 2022, https://von.gov.ng/acaosa-tasks-nigerians-on-perseverance-as-it -commissions-mosque/.

Nigerian author Olunlade Toluwalase Joshua writes that self-discipline is not only honored by Nigerians but is regarded as a "superpower" that creates important habits. "For success and happiness," he says, "to have and continuously build self-discipline is fundamental."[77] Interestingly, the other two vital virtues—perseverance and personal responsibility—are mentioned by him as enablers of self-discipline. "Train[ing] yourself in discomfort" facilitates command over one's passions.

The Nigerians take the vital virtues so seriously that they are even reflected in the constitution of Nigeria. Unlike the United States Constitution, which outlines the separation of powers and describes the rights of the individual in the Bill of Rights, the Nigerian constitution focuses on citizenship. It is not individual rights that matter most; it is individual responsibilities.

The Nigerian constitution begins by specifying the "duty of every citizen" to work for the common good. It offers explicit directives, such as the need for citizens to "abide by the Constitution, respect its ideals and its institutions, the National Flag, the National Anthem, the National Pledge, and legitimate authorities." Citizens are also called upon to "enhance the power, prestige and good name of Nigeria" and to "respect the dignity of other citizens." They are expected to "make a positive and useful contribution to the advancement, progress, and well-being of the community" and to work with "lawful agencies in the maintenance of law and order."[78]

---

[77] Olunlade Toluwalase Joshua, "Tips to Build Self-Discipline as a Nigerian," Insight.ng, https://insight.ng/lifestyle/build-self-discipline/.

[78] "Duties and Obligations of a Nigerian Citizen," Nigerian Scholars, December 30, 2018, https://nigerianscholars.com/tutorials/citizenship-and-rights/duties-and-obligations-of-a-nigerian-citizen/.

Again, the emphasis is not on exercising rights; it is on exercising duties to one's country and fellow citizens.

If there is a critical difference between Nigerian Americans and other African Americans, it is the absolute refusal of the former to see themselves as victims. If anything, Nigerian Americans share with Jews, Mormons, and Asians what Chua and Rubenfeld call a "superiority complex."[79] They relate what one business-school graduate, born in the United States to two Nigerian parents, had to say about this issue:

> Perception is important, and I think it is what holds African-Americans back. If you start thinking about or becoming absorbed in the mentality that the whole system is against us, then you cannot succeed.... Nigerians do not have this. I feel that Nigerians coming from Nigeria feel they are capable of anything.... They don't feel they can't do chemistry or engineering or anything because they are Black.[80]

Here is what another Nigerian American had to say. "Average Nigerians have moral values and have one thing or the other to pursue to give them [an] edge over others. We don't see victimisation as a limitation to our pursuit [but] rather as an inspiration to pursue more."[81]

Perceiving oneself to be a victim is perhaps the most debilitating handicap of them all. It practically assures failure in life.

---

[79]  Chua and Rubenfeld, *Triple Package*, 8.

[80]  Ibid., 81–82.

[81]  "Americans Agree Nigerians Hardworking, Most Successful Group in U.S.," Vanguard, July 5, 2019, https://www.vanguardngr .com/2019/07/americans-agree-nigerians-hardworking-most -successful-group-in-u-s/.

We know what works. Demographic groups that embody the vital virtues of self-discipline, personal responsibility, and perseverance do the best in education and in the workplace. Jews, Mormons, Asians, and Nigerians have a stunning record of success because they live by the vital virtues. If we were smart—as smart as they are—we would learn from them and practice the vital virtues. Instead, our ruling class is at war with the vital virtues—and the American dream slips away for too many.

### The Importance of Intact Families: A Personal Note

I would like to add a personal note at this point. The four groups that have achieved so much could not have succeeded without the benefit of the intact family. As we shall see, African Americans have struggled to realize the American dream, and while there are many reasons for this, the prevalence of fatherless families is a key factor. I know from experience.

A few years ago, my long-time friend Mike Mansfield ran into a classmate of ours from elementary school. He said, "Do you know what happened to Billy Donohue?" She answered, "He's in prison."

She made this assumption based on her experiences with me in school. I was always in trouble. I was not a mean kid, but I was mischievous. At Saint Anne's in Garden City, Long Island, the nuns would give grades not just for academic subjects but also for conduct. Students were assigned an S for satisfactory or a U for unsatisfactory." I never got a single S. Moreover, there was hardly a Friday afternoon when my mother wasn't summoned to meet with my teacher—or the principal.

But that didn't help. At my high school, a military boarding school, I was suspended for conduct and for grades. I was thrown out of college after one year, largely because I spent more time at the pub across the street than in the classroom.

It's not hard to understand why I was always in trouble: I came from a fatherless home. My mother, who worked nights as a nurse—my grandparents from Ireland helped raise my sister and me—thought that sending me to a military boarding school would help to straighten me up. It didn't happen. It was not until I enlisted in the actual military, the Air Force, at age nineteen that I straightened up—though the rebel is still in me.

Boys need fathers. They need to be disciplined. Though mothers can do the job a little, particularly when their boys are young, fathers are nevertheless the key.

I tell my story because some people (who are usually white) still think that race explains why black young men are more likely to commit crime. It has nothing to do with race. It has everything to do with fatherless homes.

2

# Virtue under Fire

## The Assault on Bourgeois Virtues

In the latter part of the nineteenth century, the bourgeois ethos in both England and the United States declined as a result of economic and social changes sparked by the growth of industrialism. Mass migration to urban areas resulted in a significant rise in individualism and a concomitant loss of community. Though these factors were somewhat organic—there was no concerted effort to alter the bourgeois ethos—that was about to change.

As James Q. Wilson has observed, at the turn of the century social elites began actively to seek to change the social order. "The Bloomsbury set had replaced Queen Victoria, resistance to war had replaced habitual patriotism, and writers argued that crime was the result of social injustice rather than a weak human nature."[82] Christopher Lasch dates the attack on the traditional family and bourgeois virtues to the 1920s. That is when those in the behavioral sciences took aim at the nuclear family, bemoaning

---

[82] James Q. Wilson, "Cultural Meltdown," American Enterprise Institute (AEI), September 1, 1999, https://www.aei.org/articles/cultural-meltdown/.

the "sexual repression" that was fostered by Judeo-Christian sexual ethics.[83]

These assaults on the traditional moral order reached new heights in the 1960s. The sexual revolution, made technologically possible by the advent of the birth control pill in 1960, blew through American society like a tornado, quickly destroying social and cultural norms and values that had existed since time immemorial. Intellectuals and academics who hated the bourgeois ethos were only too happy to help decimate the existing moral order.

Today, conditions are even worse. Not only does the smart class have nothing but contempt for the vital virtues; it also loathes any academic who defends them. Consider the experience of Amy Wax, a professor at the University of Pennsylvania Law School. In 2017, she co-authored an op-ed in the *Philadelphia Inquirer* with Larry Alexander, a professor at the University of San Diego School of Law. They argued that the cultural meltdown that took place in the 1960s was aided and abetted by "the chattering classes—academics, writers, artists, actors, and journalists—who relished liberation from conventional constraints and turned condemning America and reviewing its crimes into a class marker of virtue and sophistication." They called for the restoration of bourgeois norms. "But restoring the hegemony of the bourgeois culture will require the arbiters of culture—the academics, media, and Hollywood—to relinquish multicultural grievance polemics and the preening pretense of defending the downtrodden. Instead of bashing the bourgeois culture, they should return to the 1950s posture of celebrating it."[84]

[83] Christopher Lasch, *Haven in a Heartless World* (New York: Basic Books, 1977).
[84] Amy Wax and Larry Alexander, "Paying the Price for Breakdown of the Country's Bourgeois Culture," *Philadelphia Inquirer*, August

Everything that Wax and Alexander said was true. No matter; it was enough to set off an explosive reaction. The day after the eight-hundred-word op-ed appeared, a student newspaper on Penn's campus went after Wax. The newspaper quoted a Middlebury College sociologist who claimed that his school's "students of color were being attacked and felt attacked" by a lecture Wax gave at the college—four years earlier—on the breakdown of the black family. The campus paper also cited a 2005 criticism of her by Penn's Black Law School Students Association after she published a *Wall Street Journal* op-ed on black self-help.[85]

When the paper interviewed Wax, she held her ground. But then a Penn graduate students' union attacked her and claimed that she was responsible for the "presence of toxic racist, sexist, homophobic attitudes on campus," even though the Wax-Alexander piece had said nothing about any of those issues.[86] More columns followed; more denunciations.

But the most significant reaction came from Wax's colleagues. Nearly half of them—thirty-three law professors—signed an open letter stating that they "categorically reject[ed] Wax's claims." The far-left National Lawyers Guild, which has a history of supporting communist totalitarian regimes, asked about punishing her and suggested that it was not appropriate for her to teach

---

9, 2017, https://inquirer.com/philly.com/philly/opinion/commentary/paying-the-price-for-breakdown-of-the-countrys-bourgeois-culture-20170809.html.

[85] Heather Mac Donald, "Scandal Erupts over the Promotion of 'Bourgeois' Behavior," *National Review*, August 29, 2017, https://www.nationalreview.com/2017/08/bourgeois-values-scandal-tars-law-prof-amy-wax-racism-charge/.

[86] Ibid.

a course required for first-year law students.[87] The Ivy League law professors were all discombobulated simply because one of their colleagues had made some commonsense observations about the role virtue plays in making for success in school and in the workplace.

## The Judeo-Christian Roots of Bourgeois Virtue

The roots of the Victorian ethos in Britain and America were grounded in a shared Judeo-Christian heritage. Victorianism was itself a reaction to the social disorder evident in the early nineteenth century; its emphasis on virtue was a deliberate corrective applied to the prevailing conditions. "Many of the institutions that were responsible for its spread were overtly religious in nature," writes Francis Fukuyama, "and the change they brought about occurred with remarkable speed."[88]

Himmelfarb notes that historians generally agree that Victorian values were "Christian—Protestant, Puritan, Methodist; or perhaps not religious at all but rather secular—bourgeois, middle-class, capitalist. They were also, some Victorians discovered to their astonishment, Jewish."[89] The Catholic Church also promoted the four cardinal virtues of prudence, justice, fortitude, and temperance, as well as a cluster of other key virtues.

---

[87] Jesse Singal, "Is the U.S. Declining Because Americans Abandoned 'Bourgeois Virtues'?," Intelligencer, September 9, 2017, https://nymag.com/intelligencer/2017/09/can-an-embrace-of-bourgeois-values-revive-america.html.

[88] Francis Fukuyama, *The Great Disruption: Human Nature and the Reconstitution of Social Order* (New York: Free Press, 1999), 266–268.

[89] Gertrude Himmelfarb, *The Demoralization of Society: From Victorian Virtues to Modern Values* (New York: Vintage, 1994), 170.

Dennis Prager is one of the most astute students of the West's Judeo-Christian heritage. He identifies the belief in liberty as central to that heritage. Where Eastern religions emphasized social conformity, and Muslims prized theocracy, Western cultures emphasized equality. The belief in liberty, as highlighted in America by the phrase "In God we trust," is unique to the West. Prager contends that "the Christians who founded America saw themselves as heirs to the Old Testament, the Hebrew Bible, as much as the New." Indeed, he writes that "the words on the Liberty Bell, 'Proclaim Liberty throughout all the land …,' are from the Torah."[90]

In addition to liberty, the Judeo-Christian idea of America is based on their Judeo-Christian concepts of morality. "It is a belief in universal, not relative, morality," Prager hastens to say.[91] The Ten Commandments are the greatest exponent of this belief, proscribing behaviors that are offensive to God.

Prager is not being chauvinistic when he says that "the Judeo-Christian value system as developed on the basis of the Hebrew Bible (the Old Testament) and developed largely by Christians, and especially in America, is the best value system ever devised."[92] He is simply telling the truth.

For example, Prof. Steven D. Smith's research on paganism and Christianity led him to the conclusion that the pagan world was

---

[90] Dennis Prager, "What Does 'Judeo-Christian' Mean?," The Dennis Prager Show, March 30, 2004, https://dennisprager.com/column/what-does-judeo-christian-mean/.

[91] Ibid.

[92] Dennis Prager, "The Arrogance of Values: Judeo-Christian Values, Part XIV," The Dennis Prager Show, May 31, 2005, https://www.dennisprager.com/column/the-arrogance-of-values-judeo-christian-values-part-xiv/.

devoid of any notion of liberty and morality, as well as exhibiting an absence of a concern for truth.[93] The two value systems also have a very different history. He contends that "a fair assessment" of Christianity would likely credit it with "helping to bring about many of the features of modern civilization that are most valued—including respect for the dignity of the individual, human rights, the commitment to equality, and concern for the poor."[94] None of this would have happened without the Catholic Church, which was the only Christianity for more than a millennium.

A socially responsible understanding of liberty, coupled with a respect for moral absolutes, is the best recipe for individual and social well-being. Both liberty and morality, properly understood, depend heavily on the observation of the vital virtues. The pursuit of morally ordered liberty has made America the greatest nation in history.

## The Assault on Liberty, Properly Understood

The Judeo-Christian concept of liberty, which is embodied in the vital virtues, is based, first and foremost, on self-discipline. But America's dominant culture today rejects self-discipline in favor of self-indulgence. The two conceptions of liberty could not be more different: one is a prerequisite to achieving the American dream—and the other kills it.

"The excess of liberty, whether in States or individuals," wrote Plato, "seems only to pass into excess of slavery."[95] Madison understood this as well. He contended that "liberty may be endangered

93   Steven D. Smith, *Pagans and Christians in the City: Culture Wars from the Tiber to the Potomac* (Grand Rapids, MI: William B. Eerdmans, 2018), 146.
94   Ibid., 206.
95   Plato, *The Republic*, bk. 8, Project Gutenberg, https://www.gutenberg.org/files/1497/1497-h/1497-h.htm#link2H_4_0011.

by the abuses of liberty as well as the abuses of power."[96] Indeed, when liberty becomes license, no one wins. Libertinism, or the excess of liberty, leads inexorably to liberticide.

When we make a fetish of individual rights, we cannot help but diminish interest in their concomitant responsibilities. The link between rights and responsibilities, which was clear in times past, has long been severed—with little to show for it but adversity.

Ben & Jerry's spent big bucks to erect in New York City gigantic billboards sporting a picture of Colin Kaepernick (the failed quarterback turned left-wing activist) with his fist clenched and the inscription, "I know my rights." But Ben & Jerry's idea of freedom is backward: we need less talk about rights and more talk about responsibilities, less about entitlements and more about obligations. Good parents don't give their children "rights" just because they ask for them. They demand that their children act responsibly, and only then do they award privileges, little by little, as they prove to be responsible with the ones they have. For instance, responsible parents may allow their teenagers who have gotten their driver's licenses to drive within their zip code, or within their surrounding communities, before they give them the okay to travel afar. In other words, rights should *follow* responsibility, not *precede* it.

Ask a young person what it means to be free, and he is likely to answer, "You can do what you want." Unfortunately, many adults—especially among the elite—would agree. But Pope Leo XIII had a more considered response: he explained that no one has a natural right to do wrong and that "liberty is to be regarded

---

[96] Alexander Hamilton, James Madison, and John Jay, *The Federalist Papers*, ed. Clinton Rossiter (New York: American Library, 1961), no. 63.

as legitimate in so far as it affords greater liberty for doing good, but no farther."[97]

Furthermore, when we understand freedom properly, we realize that self-mastery is integral to being free. Are we not at our freest when we reach our potential, whether we are pitchers, painters, or piano players? Yet we must choose to restrict and govern our "freedom" in order to master those skills. Conversely, are people really free when they are addicted to drugs or are living profligate lifestyles? In an effort to be free—to do what we want—we only end up enslaved.

"The tendency of contemporary liberal democracies to fall prey to excessive individualism is perhaps their greatest long-term vulnerability," writes Fukuyama, "and is particularly visible in the most individualistic of all democracies, the United States."[98] No doubt about it: radical individualism is the great killer of virtue, and without virtue, neither individual nor social progress can be made. A free society depends on social capital, individuals who incorporate the vital virtues into their very being. There are far too few in America today.

## The Assault on Morality

In a healthy society, some percentage of individuals may have their own quirky moral compasses. But no society can exist without some moral consensus, or general agreement, about what is right and wrong. That is what it means to have a society. Furthermore, to a certain degree, the consensus must be enforced with sanctions and stigma, or the society will have no ability to protect and govern itself.

---

[97] Leo XIII, encyclical letter *Libertas* (June 20, 1888), no. 42.
[98] Fukuyama, *The Great Disruption*, 10.

A free society requires more than just any moral consensus: not all codes are consistent with freedom. The freedoms that began in Western civilization and that have spread to other parts of the world sprang from our Judeo-Christian faith and the Ten Commandments; they form the heart and soul of our moral order.

The Ten Commandments cannot be observed without the vital virtues. "Thou shalt not" demands personal responsibility, self-discipline, and perseverance because the behaviors proscribed by the commandments require the ability to slam on our moral brakes, to say no to temptation. St. John Paul II rightly said that the Ten Commandments "are the *first necessary step on the journey towards freedom*, its starting point" (italics in original). He cited St. Augustine, who said that to be free from "murder, adultery, fornication, theft, fraud, sacrilege, and so forth" was "the beginning of freedom."[99]

Unfortunately, in our society, "Thou shalt not" are the three most dreaded words in the English language. We are left with Pope Benedict XVI's "dictatorship of relativism" and the view that "recognizes nothing as definite and has as its ultimate measure only the self and its own desires."[100]

Indeed, our cultural edifice has been under attack for a long time. Historian Peter Gay contends that "the rise of modern paganism" began with the Enlightenment. A loathing for Christianity, with its moral universals, prompted the initial attack. But what

---

[99] Pope John Paul II, *The Splendor of Truth* (Boston: Pauline Books and Media, 1993), 25.
[100] Pope Benedict XVI, Address of His Holiness Benedict XVI to the Participants in the Ecclesial Diocesan Convention in Rome, June 6, 2005.

have we to show for it? Kierkegaard and Nietzsche knew that the destruction of moral confidence would result in nihilism. And yes, the moral anarchy that plagues the Western world today is a classic example of the damage that occurs when the traditional moral order is shaken. The "death of God," as Nietzsche put it, cascades into the death of morality. And then what? "If there is no God," Dostoyevsky said, "everything is permissible."

### Don't Blame the Founders

If the assault on our moral patrimony began in the Enlightenment, it has continued apace. But don't blame the Founding Fathers of America. Though some scholars have suggested that the Founders' vision of liberty and morality laid the groundwork for the moral nihilism of our day, a more accurate interpretation is afforded by Robert R. Reilly.[101] He maintains that America was founded on solid principles, on ideas that are true and just and deserving of our support. It is not the fault of the Founders that we have strayed from—and even corrupted—their noble principles. The Founders treasured virtue; today we trash it.

Himmelfarb nicely captures what the Founders believed. "Republican government means self-government—self-discipline, self-restraint, self-reliance—'republican virtue,' in short." Madison, for instance, said that "the people will have virtue and intelligence to select men of virtue and wisdom.... To suppose that any form of government will secure liberty or happiness without any virtue in the people is a chimerical idea."[102]

---

[101] Robert R. Reilly *America on Trial: A Defense of the Founding*, expanded ed. (San Francisco: Ignatius Press, 2021).

[102] Gertrude Himmelfarb, *One Nation, Two Cultures* (New York: Alfred A. Knopf, 1999), 85.

John Adams also stressed the role of virtue. "The only foundation of a free constitution, is pure virtue, and if this cannot be inspired into our people, in a greater measure than they have it now, they may change their rulers, and the forms of government, but they will not obtain a lasting liberty. They will only exchange tyrants and tyrannies."[103]

The Founders understood that religion—by which they meant our Judeo-Christian faith—is the basis of virtue. Franklin opined that, were it not for religion, men would be even more wicked than they are. Adams insisted that only "a moral and religious people" was capable of establishing a free society. Washington named "religion and morality" as the "indispensable supports" of what he called "political prosperity." Even Jefferson, who is often perceived to be a fair-weather Christian, insisted that, as president, he was required to give public recognition to the Christian religion.[104] These were men who defended freedom and morality, properly understood. It is for these reasons that Reilly argues that "the reason for our current decline is not that the nation's original principles have finally reached fruition, but that the Christian and natural law perspective that animated its Founders is being lost" and, with it, a respect for the vital virtues.[105]

If the Founders are not responsible for the cultural rot we see in America today, who is? And when did things really start falling apart?

[103] Terence P. Jeffrey, "Will America Remain Virtuous Enough to Be Free?," CNSNews, June 1, 2022, https://cnsnews.com/commentary/terence-p-jeffrey/will-america-remain-virtuous-enough-be-free.

[104] Himmelfarb, *One Nation*, 86.

[105] Reilly, *America on Trial*, 7.

## The "Blame America" Campaign

Fukuyama characterizes the 1960s and 1970s, when traditional moral values were relentlessly criticized, as the period in which the "Great Disruption" took place. But much has changed since his book on this subject was published at the end of the last century. Today, a sustained campaign to "blame America" has begun. It is one thing for traditional social norms and values to be upended, inadvertently and unintentionally, by technological changes. It is quite another when elite intellectuals set out to destabilize and sabotage American society. How can virtue flourish in such a toxic environment?

There are three stages to the "blame America" movement:

Stage 1 flowered in the aftermath of World War II, when the baby boomers came of age. It was a time of unprecedented affluence and domestic strife. The civil rights movement, the war in Vietnam, and the sexual revolution wrought chaos and confusion. College students were taught that our country was racist and sexist and that our foreign policy was imperialistic. "Amerikkka" was called the land of oppression. Parts of many urban areas, particularly on the East and West Coasts, were overtaken by left-wing activists, many of whom were preaching love while throwing Molotov cocktails at the police.

Stage 2 was born in the 1980s. Once again, college campuses were the epicenter of challenges to America. Multiculturalism was the principal tool. This pedagogical tool was never about teaching students to appreciate diverse cultures; rather, it was used as an ideological weapon to trash Western civilization and its Judeo-Christian core.

Pope Benedict XVI wasn't fooled. Multiculturalism, he observed, has led to "a peculiar Western self-hatred that is nothing short of pathological." The distinguished historian Arthur

M. Schlesinger Jr. was more specific: "There is surely no reason for Western civilization to have guilt trips laid on it by champions of cultures based on despotism, superstition, tribalism, and fanaticism."[106]

In 1984, UN Ambassador Jeane J. Kirkpatrick noticed that a hypercritical vision of America had seeped into parts of the Democratic party, what she called the "San Francisco Democrats." The former Democrat was not shy about stating her concerns. "When Marxist dictators shoot their way into power in Central America, the San Francisco Democrats don't blame the guerillas and their Soviet allies," she said. "They blame the United States policies of 100 years ago. But then they always blame America first."[107]

What she observed was a harbinger of what was to come. Stage 3 of the "blame America" campaign is not confined to students, faculty, and campus administrators: it has spread to virtually every segment of the ruling class. That is why our current situation is so perilous and pernicious—radical ideologies, particularly those governing race and sexuality, have made their way into every elite quarter in the country.

It is no longer just artists, entertainers, reporters, and professors who blame America first. Members of the Fortune 500, the health-care industry, and the military top brass have joined the chorus. While some are reluctantly bowing to public pressure,

---

[106] Bill Donohue, " 'Hate America' Campaign Is in High Gear," Catholic League for Religious and Civil Rights, April 27, 2021, https://www.catholicleague.org/hate-america-campaign-is-in-high-gear/.

[107] Johanna Neuman, "Jeane J. Kirkpatrick, 80: First American Woman to Serve as U.N. Ambassador," *Los Angeles Times*, December 9, 2006, https://www.latimes.com/archives/la-xpm-2006-dec-09-me-kirkpatrick9-story.html.

others are true believers and are fully engaged. Never before in American history have we seen anything like this. The American dream cannot be successfully maintained when the people who rule America despise their own country.

## The Superiority of the Ruling Class

No one chronicled the antics of the ruling class better than Angelo Codevilla. He noted that its members are both Republicans and Democrats, though there are more Democrats than Republicans. Importantly, elites "think, look, and act as a class." They are "formed by an educational system that exposed them to the same ideas and gave them remarkably uniform guidance, as well as tastes and habits."[108]

They are decidedly not like the rest of us. They believe themselves "the best and brightest while the rest of Americans are retrograde, racist, and dysfunctional unless properly constrained."[109] They are patricians; we are the plebes. They condescend toward Americans who value bourgeois virtues; they value only their own power.

David Halberstam authored *The Best and the Brightest*, a brilliant study of the ruling class. Stephen Marche captured the essence of his work, saying that these well-educated people ironically create "elaborate policies that misunderstand the most basic facts about the world, leading to immense suffering for ordinary people. That is the Ivy League way— 'brilliant policies that defied common sense,' in Halberstam's phrasing."[110]

---

[108] Angelo Codevilla, "America's Ruling Class," *American Spectator*, July 16, 2010, https://spectator.org/americas-ruling-class/.

[109] Ibid.

[110] Stephen Marche, "How Ivy League Elites Turned against Democracy," *Atlantic*, January 5, 2022, https://www.theatlantic.

Victor Davis Hanson notes that the ruling class comprises the "transnational mega-wealthy, who have been enriched by globalization." They are defined by

> education (preferably Ivy League and its coastal counterparts), residence (primarily between Boston and Washington on the East Coast and from San Diego to Berkeley on the Pacific), profession (executive positions in government, media, law, foundations, the arts and academia), celebrity (name recognition from television, Hollywood, network news, finance, etc.), and ideology, such as those prominent in the progressive movement.[111]

What drives the ruling class is power. While the ruling class "stakes its claim through intellectual-moral pretense," says Codevilla, "it holds power by one of the oldest and most prosaic of means: patronage and promises thereof." It functions the way left-wing parties always have, like a "machine" that provides "tangible rewards to its members."[112] When some of its institutions falter—such as in the investment-house collapse of 2008—Republicans and Democrats rush to the rescue with bailouts and "stimulus" packages. If they believed in personal responsibility, they would have insisted that their elitist colleagues bear the full burden of their own inept decision-making.

It is not actually wealth that distinguishes the ruling class, despite what F. Scott Fitzgerald may have said. There are plenty

---

com/ideas/archive/2022/01/ivy-league-apologists-january-6-gop-elitism-populism/621153/.

[111] Victor Davis Hanson, "Who Are the Elites Who Have So Upset the Middle Class?," *Newsweek*, September 17, 2016, https://www.newsweek.com/who-are-elites-who-have-so-upset-middle-class-497945.

[112] Codevilla, "America's Ruling Class."

of Texas oilmen who are quite rich but don't necessarily qualify as members of the ruling class. Academic achievement is also not a determinative factor. Lots of students do well in school. "What really distinguishes these people demographically," argues Codevilla, is that "their careers and fortunes depend on government."[113]

The ruling class has long looked down its nose at the average American. In 1993, *Washington Post* reporter Michael Weisskopf labeled evangelical Christians "poor, uneducated and easy to command."[114] In 2008, presidential candidate Barack Obama opined that small-town Americans like to "cling to their guns or religion."[115] When Hillary Clinton was running for president in 2016, she famously referred to Trump supporters as a "basket of deplorables."[116] None of these statements was insincere or a mistake: they were accurate depictions of the way these illustrious people think.

## The Composition of the Ruling Class

The nineteenth-century business tycoons who drove the economy were grateful for the opportunities that America afforded them.

113  Ibid.
114  William A. Galston, "God in the Public Square," *America*, April 21, 2008, https://www.americamagazine.org/issue/culture/god-public-square.
115  Janell Ross, "Obama Revives His 'Cling to Guns or Religion' Analysis—for Donald Trump Supporters," *Washington Post*, December 21, 2015, https://www.washingtonpost.com/news/the-fix/wp/2015/12/21/obama-dusts-off-his-cling-to-guns-or-religion-idea-for-donald-trump/.
116  Domenico Montanaro, "Hillary Clinton's 'Basket of Deplorables,' in Full Context of This Ugly Campaign," NPR, September 10, 2016, https://www.npr.org/2016/09/10/493427601/hillary-clintons-basket-of-deplorables-in-full-context-of-this-ugly-campaign.

They would never have blamed America. Most elites in other segments of society were also patriotic. But this is no longer the case. We can thank the professors who specialize in the humanities and the social sciences for this new development. We can also credit those who work in the media and the entertainment industry with playing a key role in crafting and disseminating a hypercritical vision of America and its history.

At the start of the academic year in 2021, a teacher at Alexander Hamilton High School in Los Angeles took down the American flag in his classroom. In its place, he hung a Palestinian flag, the transgender flag, a Black Lives Matter flag, and "the modern PRIDE flag." He also displayed wall posters saying, "F*** the police" and "F*** Amerikkka. This is native land."

While this teacher's behavior may not be representative of most teachers, the incident is nonetheless a reflection of thinking that is all too common in schools today. We no longer teach students about the innumerable virtuous men and women who made America the envy of the world. Instead, we fixate on America's weaknesses, real and contrived.

A survey of the most prominent history and government textbooks used in elementary and secondary schools found that much of the coverage is negative.[117] To be sure, America's history has many imperfections—as does the history of every other country. There are certainly incidents, episodes, and policies that are cause for criticism, even condemnation. But fairness demands that students learn why immigrants continue to charge our borders. They do not struggle and suffer so they can experience oppression.

---

[117] Michael McDonald, "Battle of the Textbooks," Catholic League for Religious and Civil Rights, September 21, 2021, https://www.catholicleague.org/battle-of-the-textbooks/.

They come dreaming of a better life, and they expect to find it in America.

In these textbooks, Christianity—and especially Catholicism—is derided. Students do not learn about the catalogue of contributions that the Church has made to natural rights and natural law or to the creation of human rights in general. They are not told that it was the Catholic Church that first insisted upon the equal dignity of all people, regardless of race or sex. The spectacular achievements in the arts and sciences that the Church bequeathed to humanity are never mentioned, nor is there a discussion of the role the clergy played in the civil rights movement.

A fair account of Catholicism would explore why virtue occupies such a special place in its understanding of reality. The incredible acts of charity and self-sacrifice performed by faithful Catholics—many of whom gave their lives to serve others—are ignored. Sacrifice depends on perseverance, on the ability to tough it out during times of adversity. We should be celebrating people who modeled these virtues, to give young people the strength to follow them.

If we are serious about instilling virtue in students, we cannot create an environment that constantly disdains America, past, present, and future. Why would a young person aspire to contribute to a morally debased society? Personal responsibility, self-discipline, and perseverance take hard work. If the effort is not valued, why bother?

The Smithsonian's National Museum of African American History and Culture is well positioned to portray and promote the many achievements of African Americans. While some of its programs do that, many others lash out at the vital virtues as if they were a scourge on black America. In 2021, the museum featured an exhibit that defined "whiteness" as "self-reliance," "the nuclear family," "the scientific method," "objectivity," "hard work," "Christianity," "delayed gratification," and "respect for authority."[118]

Is this what black Americans should be taught? That to be self-reliant is to be like whitey? The intact nuclear family explains why Mormons, Jews, Asians, and Nigerians end up on top. Why denigrate it? If hard work is disparaged, do we not necessarily glorify laziness? If Christianity is rejected, what beliefs should we endorse? Delayed gratification is something we should nourish—if it is condemned, should we advocate for immediate gratification?

Personal responsibility, self-discipline, and perseverance are the virtues that make for success, not failure. One would never know this from the Smithsonian exhibit. It seems the goal of the ruling class is to destroy the American dream for black Americans. Why else do they promote exhibits like this?

If the Smithsonian exhibit were an anomaly, it wouldn't matter very much. But it is not an anomaly. Many of the most influential foundations have long funded programs that threaten virtue. For example, the John D. and Catherine T. MacArthur Foundation annually present a fellowship known as their "genius" award. The winners in 2021 had much in common: 72 percent of them were hard-core left-wing writers, artists, and activists. Almost all were consumed with race; almost none looked kindly on America. Indeed, many of the winners were self-described socialists—but that did not stop them from collecting the $625,000 grant made possible by the capitalist system that they abhor.[119]

---

[118] Miranda Devine, "Biden's 'Bigot' Smear vs. Trump Voters," *New York Post*, June 2, 2021, https://www.nypost.com/2021/06/02/bidens-bigot-smear-vs-trump-voters-devine/.

[119] Bill Donohue, "Left-Wing Radicals Win 'Genius' Awards," Catholic League for Religious and Civil Rights, October 4, 2021, https://www.catholicleague.org/left-wing-radicals-win-genius-awards/.

There are several foundations that seem to specialize in undermining American norms and values. The Tides Foundation, the Ford Foundation, and the Hewlett Foundation are among the most prominent. None is more effective than the Open Society Foundations sponsored by atheist billionaire George Soros.

There is hardly a radical cause that Soros's foundations have not funded. The institutions he has tried to influence, and corrupt, range from the Catholic Church to the criminal justice system. For example, Soros funded Catholics in Alliance for the Common Good and Catholics United, both of which were dummy Catholic entities designed to create a "Catholic Spring" revolution in the Church. Not surprisingly, several men and women who worked at Soros's Open Society Foundations landed senior positions in the Biden administration.

The corporate world has also gone woke. The Fortune 500 companies have given generously to an array of "social justice" causes, most of which are antagonistic toward the vital virtues. Moreover, given the great good performed by so many religious organizations—particularly in molding students to be virtuous—it is scandalous that the big corporations provide so few grants to them. Indeed, in the name of social justice, some corporations have adopted anti-Christian policies that, in fact, smack of authoritarianism.

In 2021, Cigna devised a "Societal Norms" checklist that asked employees to "Check Your Privilege." Among the choices were "Christian," "White," and "Cis-Male" (by which they mean biological males).[120] It seems billionaire entertainer Oprah Winfrey

---

[120] Bill Donohue, "Cigna's Top Officers Should Resign," Catholic League for Religious and Civil Rights, March 24, 2021, https://www.catholicleague.org/cignas-top-officers-should-resign/.

would not be a member of the "privileged class"—but low-ranking members of the army who are white Christian men would be.

Telling Christians that they are beneficiaries of "religious privilege"—and that they need to admit this, as in a novel about a totalitarian state—is false and demeaning. Are Hispanic Catholics who work in housekeeping at Cigna "privileged"? What about African American Christians who work in security? And why would filthy rich atheist executives not be considered "privileged"? Creating a hostile workplace for Christians is repulsive as well as counterproductive. Why would anyone strive to perform, endeavor to go the extra mile, or demonstrate the virtue of perseverance in such a milieu?

The hypocrisy of the ruling class never ends. The National Football League and Nike are two of the most vociferous advocates for social justice in the nation, especially for causes that purport to combat racism. Both of them have stridently denounced human rights abuses in America. Yet both invest heavily in China, a nation that is guilty of some of the most egregious human rights abuses in the world. The same is true of Apple, Coca-Cola, and many other corporate giants.

In 2019, NFL commissioner Roger Goodell bragged about his relationship with the Chinese Communist government. "China is a priority market for the NFL. We believe that our game has a great deal of potential to expand to grow and bring new fans into our game." John Donahoe, Nike's CEO, was just as exuberant. "Nike is a brand that is *of* China and *for* China" (my italics).[121]

The NFL and Nike are joined at the hip. In 2018, they announced "a long-term extension to their on-field rights partnership.

[121] Bill Donohue, "NFL and Nike Lose on Anti-Slave Bill," Catholic League for Religious and Civil Rights, December 17, 2021, https://www.catholicleague.org/nfl-and-nike-lose-on-anti-slave-bill/.

Central to the extension, Nike will continue to provide all 32 NFL Clubs with uniforms and sideline apparel bearing the Nike brand for use during the games."[122]

The degree of oppression in China, especially among religious minorities, is not disputed. On July 1, 2021, the U.S. State Department released a damning assessment of conditions there. The report listed physical and sexual violence, forcible drug intake, mass detention, and political indoctrination. Even the liberal-leaning media outlet Politico cited evidence that "the Chinese Communist Party is perpetuating a genocide against the religious minority [the Uyghurs, a Muslim ethnic group], including slave labor, forced sterilizations and concentration camps."[123]

The genocide and slave labor in China are made possible because of organizations such as the NFL and Nike. Add Major League Baseball (MLB) to the list as well. Robert Manfred, the MLB commissioner, moved the All Star Game in 2021 from Atlanta to Denver because he disagreed with a voting reform law in Georgia. Never mind that Atlanta had fairer voting rules than Denver. But Manfred's interest in human rights was a farce: MLB invests heavily in China. Even worse is Chamath Palihapitiya, co-owner of the Golden State Warriors NBA team. In 2022, he belittled the ongoing genocide against the Uyghurs, saying, "Nobody cares about what is happening to the Uyghurs."[124]

These members of the ruling class are too busy screaming about racism at home to be worried about blatant human rights violations

[122] Ibid.

[123] Ibid.

[124] Joel B. Pollak, "NBA Owner Who Said 'Nobody Cares' about Uyghurs Is Democrat Mega-donor," Breitbart, January 17, 2022, https://www.breitbart.com/politics/2022/01/17/nba-owner-who -said-nobody-cares-about-uyghurs-is-democrat-mega-donor/.

in a communist country. As Nathanael Blake put it, "Woke capital's CEOs wave rainbow flags and Black Lives Matter banners at home while using slave labor abroad."[125]

Ironically, the captivating achievements of the NFL and MLB players that they invest in are the direct consequence of years of personal responsibility, self-discipline, and perseverance on the part of athletes. But instead of funding programs, projects, and policies that encourage these virtues, corporate America works against them.

## The Virtue of Patriotism

Bill Bennett lists patriotism as an example of the virtue of personal responsibility; Tom Wolfe and Gertrude Himmelfarb saw patriotism as a virtue in its own right. Either way, patriotism requires taking ownership of our lives and realizing that we matter. It is in that capacity that it functions as a vital virtue.

No one is better known for defending the virtue of patriotism than Alasdair MacIntyre. He understood both its moral dynamics and its ability to provide for a sense of community.

According to MacIntyre, patriotism involves "a peculiar regard not just for one's nation, but the particular characteristics and merits and achievements of one's own nation."[126] From the nineteenth century until the 1960s, national pride was taken for granted.

But what happens when patriotism is in decline? That is exactly what has been happening since the 1960s, and the ruling class bears much of the responsibility for it. When a nation

---

[125] Nathanael Blake, "Why America's Ruling Class Is So Incompetent," *Federalist*, January 7, 2022, thefederalist.com/2022-01/07/why-americas-ruling-class-is-so-incompetent/.

[126] Alasdair MacIntyre, "Is Patriotism a Virtue?," The Lindley Lecture, University of Kansas, March 26, 1984.

systematically disowns its own history, MacIntyre points out, patriotism ineluctably becomes perceived as an irrational feeling. The consequences of this mind shift are dramatic. For example, if those who serve in the armed forces—who are typically not from ruling-class families—become convinced that their country is unjust and oppressive, why would they want to lay down their lives to preserve it?

It was heartening to read that, in 2017, 85 percent of Americans said either that the United States "stands above all other countries in the world" (29 percent) or that it is "one of the greatest countries, along with some others" (56 percent).[127] But just three years later, the numbers declined dramatically. A majority of adults still said they were "extremely proud" (42 percent) or "very proud" (21 percent) to be an American, but these were the lowest readings posted by Gallup since this question was first asked in 2001.[128] While the cause of the drop-off is not certain, the steady drumbeat of criticism of our nation's past on college campuses surely explains part of it.

Who are the most patriotic and the least patriotic citizens? In terms of political affiliation, Republicans are the most patriotic. As far as economic class, those at the bottom—the poor and the working class—are the most patriotic. With respect to age, the elderly come out on top; young people are the least patriotic.[129]

---

[127] A. W. Geiger, "How Americans See Their Country and Their Democracy," Pew Research, July 4, 2018.

[128] Megan Brenan, "U.S. National Pride Falls to Record Low," Gallup, June 15, 2020, https://news.gallup.com/poll/312644/national-pride-falls-record-low.aspx.

[129] Public Religion Research Institute (PRRI), *Competing Visions of America: An Evolving Identity or a Culture Under Attack? Findings from the 2021 American Values Survey* (Washington, D.C.: PRRI,

It should come as no surprise that young people are the least likely to be patriotic. It used to be that the "blame America" theme was confined to higher education, but today it has infected students in the elementary and secondary schools as well. In 2018, a survey found that one out of five Americans under the age of thirty-seven do not think Americans should be proud of their country. One in five millennials sees the flag as a symbol of intolerance; this explains why two out of five think it is okay to burn it. Importantly, the survey also found that no segment of America is more ignorant about the Bill of Rights than millennials.[130]

In a 2021 American Values survey, respondents were asked whether "America has always been a force for good in the world." Among Republicans, 92 percent agreed, but only 67 percent of Democrats did. Republicans and Democrats also disagree on whether schools ought to do more to teach students to love their country: 88 percent of Republicans thought they should, but only 40 percent of Democrats did.[131]

In a 2019 General Social Survey, more than 90 percent of the poorest Americans—a higher percentage than the working class, the middle class, and the upper class—said they would rather be citizens of the United States than of any other nation. Data from the World Values Survey were even more impressive. This survey

---

2022), https://www.prri.org/wp-content/uploads/2021/10/PRRI-Oct-2021-AVS.pdf. See also Daniel A. Cox and Nat Malkus, "Controversy and Consensus: Perspectives on Race, Religion, and COVID-19 in Public Schools," American Enterprise Institute, September 22, 2021, https://www.americansurveycenter.org/research/august-2021-aps/.

[130] Daniel Davis, "Pulling Young Americans Back from the Brink," *Daily Signal*, December 20, 2018, https://www.dailysignal.com/2018/12/20/pulling-young-americans-back-from-the-brink/.

[131] Ibid.

found that 100 percent of those who belong to the lowest income group were either "very" or "quite" proud of their country.[132]

These results are striking. It is not members of the pampered ruling class who are the most patriotic—it is the poor. It is ironic that the education elite constantly portray the poor as oppressed. If they are, why do they love America so much? The "experts" have no answer.

Joan C. Williams is a professor at the University of California, Hastings College of the Law, and the author of an important book on the working class. "Flag waving went out of fashion in the 1970s among the college-educated, particularly progressives," she says, "not least because of their objections to the Vietnam War. But overt love of country remains robust in the group called the white working class."[133] These men and women also have great respect for the military, and they tend to value religion.

Williams notes perceptively that "respect for the military also reflects working-class whites' focus on self-discipline and personal responsibility," two of the vital virtues. Religion, she observes, is another institution that aids self-discipline. "For non-elites," she writes, "religion often provides the mental exercise, stability, hopefulness, impulse control and social safety net that elites get from their therapists, jobs and bank accounts."[134] She's right. The

---

[132] Francesco Duina, "Why Are Poor Americans More Patriotic Than Their Wealthier Counterparts?," *Guardian*, November 20, 2019, https://www.theguardian.com/commentisfree/2019/nov/20/poor-americans-patriotic-than-their-wealthier-counterparts.

[133] Joan C. Williams, "Even on July 4, the Working Class and the Elites Don't See Eye to Eye," *Los Angeles Times*, July 4, 2017, https://latimes.com/opinion/op-ed/la-oe-williams-patriotism-and-the-white-working-class-20170704-story.html.

[134] Ibid.

ruling class would prefer to take their moral cues from psychologists than from clergy.

May 8, 1970, was the day of the Hard Hat Riot in New York City. A few days earlier, National Guardsmen had opened fire on Kent State University students and outside activists who had expressed their love of country by burning down the ROTC building on campus. This was a classic showdown between the working class and the pampered class. But it was small potatoes compared with what happened when about a thousand left-wing students took to the streets in downtown New York City to protest the Kent State shootings.

The working-class construction workers, about four hundred of them, along with eight hundred office workers, did not take kindly to the young radicals' American-flag burning, so they went on the attack. Eventually, more than twenty thousand people poured into the streets, and that led to a siege of New York City Hall. Many people were injured on both sides, though the flag burners got the worst of it.

The working class is heavily composed of veterans, policemen, and firefighters, almost all of whom have suppressed contempt for the ruling class. They do not take kindly to those who call them white supremacists or Christian nationalists. Not surprisingly, they rallied to President Trump's side, largely because he embraced them. Trump himself was hated by the ruling class precisely because he was comfortable being an outsider, despite his wealth and elite connections.

Starting in 2020, the pace of anti-Americanism quickened, mostly as a result of a series of violent interactions between the police and African American men. This led to "mostly peaceful protests," many of which turned violent, and it even led to professional athletes' refusal to stand for the national anthem. Hundreds of monuments were defaced or torn down by indoctrinated mobs who knew little about American history. Statues of Columbus were the most frequently destroyed, followed by monuments of Robert E. Lee and Thomas Jefferson. Statues of Junípero Serra, the eighteenth-century priest who was declared a saint by Pope Francis for his heroic efforts to defend the rights of Indians, were smashed by those who had no idea who he was.

On November 22, 2017, I testified before the New York City Mayoral Advisory Committee on Art, Monuments, and Markers. The anger of the audience was striking. They hated the country. But even worse was the attitude of the ruling-class bureaucrats and educators: they were quite at home listening to speakers who viciously attacked America.

Does any of this matter? And what does it mean with respect to the vital virtues? In 2020, the Carr Center for Human Rights Policy at the Harvard Kennedy School issued a major report on civic education. The results were very concerning. Americans are largely ignorant about their own government.[135] This is important because civic education is intimately associated with active citizenship: people are less likely to be engaged with the organizations of civil society if they are badly educated about their government.

Stanford University professor William Damon faults the public schools for their refusal to provide for citizenship education. He notes that the Obama administration "closed down the Department of Education's character education desk as soon as it took office."[136]

---

[135] Carr Center for Human Rights Policy, *Reimagining Rights and Responsibilities in the United States,* Harvard Kennedy School, Fall 2020, issue 2020-004, https://carrcenter.hks.harvard.edu/files/cchr/files/201007_rr-executive-summary.pdf.

[136] William Damon, "Restoring Purpose and Patriotism to American Education," in Michael J. Petrilli and Chester E. Finn Jr., eds., *How to Educate an American: The Conservative Vision for Tomorrow's Schools* (West Conshohocken, PA: Templeton Press, 2020), 80–81.

Why would members of the ruling class do this? "Although most parents would like to see schools impart virtues such as honesty and responsibility to their children," Damon writes, "character education in public education has been hindered by progressive resistance to instruction that makes claims about right and wrong in the face of cultural variation (even when such claims focus on values such as truth and obligation that virtually all cultures respect)."[137]

In other words, it is the ruling class, not parents, that opposes character education in schools. Character development, of course, means teaching about the intrinsic worth of virtue — and perhaps that is uncomfortably close to endorsing Christianity. Members of the ruling class seem to regard personal responsibility, self-discipline, and perseverance as quaint attributes best confined to another era.

The American dream can still be realized by those fortunate enough to trust the vital virtues. But those who succeed do so in spite of the ruling class.

---

[137] Ibid., 81.

3

# Promoting Racism

## Perception and Reality

The Catholic Church calls racism "intrinsically evil."[138] Moreover, the Church has a long and proud history of opposing slavery. The first person in history to condemn slavery publicly was St. Patrick, who was himself a slave. And although racism was not intrinsic to slavery in most parts of the world, the Church has rejected racism in all of its manifestations for centuries. Slavery is no longer a legal issue in the United States, but alas, racism continues to plague us.

One of the great ironies of our time is that those who claim to be most opposed to racism are often the ones most responsible for promoting it. The ruling class is persuaded that the best way to combat racism is to adopt a racist agenda. Worse, their efforts do little to help traditional victims of racism.

If there is one demographic group that has struggled to achieve the American dream, it is African Americans. Slavery and

---

[138] United States Conference of Catholic Bishops, *Forming Consciences for Faithful Citizenship* (June 2, 2020), no. 23, https://www.us-ccb.org/issues-and-action/faithful-citizenship/upload/forming-consciences-for-faithful-citizenship.pdf.

discrimination are partly responsible. Though nothing can be done about the legacy of slavery, discrimination can be checked—and indeed, much progress has been made. But if more progress is to be made by blacks, the vital virtues must play a more prominent role in their lives. Unfortunately, there is little sign that the ruling class is going to facilitate this. The black community will have to do this on its own, without looking to elites for assistance.

It seems as if the socioeconomic status of blacks should reflect the state of race relations in the country, at least to a certain extent: that is, if blacks are doing better economically, race relations must be improving. But as it turns out, that is not the case: economic status is an objective measure; race relations are, at least partly, a subjective matter.

For example, in 1964, the year of the Civil Rights Act, 81 percent of Americans believed that life was improving for blacks.[139] Yet in 2020, after decades of progress, both legally and economically—to say nothing of the election of America's first black president—81 percent of Americans still said that racial and ethnic discrimination was a big problem.[140] How could this be?

The 2020 survey was taken midway through the year, after violent protests had broken out because of several controversial interactions between police and black men. Kathleen Brush, whose scholarship includes race relations, explains what happened. "When people are fed a steady uncontested diet of racism, racism, racism, and the nation's cities are experiencing nightly BLM

---

[139] Mona Charen, *Do-Gooders: How Liberals Hurt Those They Claim to Help—and the Rest of Us* (New York: Sentinel, 2004), 11.

[140] Dr. Harry Wilson, "The Reconnect Research/Roanoke College Poll on Race and Police," Roanoke College, July 7, 2020, https://www.roanoke.edu/about/news/reconnect_research_roanoke_college_poll.

(Black Lives Matter) protests it would be hard for people not to perceive racism as a big problem." Importantly, she points out what the surveys did not say: they did not say that Americans are racist, that America is systematically racist, or that racism is on the rise. "It could not say that," she writes, "because the data does not support that."[141]

All the objective indices say that blacks are not being held back because of racism, despite the widespread perception otherwise. The "steady uncontested diet" of media reports on racism are a factor, as Brush says. But why do the big media outlets incessantly harp on this theme? To understand, we need to understand the mindset of the ruling class.

The ruling class is convinced that personal characteristics, such as the vital virtues, do not explain why some religious and ethnic groups do better than others. They prefer to blame prejudice and discrimination, rather than behavioral factors, for failure. It is not a coincidence that most elites are white. They are desperately afraid of being accused of racism, so they have a vested interest in condemning racism. Not only does that deflect personal guilt; it erects a high moral platform on which to preach.

Jason Riley is an African American columnist for the *Wall Street Journal*, and what he had to say about the death of George Floyd—the Minneapolis black man who died after a white police officer knelt on his neck after subduing him—was very different from most media accounts. "The protests that followed Floyd's death rested on two assumptions," Riley said. "The first is that Floyd, career criminal and drug addict, was somehow representative of black America, which is not only false, but insulting.

---

[141] Kathleen Brush, *Racism and Anti-Racism in the World: Before and After 1945* (Middletown, DE: Bowker, 2020), 74.

The second is that police acted out of racial animus, which has never been proven. This is what happens when racial identity becomes the centerpiece of politics and public life in a multiracial society."[142]

What Riley said is not merely his opinion. Floyd had, in fact, served nine separate jail sentences for crimes ranging from armed robbery to drug dealing. The Minnesota attorney general in charge of the prosecution of policeman Derek Chauvin was a left-wing African American, Keith Ellison, and even he concluded that what happened was not a "hate crime." He said, "I wouldn't call it that because hate crimes are crimes where there's an explicit motive and bias." He could not have been clearer about his assessment. "We don't have any evidence that Derek Chauvin factored in George Floyd's race as he did what he did."[143]

David Horowitz covered this case extensively, and after quoting Ellison, he addressed the riots that followed Floyd's death. "All the outrage against police racism," he wrote, "and all the mayhem fueled by that outrage, was based on no evidence whatsoever. It was based on a lie." The lie, perpetuated by Black Lives Matter, "inspired over 600 attacks on 220 American cities."[144]

Riley punctuates his argument by contrasting the media's reaction to Floyd to that of Darrell Brooks. Brooks is a black man who was charged with driving his car through an annual Christmas parade in 2021 in Waukesha, Wisconsin. He killed six people, all of whom were white, including an eight-year-old boy. "Given the

---

[142] Jason Riley, "It's Reckless for the Left to Selectively Cry Racism," *New York Post*, December 1, 2021, https://nypost.com/2021/12/01/its-reckless-for-the-left-to-selectively-cry-racism/.

[143] David Horowitz, *I Can't Breathe: How a Racial Hoax Is Killing America* (Washington, D.C.: Regnery Publishing, 2021), 60.

[144] Ibid.

suspect's history of posting messages on social media that called for violence against white people and praised Hitler for killing Jews," says Riley, "you'd think that his race and the race of his victims would be relevant to reporters. Race is all anyone would be talking about if a white man had slammed his vehicle into a parade full of black people."[145]

Though left-wing writers and activists, as well as members of the ruling class, continue to sound racial alarms at every opportunity, much evidence indicates that race relations are much better than they would have us believe. For example, one measure of racial progress is the approval rate of white people toward interracial marriages. In 1958, the figure was 4 percent; in 2021, it was 94 percent.[146] Another measure is how blacks think they fare vis-à-vis their parents. Black Americans (61 percent) are more likely than white Americans (51 percent) to believe that their generation is better off than that of their parents; 56 percent of Hispanics feel this way.[147] In short, the perception that racism is getting worse doesn't reflect the current reality.

## The Racism of the Ruling Class

The ruling class projects moral superiority, especially with respect to race, as a means of justifying its rule and maintaining authority. It presents itself as a beacon of tolerance, without prejudice, to create moral pressure for the rest of us to fall into line with its "progressive" initiatives. But it is also not afraid to use genuinely coercive tactics, from imposing quotas to censoring speech on campus.

[145] Riley, "It's Reckless for the Left to Selectively Cry Racism."
[146] Justin McCarthy, "U.S. Approval of Interracial Marriage at New High of 94%," Gallup, September 10, 2021, https://news.gallup.com/poll/354638/approval-interracial-marriage-new-high.aspx.
[147] PRRI, *Competing Visions of America*, 27.

The truth of the matter is that those who make up the ruling class are among the most racist members of American society. How so? To all appearances, they do not believe that blacks are capable of competing with whites, and indeed, the ruling class seems to have all but given up on blacks. In America today, it is not white supremacists whom blacks need to fear. It is the ruling class.

The roots of ruling-class racism go deep. George Fitzhugh was America's first sociologist. He is the author of the 1854 book *Sociology for the South*. He was a man of considerable affluence and intellect, and like most sociologists today, he was a man of the Left who railed against what he perceived to be the exploitative nature of capitalism. He was also a strong proponent of slavery. Why would a "progressive" support slavery? He said that blacks were not capable of competing with white people in a capitalist economy, and it was therefore preferable for them to remain as slaves for their own welfare.

In his work "The Universal Law of Slavery," written in 1850, Fitzhugh explained his view that "the Negro is but a grown up child and must be governed as a child, not as a lunatic or criminal. The master occupies toward him the place of parent or guardian." He noted that slavery had a positive effect. "The negro slaves of the South are the happiest, and, in some sense, the freest people in the world." Everything was taken care of for them, which would not be the case in a market economy. "The master labors for the slave, they exchange industrial value. But the capitalist, living on his income, gives nothing to his subjects. He lives by mere exploitations."[148]

[148] George Fitzhugh, "The Universal Law of Slavery" (1850) PBS, https://www.pbs.org/wgbh/aia/part4/4h3141t.html.

African Americans, Fitzhugh argued, were inferior to white people:

> The negro is improvident [and] would become an insuffer-able burden to society. Society has the right to prevent this, and can only do so by subjecting him to domestic slavery. In the last place, the negro race is inferior to the white race, and living in their midst, they would be far outstripped or outwitted in the chaos of free competition. Gradual but certain extermination would be their fate.[149]

This inability to compete with whites, Fitzhugh wrote, was known to even "the maddest abolitionist." "This defect of char-acter would alone justify enslaving him, if he is to remain here. In Africa or the West Indies, he would become idolatrous, savage and cannibal, or be devoured by savages and cannibals. At the North he would freeze or starve."[150] Of course, Fitzhugh's views sound cruel to us today. But in fact, they are justified by the same logic that supports many of the policies of our modern ruling class with respect to race.

During the Progressive Era, in the late nineteenth and early twentieth centuries, Richard T. Ely was one of the most prominent leaders in the social-justice crusade. He co-founded the American Economic Association and was considered to be sympathetic to blacks. But he was also a racist who expressed exactly the same ideas as Fitzhugh: "Negroes, are for the most part grownup children, and should be treated as such."[151]

---

[149]  Ibid.

[150]  Ibid.

[151]  Bradley Thomas, "The Progressive Ideas That Fueled Ameri-ca's Eugenics," FEE, March 7, 2019, https://fee.org/articles/the-progressive-ideas-that-fueled-america-s-eugenics-movement/.

In 1988, Charles Murray captured the essence of this mindset better than anyone. He predicted the "coming of custodial democracy"—and his prediction has come true. He said that "what is now a more or less hidden liberal condescension toward blacks in general, and toward the black underclass in particular, will have worked its way into a new consensus."[152]

Murray maintained that liberal intellectuals and policy makers would come to terms with their view that "inner-city blacks are really quite different from you and me, and the rules that apply to us cannot be applied to them." Furthermore, he said that progressives will conclude that it is "futile to seek solutions that aim at bringing them into participation in American life." Therefore, "the humane course" is to generously supply them with "medical care, food, housing, and other social services—much as we do for American Indians who live on reservations." This is the face of custodial democracy, treating inner-city blacks as "wards of the state."[153]

This is an accurate description of the way that ruling-class men and women think about black Americans. If they truly believed that black people were just as capable of exercising personal responsibility, self-discipline, and perseverance as white people, they would never give up on them. But they have given up. The dirty little progressive secret is that the ruling class believes that blacks can't make it on their own, and that is why progressives are always looking to implement new racist government policies.

Shelby Steele, a brilliant black social scientist, recalls listening to the black entertainer and activist Dick Gregory when he was

---

[152] Charles Murray, "The Coming of Custodial Democracy," *Commentary*, September 1988, https://www.commentary.org/articles/charles-murray/the-coming-of-custodial-democracy/.
[153] Ibid.

a young man. Gregory was upset that blacks were being called to practice personal responsibility, an expectation that he saw as fundamentally illegitimate. "Responsibility made fools of us."[154] That was the bottom line for Gregory. This infuriated Steele, who correctly observed that such talk would never have been countenanced by black militants such as Malcolm X.

"If Malcolm X railed ferociously against white America," Steele says, "he never called for a redistribution of responsibility for black uplift to whites or American institutions. His was a self-help black militancy that was naturally skeptical about what others would actually do for blacks." In fact, Steele's description of Malcolm X's stance shows Malcolm's firm support for the vital virtues. "You might call it 'hard-work' militancy, delayed gratification, family unity, individual initiative, entrepreneurialism, and so on."[155]

Steele knows that this is the surest path to success. Speaking of blacks, he notes that "we are good at sports and music because we subject ourselves to unforgiving standards of excellence and then work ferociously to meet those standards. Ruthlessly, we allow absolutely no excuses."[156]

Blacks don't need ruling-class custodians to take care of them. They certainly do not need elites throwing in the moral towel. They need high expectations. Of course they can achieve the American dream. There are many examples of extraordinary success in the black community, in virtually every walk of life. Moreover, the growth of the black middle class suggests that the American dream is a reality for millions of African Americans.

---

[154] Shelby Steele, *White Guilt: How Blacks and Whites Together Destroyed the Promise of the Civil Rights Era* (New York: Harper Perennial, 2006), 52.

[155] Ibid., 59.

[156] Ibid., 64–65.

## Overcoming Adversity

Glenn Loury is a black intellectual who is a descendant of slaves and was reared in Chicago's South Side in the 1950s and 1960s. He knows how racial inequality has created barriers to success; yet he wound up teaching in the Ivy League at Brown University. He wants what all blacks want. "We want a shot at the American Dream." But he knows that to succeed, blacks must resist internalizing the nonstop talk about how unjust America is and must get on with making their lives better. Divisive rhetoric, he notes aptly, is the work of those who "make their living by focusing on our differences."[157]

Loury is proud to be an American. "On our shores," he says, "we have witnessed the greatest transformation in the status of an enserfed people that is to be found anywhere in world history. Some 46 million strong, we black Americans have become by far the richest and most powerful large population of African descent on the planet." Instead of telling tales of woe, he contends, it is time to recognize that America is "the greatest force for human liberty" anywhere in the world.[158]

Loury blames the ruling class for promoting "the woke racialism [that] gives the lie to the notion that the American Dream doesn't apply to blacks." In particular, he names "the cultural barons and elites of America—who run the *New York Times* and the *Washington Post*," as well as those "who give out Pulitzer Prizes and National Book Awards." He includes those "who make grants for the MacArthur Foundation [and] who run the human resource departments of corporate America." They are responsible, he says,

---

[157] Glenn Loury, "The Case for Black Patriotism," *First Things* (January 2022): 44.
[158] Ibid., 47.

for robbing blacks of "self-determination" and for the "patronizing lie" that blacks lack the attributes necessary for success.[159] He sees right through their agenda.

The ruling class has set the table for numerous black leaders, many of whom have bought into the idea that blacks are not capable of succeeding. "The majority of black leaders today have chosen to play the race card rather than call for personal responsibility in their own community," notes Manhattan Institute scholar Heather Mac Donald. Instead of promoting racist quotas in colleges to push blacks ahead, she says, they should urge students to "crack the books in order to close the academic achievement gap."[160]

In addition to encouraging personal responsibility, we need to promote the virtue of perseverance. Black journalist Clarence Page knows that perseverance is what accounts for success in the black community. "We must disrupt the long-held stereotypes of black people as helpless bystanders in their own history. We have had entrepreneurs, skilled tradesmen, military officers, inventors, organizers, and many others" who have weathered adversity. He emphasizes how "we persevered to build businesses that included banks, hotels, small factories, and a black-owned railroad."[161] Unfortunately, schoolchildren, black and white alike, are not learning about these black role models. Instead, they are only learning about the racist barriers that have been instituted to block black progress.

[159]  Ibid., 48.

[160]  Heather Mac Donald, "Race, Discipline, and Education," in Petrilli and Finn, *How to Educate an American*, 95.

[161]  Clarence Page, "'A Dream as Old as the American Dream': Embrace Black Patriotism over Victimization," February 13, 2020, https://www.washingtonexaminer.com/opinion/op-eds/clarence-page-a-dream-as-old-as-the-american-dream-embrace-black-patriotism-over-victimization-and-learned-helplessness.

Contemporary black scholars, such as John Sibley Butler, also recognize the role that bourgeois virtues play. They are what made the first "black bourgeoisie." Faced with tremendous odds, "the black bourgeoisie persevered," setting a role model for future generations.[162] It emerged during slavery, among free blacks who created new business opportunities by drawing on the strengths of their families and communities. Butler credits his success to these same sources, and he has built on his experience to help other blacks. "Since I wear the success of my bourgeoisie group on my sleeves," he opines, "one of my goals has been to create an analog of bourgeois: self-help structures that produce excellent black communities—some of which are now troubled."[163]

If only the ruling class would embrace the vital-virtues approach embodied by Butler. If only they followed black leaders such as Robert Woodson—one of our nation's most ardent believers in black self-help—there would be far fewer problems in the black community.

Critics charge that people such as Butler and Woodson do not understand the degree to which racist policies have hurt blacks. That is not so: they never deny the facts about the past; they just refuse to wallow in them. The past is gone; the future is what you make of it—even if the path is harder than it should have been.

Even black leaders such as Eldridge Cleaver, a militant who was never hesitant about attacking white racists—he adored Malcolm X—came to understand that hating all white people was pointless. He credits his hero with changing his mind and said he was "glad

---

[162] John Sibley Butler, "Straight out of the Black Bourgeoisie: Lessons for the Twenty-First Century," in Robert L. Woodson Sr., ed., *Red, White, and Black: Rescuing American History from Revisionists and Race Hustlers* (New York: Emancipation Books, 2021), 151.
[163] Ibid., 155.

to be liberated from the doctrine of hate and racial supremacy." "If a man like Malcolm X could change and repudiate racism," Cleaver says, "if I myself and other former Muslims can change, if young whites can change, then there is hope for America."[164] He shows how critically important it is to have the right mindset.

No black leader was more optimistic than Rev. Martin Luther King Jr. It is a sad commentary on our society that his noble legacy is dishonored every day. Who dishonors it? Not racist white rednecks but members of our own ruling class who embrace racism in the name of fighting racism. King would be appalled.

King's 1963 "I Have a Dream" speech articulated his vision of America. While he made several references to serious problems that confronted blacks—ranging from discrimination in public accommodations to police brutality—he did so against the backdrop of profound respect for the American commitment to liberty, equality, and justice for all. Indeed, his "dream" was based on his conviction that these goals would eventually be reached.

Just recently, street anarchists and professional agitators were busy tearing down statues of American icons. But King celebrated the heroic figures those statues represented. He opened his speech by referencing the Emancipation Proclamation, calling its author, Abraham Lincoln, "a great American." He credited the Founders, "the architects of our republic," with writing "the magnificent words of the Constitution and the Declaration of Independence."[165]

King knew that the goals of those documents were aspirational and had not been fully realized. But he was wise enough to know

---

[164] Eldridge Cleaver, *Soul on Ice* (New York: Delta, 1968), 79, 106.

[165] Bill Donohue, "Dishonoring Martin Luther King's Legacy," Catholic League for Religious and Civil Rights, May 24, 2021, https://www.catholicleague.org/dishonoring-martin-luther-kings-legacy/.

that the Founders gave us "this promissory note," so that appeals to liberty, equality, and justice would be given strength and power. "America has given the Negro people a bad check," he noted, but "we refuse to believe the bank of justice is bankrupt. Now is the time to make justice for all of God's children."[166] What a very Christian response!

Contrast what King said with the words of the Biden-appointed U.S. ambassador to the United Nations, Linda Thomas-Greenfield, in 2021. She told reporters in New York City that "the original sin of slavery weaved white supremacy into our founding documents and principles."[167] Wrong. It was our inalienable rights that were weaved into our founding documents and principles and that ultimately abolished slavery in America.

King had nothing but praise and admiration for our founding documents and principles. His problem was the American people's failure to make good on what those documents and principles embodied, our failure to live by the noble contents of the American creed.

### Hating Whitey

Martin Luther King criticized the policies of white officials, and the racist behavior of some whites, yet he never engaged in a sweeping condemnation of all white people. Those distinctions are all too frequently ignored these days, most often by the ruling class.

It seems odd that the mostly-white ruling class would participate in a campaign to demonize white people. But as they don't see themselves as part of the guilty class, they feel exempt from their own gross generalizations.

[166] Ibid.
[167] Ibid.

"I think white people are committed to being villains in the aggregate." This is what Brittney Cooper teaches her students. She is a professor of women's and gender studies at Rutgers University. What does she advise? "The thing I want to say to you is we got to take these [expletive deleted] out."[168] She is more of an activist, and a treacherous one at that, than a professor.

Dr. Aruna Khilanani spoke at Yale in 2021 about race relations:

> This is the cost of talking to white people at all—the cost of your own life, as they suck you dry. There are no good apples out there. White people make my blood boil.... I had fantasies of unloading a revolver into the head of any white person that got in my way, burying their body and wiping my bloody hands as I walked away relatively guiltless with a bounce in my step, like I did the world a favor.[169]

To say that she is consumed with thoughts of violence is an understatement.

Many of these racists have a particular hatred of white Christians, especially white Christian men. African American professor Anthea Butler, who teaches at the University of Pennsylvania, says, "White Christianity is a Christianity that is based on the following: Jesus is white. Jesus privileges white culture and white supremacy, and the political aspirations of whiteness over and

---

[168] Jackie Salo, "'We Got to Take These Motherf—kers out': Rutgers Professor Calls White People 'Villains,'" *New York Post*, October 29, 2021, https://nypost.com/2021/10/29/rutgers-professor -calls-white-people-villains/.

[169] She made her comments at Yale, June 4, 2021. See Bill Donohue, "Hating Whitey Is Chic," Catholic League for Religious and Civil Rights, January 7, 2022, https://www.catholicleague.org/ hating-whitey-is-chic/.

against everything else."[170] What she said is what we would expect from someone who says she believes that Christians worship "a white racist god."[171] Like Cooper and Khilanani, Butler is prone to making incendiary remarks. White Evangelicals, she warns, "may end up killing us all."[172]

Robert P. Jones is a white Christian author and one of the nation's most well-known critics of white Christians. "Practically, we must reject what have, for too long, been three articles of our faith: that the Bible is a blueprint for a white Christian America; that Jesus, the son of God, is a white savior; and that the church is a sanctuary of white innocence."[173]

Jones is also the CEO of the Public Religion Research Institute (PRRI) and has frequently used his perch to say that racism is built into the DNA of white people. White Christians, he says, "have constructed and sustained a project of perpetuating white supremacy that has framed the entire American story. The legacy of this unholy union still lives in the DNA of white Christianity today, and not just among white evangelical Protestants in the South, but also among white mainline Protestants in the Midwest and white Catholics in the Northeast."[174] He always exempts himself.

[170] Ibid.
[171] Anthea Butler, "The Zimmerman Acquittal—America's Racist God," History News Network, July 14, 2013, https://www.historynewsnetwork.org/article/152638.
[172] Jason Lemon, "University Professor Argues White Evangelicals 'May End Up Killing Us All' during Racism Panel," Newsweek, May 27, 2021, https://www.newsweek.com/university-professor-argues-white-evangelicals-may-end-killing-us-all-during-racism-panel-1595543.
[173] Donohue, "Hating Whitey Is Chic."
[174] Robert P. Jones, "Racism among White Christians Is Higher Than among the Nonreligious. That's No Coincidence,"

These deep thinkers are convinced that there is something brewing inside white Christians that is a threat to liberty. Author Katherine Stewart specializes in writing about white Christian "nationalists." She is convinced that they are a menace to society. In fact, she says they are "running the country." Her proof? A remark made by President Trump in the late winter of 2020 that "by Easter" the Covid crisis would ease. That was all the evidence she needed—he used the "E-word."[175]

Andrew Whitehead and Samuel Perry are sociologists who also write about Christian nationalists. Whitehead believes that these people "think you have to be Christian to be truly American."[176] He did not quote anyone to that effect and would have a hard time finding anyone of significance who believes this to be true. No matter; both Whitehead and Perry argue that anyone who believes that the Declaration of Independence and the Constitution are divinely inspired documents—a defensible view for anyone who believes that God can act for our good—proves that he is a Christian nationalist.

Thomas Jefferson was no Christian nationalist. Indeed, he was barely a practicing Christian. But the author of the Declaration made a number of references to God in our founding document. He spoke of "the laws of nature and nature's God"; "the Creator"; "the supreme judge of the world"; and "the protection of Divine Providence." And, of course, he said our rights come from our "Creator," not from government.

---

Think, July 28, 2020, https://www.nbcnews.com/think/opin-ion/racism-among-white-christians-higher-among-nonreligious-s-no-coincidence-ncna1235045.

[175] Bill Donohue, "Inventing the Enemy," *Catalyst*, October 2021, https://www.catholicleague.org/inventing-the-enemy/.

[176] Ibid.

Demonizing white people has consequences. On October 18, 2021, New York City officials voted unanimously to remove a seven-foot-tall statue of Thomas Jefferson from the chambers of the New York City Council in City Hall. Perversely, the person most responsible for declaring Jefferson a racist was himself an anti-Semite. In fact, New York State Assemblyman Charles Barron, who said about the statue, that it "should be put in storage or destroyed or whatever," has a long record of anti-Semitism.[177] If he knew anything about Jefferson, he would know that he wrote into the Declaration the very principles that led to the end of slavery. Moreover, the Constitution itself required that the international slave trade would end on January 1, 1808. The president who made good on that pledge? Thomas Jefferson.

The cultural environment that demonizes whites has led to public policies that discriminate against them. On December 27, 2021, the New York State Department of Health issued a new policy on the distribution of anti-Covid treatments. To be a recipient, the patient must "have a medical condition or other factors that increase their risk for serious illness." One of the risk factors was being of a "non-white race or Hispanic/Latino ethnicity." So white people were shoved to the back of the line.[178]

At the federal level, the Biden administration had been in office for just a month before it started going after white people. The Covid-19 relief bill offered debt forgiveness to farmers—provided

---

[177] Bill Donohue, "Is NY Assemblyman Barron the Most Ironic Person to Brand Jefferson Racist?," CNSNews, October 19, 2021, https://www.cnsnews.com/commentary/bill-donohue/ny-assemblyman-barron-most-ironic-person-brand-jefferson-racist.

[178] Bill Donohue, "Justifying Racism," Catholic League for Religious and Civil Rights, January 5, 2022, https://www.catholicleague.org/justifying-racism/.

they were not white. Recipients had to be "Black/African American, American Indian or Alaskan native, Hispanic or Latino, or Asian American or Pacific Islanders."[179]

Biden also punished white business owners for their whiteness by putting them at a competitive disadvantage. He explicitly said that his "priority will be black, Latino, Asian and Native-American-owned businesses" and "women-owned businesses." Biden also said that restaurant owners would get priority in receiving federal funds if they were women, veterans, or members of "socially and economically disadvantaged" groups.[180]

Those who truly abhor racism do not make policies that pit one race against another. But that is exactly what happens in America today.

## Critical Race Theory

In 2021, a six-year-old girl from Virginia came home from school and asked her mother if she was "born evil." She had been told in her history class that she was born evil—because she was white. Her mother pulled her out of the public school and enrolled her in a private one.[181]

But private schools, especially rich ones, are not immune from institutionalized racism. Former Fox News TV star Megyn Kelly pulled her kids out of an expensive school in New York City after she learned about a letter that was circulated that accused white

[179] Ibid.

[180] Ibid.

[181] Joshua Rhett Miller, "Virginia Mom Claims White Daughter Asked If She Was 'Born Evil' after History Lesson," *New York Post*, November 1, 2021, https://nypost.com/2021/11/01/mom-says-white-daughter-asked-if-she-was-evil-after-history-class/.

people of "reveling in state-sanctioned depravity" and comparing white children to "killer cops."[182]

If these schools were truly interested in combating racism, they would help black students to excel. Social scientists have known for a long time that when middle-class whites interact with middle-class blacks, race relations are usually positive. The key, then, is to make sure more blacks get into the middle class—which means, once again, the inculcation of the vital virtues. But instead, the ruling-class white people lecture others about their inherent racism.

The thinking that dominates the Virginia public school and the private New York City school is the fruit of critical race theory (CRT). CRT rejects Martin Luther King's dream of judging people based on the content of their character rather than on the color of their skin. Its proponents see white racism everywhere, and they see every disparity between blacks and whites as a reflection of racism, even when it is clear that racism is irrelevant. Mark Levin explains it well when he says, "Minorities are relentlessly victimized as individuals and a class, and in all manners, by white dominance. And short of eradicating society, there is no cure. That's the mindset, that's the doctrine."[183]

Ibram X. Kendi is one of the gurus of CRT. The ruling class loves him and made him the youngest person ever to win the National Book Award for Nonfiction. He was also named a Guggenheim Fellow—and a MacArthur Fellow for 2021. In fact, his Center for Antiracist Research at Boston University is lavishly

[182] Lia Eustachewich, "Megyn Kelly Pulls Sons From 'Woke' UWS School Over Anti-White Letter," New York Post, November 18, 2020, https://nypost.com/2020/11/18/megyn-kelly-pulls-sons-from-woke-uws-school-over-anti-white-letter/.

[183] Mark Levin, American Marxism (New York: Threshold Editions, 2021), 93.

funded by big philanthropy. Twitter funds him as well, as does the Rockefeller Foundation, which awarded him $1.5 million. The Ford Foundation, the Marguerite Casey Foundation, George Soros's Open Society Foundations, and the Bill and Melinda Gates Foundation have all contributed mightily to the "anti-racist" cause of Kendi.[184]

But what does Kendi say? "When I see racial disparities," he says, "I see racism."[185] But surely he does not see racism at work in the NBA: most professional basketball players are black. Does he see the disparate success of West Indians and Nigerians as the result of racism? Thomas Sowell sees it clearly: "The West Indian experience itself seriously undermines the proposition that color is a fatal handicap in the American economy."[186]

But for Kendi, racism is ubiquitous. He believes that "there is no such thing as a not-racist idea," only "racist ideas and antiracist ideas." That explains why he believes that "every policy in every institution in every community in every nation is producing or sustaining either racial inequity or equity." He even blames racism for causing "arms races" and "climate change."[187] He offers no evidence to support his baseless claims. But that doesn't matter

---

[184] Michael Watson, "Courage Is Not Enough to Overcome Woke-Progressivism," *Capital Research* 7, no. 1 (January 2022): 13, https://capitalresearch.org/app/uploads/Capital-Research-2022-1.pdf.

[185] Christopher F. Rufo, "Ibram X. Kendi Is the False Prophet of a Dangerous and Lucrative Faith," *New York Post*, July 22, 2021, https://nypost.com/2021/07/22/ibram-x-kendi-is-the-false-prophet-of-a-dangerous-and-lucrative-faith/.

[186] Thomas Sowell, *Ethnic America: A History* (New York: Basic Books, 1981), 220.

[187] Coleman Hughes, "How to Be an Anti-Intellectual," *City Journal*, October 27, 2019, https://www.city-journal.org/how-to-be-an-antiracist.

to his ruling-class fans. They like what he says, and that's all that matters. Data be damned.

If there is one of Kendi's ideas that endears him most to the ruling class, it is his solution to racial inequalities: "The only remedy to past discrimination is present discrimination. The only remedy to present discrimination is future discrimination."[188] The hatred for Martin Luther King's legacy is stunning.

Catholic social teaching regards CRT as anathema. In 1988, before CRT became popular, the Pontifical Council for Justice and Peace issued an important document: *The Church and Racism*. It unequivocally condemns racism, and unlike CRT advocates, it makes no exceptions. It maintained that "all racist theories are contrary to Christian faith and love." It also says that "all forms of discrimination must be firmly opposed."[189]

CRT is incompatible with Catholic social teaching because it is designed to divide people. In 2001, members of the Pontifical Council for Justice and Peace attended a world conference on racism. They emphasized that while fighting racism is critical, it is also important to note that "there must be a specific effort to present—especially to the young—certain major values such as the unity of the human race, the dignity of every human being, the solidarity which binds together all member of the human family."[190] These are words that advocates of CRT could never say.

[188] Ibid.
[189] Pontifical Council for Justice and Peace, *The Church and Racism: Towards a More Fraternal Society*, (November 3, 1988), no. 33, EWTN, https://www.ewtn.com/catholicism/library/church-and-racism-towards-a-more-fraternal-society-2426.
[190] Pontifical Council for Justice and Peace, *Contribution to World Conference against Racism, Racial Discrimination, Xenophobia and Related Intolerance*, Durban, August 31–September 7, 2001, no.

To be clear, the Catholic Church is not opposed to all affirmative-action policies designed to help those who have been victims of racism and discrimination. At the world conference on this subject, the Pontifical Council for Justice and Peace recognized the utility of "voluntary measures." But it hastened to add that quotas were fraught with difficulty. "There is a real risk that such measures will crystallize differences rather than foster social cohesion."[191] Unfortunately, this is exactly what CRT does: it crystallizes differences that undermine social cohesion.

The ruling class rejects Catholic wisdom and seizes on CRT to justify racial discrimination. And not just against whites: Asians are also routinely discriminated against because they are too successful.

Further proof that Kendi's thesis fails to resolve racial inequality—and indeed, exacerbates it—is apparent in his insistence that the educational achievement gap between white and black students is itself a "racist idea."[192] In other words, when test results show that blacks are performing well below grade level, we should not work to close the gap. This is a recipe for doing nothing, which works against black interests.

CRT plays out in the schools in an insidious way. In 2019, the school board in Albemarle County, Virginia, unanimously voted to adopt an "anti-racism" policy designed to build "racial consciousness" by requiring students to deconstruct their racial and sexual identities. This was necessary, the school board argued, because we need to "dismantle the individual, institutional, and structural racism that exists." Students learned a central tenet of

---

15, https://www.vatican.va/roman_curia/pontifical_councils/justpeace/documents/rc_pc_justpeace_doc_20010829_comunicato-razzismo_en.html.

[191]  Ibid., no. 19.

[192]  Hughes, "How to Be an Anti-Intellectual."

CRT—namely, that "white people are inherently and irredeemably racist and benefit from various systematically racist power structures that white people have put in place and perpetuate."[193]

If these educational elites were honest, they would simply resign. After all, it is not the working class that instituted these alleged "power structures." It is the ruling class that did so.

Instead, it is only honest white teachers who are quitting. In 2021, a teacher in the Loudoun County Public Schools in Virginia couldn't tolerate one more of the mandatory antiwhite CRT training sessions, so she quit. Laura Morris showed up at a school board meeting to make her announcement. "School board, I quit. I quit your policies. I quit your training, and I quit being a cog in a machine that tells me to push highly politicized agendas to our most vulnerable constituents: the children. I will find employment elsewhere. I encourage all parents and staff in this county to flood the private schools."[194]

But of course, it is not just educational elites who are instituting racist policies against white people; private businesses and ruling-class-dominated corporate America are also playing this game.

AT&T literally tells white people that all of them are racists. "American racism is a uniquely white trait" says the company's

---

[193] Breccan F. Thies, "Exclusive—Critical Race Theory: Inside a Virginia County's Curriculum for Racial Indoctrination," Breitbart, May 28, 2021, https://www.breitbart.com/education/2021/05/28/exclusive-critical-race-theory-inside-virginia-countys-curriculum-racial-indoctrination/.

[194] Alana Mastrangelo, "Loudoun County Teacher Resigns over District's 'Highly Politicized' Critical Race Theory 'Agendas,'" Breitbart, August 11, 2021, https://www.breitbart.com/tech/2021/08/11/loudoun-county-teacher-resigns-over-districts-highly-politicized-critical-race-theory-agendas/.

Listen Understand Act initiative. All the racist buzz words are there: "intersectionality," "white privilege," "white fragility," etc. They don't mince words. "White people, you are the problem. Regardless of how much you say you detest racism, you are the sole reason it has flourished for centuries." White workers also learn that "black people cannot be racist."[195]

Walmart has gotten into the act. In 2018, it adopted a radical training program that was mandatory for executives and recommended for hourly workers. It taught that the United States is a "white supremacy system" that oppresses people of color. Whites, Walmart employees learned, are guilty of "white privilege" and "internalized racial superiority." The "white supremacy culture" comprises such elements as "individualism," "objectivity," "paternalism," "right to comfort" and "worship of the written word." These nefarious qualities are "damaging to both people of color and to white people."[196]

This line of thinking implies that it would be racist to teach African American students to learn how to read and write, as that would mean "worship of the written word." No doubt the Klan would approve.

When I learned about this program in 2021, I checked on the racial composition of Walmart. Of the nine members on the executive committee, eight were white, one was black; there were no Hispanics or Asians. According to their logic, Walmart is a racist institution. If the members of the exeutive committee had

195  Christopher F. Rufo, "White People, You Are the Problem," *City Journal,* October 28, 2021, https://www.city-journal.org/att-racial-reeducation-program.

196  Christopher F. Rufo, "Walmart vs. Whiteness," Christopher Rufo, October 14, 2021, https://christopherrufo.com/walmart-vs-whiteness.

any decency, I said at the time, they should resign.[197] Instead, they collected huge salaries while lording it over their minimum-wage workers, no doubt prizing their "right to comfort" from the decks of their yachts.

These pernicious ideas have made their way even into the military. Books about CRT are assigned reading in many branches of the armed forces. Men and women learn how corrupt the Founding of America was and how inherently racist white people are. Lt. Col. Matthew Lohmeier was so incensed by what was being taught that he wrote a book about it, arguing that the ideas were Marxist. He was fired as commander of a U.S. Space Force unit.[198]

CRT has even invaded the Salvation Army. In 2021, the International Salvation Army issued the lengthy report *Let's Talk about Racism*. This discussion guide was aimed at everyone associated with the organization. Part of it was commendable—Scripture was cited on the need to treat everyone equally—but CRT polemics were interposed throughout. When the elites in the organization experienced pushback, they took the report off the Internet. But they did not back down altogether. They issued a statement, "The Salvation Army's Response to False Claims on the Topic of Racism." Instead of apologizing for adopting the politics of the hard-core Left, the elites lashed out at the critics. They said the critics were wrong when they said that "the Salvation Army believes America is an inherently racist society." But on page 3 of appendix D, the

---

[197] Bill Donohue, "Corporate Elites Are Playing Blacks," Catholic League for Religious and Civil Rights, February 22, 2022, https://www.catholicleague.org/corporate-elites-are-playing-blacks/.

[198] Dakota Wood and Mike Gonzalez, "The Woke Takeover of the US Military Endangers Us All," *New York Post*, May 24, 2021, https://nypost.com/2021/05/23/the-woke-takeover-of-the-us-military-endangers-us-all/.

report explicitly says of America that "our foundations were built on racism, and it is strongly felt in every aspect of American life."[199]

The report also noted that a person cannot be a racist unless he belongs to "a dominant or privileged group." In May 2021, Lori Lightfoot, the African American mayor of Chicago, expressly said that she would not grant interviews to white reporters (though she rescinded the rule two days later amid a backlash).[200] Nevertheless, what she tried to do was racist, and there is no getting around it.

The authors of the report showcased their sociological ignorance when they maintained on page 6 of the glossary that "Whiteness and White racialized identity refer to the way that White People, their customs, culture and beliefs operate as the standard by which all other groups are compared."[201] This is an exquisite example of racism. Not only is "Whiteness" a contrived term designed to denigrate all Caucasians, but there is also no such thing as white "customs, culture and beliefs." The customs, culture, and beliefs of the Irish are not those of the Ukrainians. For that matter, customs vary even within countries where the ethnic stock is the same. The authors' racism is right there in black and white.

## The 1619 Project

One of the favorite resources for woke educators is the 1619 Project. It is a proposed curriculum disseminated by the *New York Times* that seeks to revise American history. According to this version of history, America was not founded in a revolution in 1776; it was founded in slavery in 1619.

---

[199] Bill Donohue, "Salvation Army Elites Turn Left," Catholic League for Religious and Civil Rights, December 6, 2021, https://www.catholicleague.org/salvation-army-elites-turn-left/.

[200] Ibid.

[201] Ibid.

Nikole Hannah-Jones is the person responsible for this initiative. She is neither a historian nor a professor. She is a journalist. While she complains of systemic racism, she insists that no white people work with her on the project (although her mother is white and her father is black). As we would expect, Hannah-Jones turned to Kendi for advice. Jake Silverstein, the editor of Hannah-Jones's book, *New York Times' 1619 Project: A New Origin Story*, said the aim of the volume was "to reframe American history, making explicit that slavery is the foundation on which this country was built."[202]

As expected, Hannah-Jones received massive funding from the guilt-ridden ruling class. Like Kendi, she was awarded a "genius grant" by the John D. and Catherine T. MacArthur Foundation: it provided $1.8 million to the Pulitzer Center for Crisis Reporting, which, in turn, made sure the project made its way into school curriculums.[203]

Peter Wood, president of the National Association of Scholars, writes, "The larger aim of the 1619 Project is to change America's understanding of itself." This reworking of history, he says "aligns with the views of those on the progressive left who hate America and would like to transform it radically into a different kind of nation."[204] Wood is correct in his assessment, but there is a curious dimension to this story that needs to be told.

The family that owned the *New York Times* were slaveholders. In fact, Bertha Levy Ochs, the mother of the paper's patriarch, Adolph S. Ochs, was a zealous advocate of slavery who followed the family tradition of advocating for slavery set by her slave-owning

---

[202] Chris Stirewalt, "The 1619 Project Book, a Pew Bible for a New Religion," *Dispatch*, November 22, 2021, https://thedispatch.com/p/the-1619-project-book-a-pew-bible.

[203] Watson, "Courage Is Not Enough."

[204] Levin, *American Marxism*, 108.

uncle. She had lived with her father's brother, John Mayer (who had dropped the surname Levy), for several years in Natchez, Mississippi, before the Civil War. Mayer owned at least five slaves.

Ochs's parents, Julius and Bertha Levy, were German Jewish immigrants who met in the South before moving to Ohio, where Adolph was born. When the Civil War broke out, Bertha moved to Memphis to support her Confederate-fighting brother (Julius was on the Union side).

When Bertha died, the United Daughters of the Confederacy, to which she belonged, draped a Confederate flag over her coffin. Adolph donated a thousand dollars to have her name engraved on the founders' roll of the Stone Mountain Confederate Memorial. He sent a note saying, "Robert E. Lee was her idol."[205]

Adolph was raised in Knoxville, Tennessee, and at age twenty he became the publisher of the *Chattanooga Times*. In 1900, the paper ran an editorial saying that the Democratic Party, which he supported, "may justly insist that the evils of negro suffrage were wantonly inflicted on them." After he purchased the *New York Times* in 1896, he moved to New York. When he died in 1935, the United Daughters of the Confederacy sent a pillow embroidered with the Confederate flag to be placed in his coffin.[206]

---

[205] Bill Donohue, "New York Times Earns Spot In '1619 Project,'" Catholic League for Religious and Civil Rights, September 8, 2020, https://www.catholicleague.org/new-york-times-earns-spot-in-1619-project/. For the best source on the *New York Times* and its relations with African Americans see Susan E. Tift and Alex S. Jones, *The Trust: The Private and Powerful Family Behind the New York Times* (Boston: Little Brown, 1999).

[206] Michael Goodwin, "Why New York Times Praises 'Cancel Culture' but Skips Over Its Own Racist History," *New York Post*, July 11, 2020, https://nypost.com/2020/07/11/ny-times-praises-cancel-culture-but-skips-its-own-racist-history-goodwin/.

In 1910, the *Times* covered a heavyweight boxing match between the black heavyweight champion Jack Johnson and Jim Jeffries, the former heavyweight champion who came out of retirement for the fight. Jeffries, dubbed the "Great White Hope," was expected to win. He lost.

Many sports writers had put their money on Johnson, but not before issuing a dire warning. "If the black man wins, thousands and thousands of his ignorant brothers will misinterpret his victory as justifying claims to much more than mere physical equality with their white neighbors."[207] In other words, blacks might interpret his victory as justifying unwarranted political, economic, and social rights.

In the 1920s, after a race riot in Washington, a *New York Times* editorial waxed nostalgic, speaking about conditions prior to the Great War (World War I). "The majority of Negroes in Washington before the Great War were well behaved," it said, adding that in those happy days, "most of them admitted the superiority of the white race and troubles between the two races were unheard of."[208]

Also in the 1920s, Adolph Ochs invited a black singer, Roland Hayes, to lunch at the *New York Times*. Adolph's father, Julius, was so angry that he left the building. According to Iphigene, Adolph's daughter, Julius believed that although "we love the Negroes," it is important to "keep them in their place; they are fine as long as they stay in the kitchen."[209]

While many similar examples of this kind could be cited, it must be said that most Americans are mature enough not to blame

[207] Ibid.
[208] Ibid.
[209] Ibid.

the *New York Times* today for the racist beliefs and practices of its ancestry. But perhaps they are too generous in their assessment. According to the 1619 Project, they must be. After all, the *New York Times*'s initiative is not so forgiving.

### Liberal Racism Is Holding Blacks Back

In his eye-opening book *Liberal Racism*, Jim Sleeper recounts that a black congressman, Major Owens, told him in 1981 that "liberals are sometimes the worst racists." At first Sleeper wasn't sure he was right. But eventually he concluded that "liberal racism patronizes nonwhites by expecting (and getting) less of them than they are fully capable of achieving."[210] That is exactly what the ruling class thinks about blacks today. It has given up on them.

Long before CRT became the rage, Sleeper saw where liberal racism was headed. "Liberals who assume that one's skin color is one's destiny tend to deceive themselves and others about that belief. They behave remarkably like 'quality white folks' in the old South, who condescended sweetly to blacks while projecting contempt for inferiors onto poor whites and onto blacks who chose not to be charmed by elite gestures of affection."[211]

What drives this thinking? Once again, Shelby Steele blames white guilt. "White guilt, as a phenomenon, I think is very much underrated in American life. I think it's extremely powerful."[212] It is used by groups such as Black Lives Matter as a power tool—it allows them to trade on their victimization, convincing the ruling

---

[210] Jim Sleeper, *Liberal Racism* (New York: Viking, 1997), 3–4.

[211] Ibid., 5.

[212] Joseph (Jake) Klein, "Shelby Steele and Eli Steele on *What Killed Michael Brown?*," Capital Research Center, January 15, 2021, https://capitalresearch.org/article/shelby-steele-and-eli-steele-on -what-killed-michael-brown/.

class to give them millions of dollars. The grievance industry, he says, has been enormously successful.

Black Lives Matter is particularly good at cultivating the idea that racism is responsible for every black problem. John McWhorter does not exaggerate when he says that "being called a racist is all but equivalent to being called a pedophile." White liberals, he says, have "fallen under the impression that pious, unempirical virtue signaling about race is a form of moral enlightenment and political activism."[213] Virtue signaling has been perfected by the ruling class. It is a clear expression of its need to put its members on a moral mantel where they can judge everyone else. They are very good at that.

This thoroughly contrived sense of guilt—which does nothing to improve race relations—has actually led well-educated white liberals to confess their racial sins in public.

Kirsten Powers is a CNN contributor who suffers terribly from the pangs of white guilt. Her prescription for racial justice is for every white person—they are all racists—to repent. She prepares the way for us all with her litany of sorrow: "I'll start: I repent for my lack of action. I repent for my lack of urgency. I repent for not listening more. I repent for lacking humility."[214]

Powers is not alone in professing her sins in public. In Bethesda, Maryland, a huge crowd of white people, mostly young women, fell to their knees in an outdoor ceremony to purge themselves of

213  Tunku Varadarajan, "Book Review: 'Woke Racism' by John Mc-Whorter," *Wall Street Journal*, October 18, 2021, https://www.wsj.com/articles/book-review-woke-racism-by-john-mcwhorter-11634596283?mod=opinion_reviews_pos1.

214  Bill Donohue, "White Liberals Need to Pony Up," Catholic League for Religious and Civil Rights, June 8, 2020, https://www.catholicleague.org/white-liberals-need-to-pony-up/.

their "white privileged" status. At that 2020 event, on command they said in unison such things as, "I will use my voice in the most uplifting way possible" and will "do everything in my power to educate my community."[215]

This is the pinnacle of virtue signaling, the zenith of white guilt. But no one should take these rich white people seriously unless they have some skin in the game. Bethesda is a wealthy community: perhaps they could begin by reimbursing the black business owners whose businesses were destroyed by the urban terrorists who inflicted so much damage on so many American cities in 2020—all in the name of protesting racism.

Instead of engaging in meaningless gestures such as mass confessions, white ruling-class liberals could condemn those who despicably accuse hard-working black students of "acting white."

In the 1980s, black anthropologists John Ogbu and Signithia Fordham found that black students underperform in school partly because those who do well are teased for being "white." McWhorter relates how these students are mocked: "Why are you working so hard on that school stuff? You think you're white?" After he wrote a book that touched on this subject, McWhorter said he was "surprised by thousands of letters, including over a hundred from black people explicitly attesting that they were teased as 'white' for liking school, as well as concerned teachers wondering what to do about black kids coming to them and telling them about this happening."[216]

Liberal racism has spawned a cult of victimhood. Black journalist William Raspberry wrote a column for the *Washington Post* about

---

[215]  Ibid.

[216]  John McWhorter, "'Acting White' Remains a Barrier for Black Education," *Reason*, October 8, 2014, https://reason.com /2014/10/08/acting-white-remains-a-barrier-for-black/.

what he called "victimism." He said this idea has had a devastating effect on young blacks. "There is no more crippling an attitude than to think of yourself primarily as a victim."[217] He said it feeds the mentality that people do not have what it takes to look after themselves. This is what psychologists call "inefficacy," or a sense that personal responsibility—one of the vital virtues—doesn't matter.

Harold A. Black sees a direct connection between the ruling-class view of blacks during the time of slavery and its view of them today. "Those who insist on according blacks victim status are guilty of perpetuating the caricatures of black people made famous by Stepin Fetchit, *Little Black Sambo*, *Uncle Tom's Cabin* and *Mandingo*. Given that caricatures are parodies, victimhood is little more than an excuse."[218]

McWhorter believes that this "cult of victimology" has gripped "the entire black community." He berates his black brothers and sisters for buying into this dangerous idea. He says they "suffer from a classic post-colonial inferiority complex. Like insecure people everywhere, they are driven by a private sense of personal inadequacy to seeing imaginary obstacles to their success supposedly planted by others."[219] CRT has only amplified this perspective. As Steele notes, "This is a dark thing because if you define yourself as a victim, you define yourself as impotent."[220]

---

[217] William A. Donohue, *The New Freedom: Individualism and Collectivism in the Social Lives of Americans* (New Brunswick, NJ: Transaction Press, 1990), p. 160.

[218] Harold A. Black, "'The Cult of Victimhood,'" in Robert Woodson, ed., *Red, White, and Black*, 61.

[219] John McWhorter, "What's Holding Blacks Back?," *City Journal*, Winter 2001, https://www.city-journal.org/html/what's-holding-blacks-back-12025.html

[220] Emma Colton, "Shelby Steele Argues 'Racial Victimization' Pushed by Democrats Has Stripped Black People of Power,"

No demographic group can be expected to succeed if it is convinced of its inability to do so. The ruling class is responsible for fostering the cult of victimhood among African Americans. The virtue of perseverance will not flourish where victimhood reigns. The ruling class must start treating black people as equals.

*Washington Examiner*, October 13, 2020, https://www.washington examiner.com/news/shelby-steele-argues-racial-victimization-pushed-by-democrats-has-stripped-black-people-of-their-power.

4

# Devaluing the Family

## The Indispensable Role of the Nuclear Family

Sociologist Carle Zimmerman identified three family structures found throughout history. The strongest family type is the trustee: its strength is due to the absence of individual rights; indeed, there is almost no concept of the individual at all. The intermediate structure is the domestic family: the rights of individuals are acknowledged by the state, which begins to weaken the control of the family. The third stage is the atomistic type: individualism reaches its maximum, and it is done at the expense of the authority wielded by the family.

Zimmerman said that these family types have cycled through history; we are clearly in the third stage of the cycle in contemporary America. Indeed, the state has virtually destroyed the power of the family. Radical individualism reigns supreme, and a breakdown in the social order is everywhere apparent.

In the name of individual rights, the state has declared that every type of domestic communal arrangement is a "family," whether it is the traditional nuclear family, a one-parent family, or some novel variant. This is the ultimate triumph of moral relativism: if every social arrangement is a family, then none are; the word has no distinct meaning. It is also sociologically illiterate. When it comes to the well-being of the individual, and of society as a whole, there is no substitute for the nuclear family.

The situation is so perverse that a 1980 White House Conference on the Family had to be renamed the White House Conference on Families because the participants couldn't agree on a definition of the family. Ten years later, *Newsweek* ran a special issue titled "The American Family Does Not Exist."[221] It cited the diversity of families, noting the increasing number of out-of-wedlock births, the divorce rate, fathers and mothers working with no one attending to their children after school, homes in which unrelated adults were raising children, gay and lesbian parents, and the increase in teenagers raising children by themselves. Not surprisingly, half of all Americans told pollsters that the American family was worse off than it was ten years earlier.

If success and happiness are engendered by bourgeois virtues—especially the vital virtues—and if the nuclear family is the best vehicle for transmitting those virtues, then the precarious state of the family is alarming, to say the least. Despite what "progressive" social scientists and activists say, not all family forms are equal. The blue-chip family is the nuclear family. Sociologists Brigitte and Peter Berger have written that "the family, and specifically the bourgeois family, is the necessary social context for the emergence of autonomous individuals who are the empirical foundation of political democracy."[222] In other words, there is no historical example of a free society associated with families other than the bourgeois, or nuclear, family.

---

[221] Jerrold K. Footlick and Elizabeth Leonard, "What Happened to the Family?" in "The American Family Does Not Exist," special edition, *Newsweek* (Winter 1990/ Spring 1991): 14.

[222] Brigitte Berger and Peter Berger, *The War on the Family: Capturing the Middle Ground* (Garden City, NY: Anchor Press, 1984), 151.

Sociologist David Popenoe is one of the most prominent scholars who has studied the family. He notes that the 1950s witnessed "a major social achievement" as "greater family stability was achieved in the fifties than at probably any other time in history, with high marriage rates, low unwed birthrates, and low death rates not yet offset by sky-high divorce rates."[223] That all changed in the 1960s with the advent of the birth control pill, the relaxation of social norms, and the increase in the size of the welfare state. As the penalties for aberrant behavior and sexual experimentation waned, their prevalence soared.

Popenoe focused his work particularly on the role of the father. He argues that "the main reason children are being hurt is because fathers are more and more absent from their children's lives, with children being raised instead by lone mothers." The sociological data, he observes, makes it clear that "two married, biological parents are the gold standard for childrearing." Notice that he mentions "biological parents," maintaining that "sex differences are biologically programmed in various ways."[224] As for families headed by the mother, he said, "no other group is so poor, and none stays poor longer, and the children of mother-headed families are the very poorest of the poor."[225]

A report released in 2010 by the National Center for Health Statistics, *Family Structure and Children's Health in the United States*, examined seven family structures: "nuclear," "single-parent," "blended," "unmarried biological or adoptive families," "cohabiting," "extended,"

---

[223] Carol Iannone, "Family Matters: A Conversation with David Popenoe," *Academic Questions* (Winter 2008–2009): 20–21.

[224] Ibid.

[225] David Popenoe, *Life without Father: Compelling New Evidence That Fatherhood and Marriage Are Indispensable for the Good of Children and Society* (New York: Free Press, 1996), 54–55.

and "other" (i.e., one or more children living with related or unrelated adults who are not biological or adoptive parents). Which family form did the report say works best? The nuclear family, which is to say, "two parents who are married to one another and are each biological or adoptive parents to all children in the family."[226]

In 2020, a Social Capital Project report on the family cited research that found that "children raised by married parents do better on a wide array of outcomes. They have stronger relationships with their parents, particularly with their fathers. They are also much less likely to experience physical, emotional or sexual abuse. They have better health, exhibit less aggression, are less likely to engage in delinquent behavior, have greater educational achievement, and earn more as adults. They are also far less likely to live in poverty."[227] It also found that Asians have the strongest families, with the fewest children living with one parent, as well as the lowest divorce rate. African Americans, on average, have the weakest families.[228]

Data from 2020 show that a record 40.5 percent of babies in the United States were born to unmarried mothers. In 1940, the figure was 3.8 percent.[229] That is an amazing, and arresting,

---

[226] Ian Rowe, "Measure What Matters," in Petrilli and Finn, *How to Educate an American*, 209.

[227] *The Demise of the Happy Two-Parent Home*, Social Capital Project report no. 3-20, July 2020, p. 3, https://www.jec.senate.gov/public/_cache/files/84d5b05b-1a58-4b3f-8c8d-2f94cfe4bb59/3-20-the-demise-of-the-happy-two-parent-home.pdf.

[228] Ibid., 13–14.

[229] Terence P. Jeffrey, "CDC: 40.5% of U.S. Babies Born in 2020 Had Unmarried Mothers; 42.0% Born on Medicaid," CNSNews.com, February 14, 2022, https://cnsnews.com/article/national/terence-p-jeffrey/cdc-405-us-babies-born-2020-had-unmarried-mothers-420-born.

statistic. In 1940, America had just come out of the Depression and was on the verge of World War II—but the family was most intact across every racial and ethnic group. Eighty years later, in a time of relative peace and prosperity, the family was falling apart.

In 2020, 28.4 percent of white babies were born out of wedlock; but only 12.2 percent of Asian babies were born to unmarried parents. However, 52.8 percent of Hispanic babies and an astonishing 70.4 percent of blacks were born out of wedlock.[230] It is difficult even for two married parents to instill the vital virtues; it is many times more difficult for one parent, no matter how responsible, to do so; it is particularly hard on mothers—and it is usually a mother who manages a single-parent family.

There are some commentators, such as *New York Times* columnist David Brooks, who contend that the nuclear family "was a mistake."[231] He doesn't contend that traditional families are not the best family structures for raising children. But he hastens to say that the 1950s, when the nuclear family thrived, were atypical and that, in any event, we need to adjust to new family forms, such as "extended families." He overrates alternatives, however, refusing to acknowledge what social scientists have studiously demonstrated, and indeed, he fails to recognize what has been known at least since the work of anthropologist George Murdock in the 1940s: the nuclear family is a cultural universal. It is not related to any specific time period in any specific countries.

The nuclear family matters because it is a critical source of morality for the young. Psychologist Angela Duckworth says that

---

[230] Michelle Osterman et al., "Births: Final Data for 2020," *National Vital Statistics Report* 70, no. 17 (February 7, 2022): 5.

[231] David Brooks, "The Nuclear Family Was a Mistake," *Atlantic*, February 10, 2020, https://www.theatlantic.com/magazine/archive/2020/03/the-nuclear-family-was-a-mistake/605536/.

"morality trumps all other aspects of character in importance."[232] This is universally true, as a study from Indonesia demonstrates. Ruslin Badu's research at Gorontalo State University concluded that children will become good citizens if they are surrounded by a friendly and stable environment. What makes the work of this professor particularly significant is her emphasis on the role that religion plays in forming character. "Being close to God" is a key element in character formation. Parents can succeed in character formation, Badu says, if they stress personal responsibility—and not just to others. "Carrying out duties towards oneself, community, environment (natural, social, and cultural aspects), country and The One Almighty God" count a great deal.[233]

The *Catechism of the Catholic Church* does not base its teachings on social science. But Church teachings on the family are fully consistent with modern research. "The family is the *original cell of social life*" (italics in the original). It is the place where "from childhood, one can learn moral values, begin to honor God, and make good use of freedom" (CCC 2207, italics in the original). The moral values that matter most are the vital virtues. "The home is well-suited for *education in the virtues*. This requires an apprenticeship in self-denial, sound judgment, and self-mastery—the preconditions of all true freedom" (CCC 2223, italics in the original). Furthermore, civil society has a duty "to acknowledge the true nature of marriage and the family, to protect and foster them, to safeguard public morality, and promote domestic prosperity" (CCC 2210, quoting GS 52 § 2).

---

[232] Angela Duckworth, *Grit: The Power of Passion and Perseverance* (New York: Scribner, 2016), p. 273.

[233] Ruslin Badu, "Family as the Key to Children Character Building," *International Journal of Innovative Science and Research Technology* 4, no. 5 (May 2019): 337–340.

The practice of religion in a family has a positive effect on the children and on society. Studies have shown that the children of parents who regularly attend religious services exhibit better self-control, social skills, and approaches to learning.[234] Harvard social scientist Robert D. Putnam has done much work on this subject, and his findings are clear. "Houses of worship build and sustain more social capital—and social capital of more varied forms—than any other type of institution in America."[235] Taken together, intact families and houses of worship make for a powerful source for the advancement of the vital virtues.

Given the overwhelming evidence showing the indispensability of the nuclear family, the nauseating efforts of the ruling class to destroy it seem diabolical. For example, Black Lives Matter explicitly says that its goal is to destroy the nuclear family—and they are no obscure, fringe group: they have been generously funded by such institutional ruling-class titans as Apple, Microsoft, Amazon, and George Soros.[236]

It is true that when the official statement posted on the Black Lives Matter website condemned "the Western-prescribed nuclear family structure," it got so much blowback that it was eventually scrubbed.[237] But it had already done enormous damage: for example, a school district in Evanston, Illinois, prescribed a curriculum

---

[234] Bill Donohue, *The Catholic Advantage: Why Health, Happiness, and Heaven Await the Faithful* (New York: Image, 2015), 26.

[235] Ibid., 27–28.

[236] Horowitz, *I Can't Breathe*, 5.

[237] Jon Miltimore, "Black Lives Matter's Goal to 'Disrupt' the Nuclear Family Fits a Marxist Aim That Goes Back a Century and a Half," Fee, September 24, 2020, https://fee.org/articles/black-lives-matter-s-goal-to-disrupt-the-nuclear-family-fits-a-marxist-aim-that-goes-back-a-century-and-a-half.

for pre-K through eighth grade heralding the subversion of the nuclear family, and students were taught that it is "important to disrupt the Western nuclear family dynamics as the best/proper way to have a family."[238]

## The Ruling Class Devalues the Family

In 2010, Angelo Codevilla offered a harsh assessment of the ruling class's treatment of the family. "The ruling class is keener to reform the American people's family and spiritual lives than their economic and civic ones," he said. "It believes that the Christian family (and the Orthodox Jewish one too) is rooted in and perpetuates the ignorance commonly called religion, divisive social prejudices, and repressive gender roles," thus making it "the greatest barrier to human progress."[239] The condition since then has only grown worse.

Codevilla focused on the role that government elites have played in undermining the family. "Since marriage is the family's fertile seed," he said, "government at all levels, along with 'mainstream' academics and media, have waged war on it. They legislate, regulate, and exhort in support not of 'the family'—meaning married parents raising children—but rather of 'families,' meaning mostly households based on something other than marriage."[240] He also condemns the arrogance of government bureaucrats who think they know better than parents how to raise children and, importantly, what to teach in school.

---

238 Alana Mastrangelo, "Illinois Teacher Sues School District over CRT Training: 'Pitting Racial Groups against Each Other,'" Breitbart, June 30, 2021, https://www.breitbart.com/politics/2021/06/30/illinois-teacher-sues-school-district-over-crt-training-pitting-racial-groups-against-each-other/.
239 Codevilla, "America's Ruling Class."
240 Ibid.

Proof that Codevilla was right is not hard to find. Recall that in an earlier chapter I mentioned that the Smithsonian's National Museum of African American History and Culture lashed out at "the nuclear family," equating it with "whiteness." Thus do cultural elites sneer at blacks who aspire to live in traditional nuclear families. What would they recommend? Broken families headed by one parent? This crazy notion is indeed entertained by those who work in higher education.

In 2021, two professors conducted a webinar sponsored by the National Council on Family Relations that offered advice on how to dismantle the nuclear family. Bethany Letiecq and Antoinette Landor maintained that "family privilege" was analogous to "white privilege" and therefore it had to go. They disparaged "traditional or 'standard' nuclear families," holding that they conferred undeserved benefits on their members.[241] Though they claimed to have an interest in the welfare of blacks, they not only failed to recommend ways in which the formation and maintenance of the two-parent family could be encouraged in the black community, but they spoke with utter disdain about it. White racists could not have done a better job of inhibiting blacks from succeeding than these sages.

The belittling of marriage and the family—and of basic biology—is widely evident in the Biden administration. For example, Biden bureaucrats invented a new right in 2021: the right of "socially infertile" single persons and homosexual couples to receive fertility treatments. They maintained that these people cannot "reproduce

[241] Bethany Letiecq and Antoinette Landor, "Toward Dismantling Family Privilege and White Supremacy in Family Science," May 11, 2021, National Council on Family Relations, https://www.ncfr.org/events/ncfr-webinars/toward-dismantling-family-privilege-and-white-supremacy-family-science.

via sexual intercourse due to *social factors*" (my italics). And what might these "social factors" be? A "lack of a partner or because of a person's sexual orientation."[242] In other words, they argue that it is not biology that stops single people and homosexual couples from having babies—it is society. This bizarre form of reasoning is what happens when nature and God are thrown to the wind.

The elites show such little value for traditional moral values, as Codevilla argued, that they are not above celebrating even such perverse acts as infanticide and bestiality. The average American would not approve of the intentional killing of innocent children who are born with a disability. Nor would they approve of humans having sex with animals. But those who awarded the prestigious Berggruen Prize for Philosophy and Culture to Peter Singer in 2021 are more open-minded. Singer, who teaches at Princeton University, was the recipient of the $1 million prize, the world's most coveted philosophy award. As Wesley J. Smith observed, Singer defends selective infanticide and bestiality. More telling, "he was brought from Australia to Princeton to assume the world's most prestigious chair in bioethics *because of these views*, not in spite of them (his italics)."[243] Such is the mindset of the ruling class.

Some members of the ruling class are not so much determined to upend the nuclear family as they are to devalue it. They do not practice what they preach, however, and they direct their sermonizing only toward unfortunate others. W. Bradford Wilcox and

242  Bill Donohue, "Biden's War on Religious Liberty Spikes," Catholic League for Religious and Civil Rights, November 18, 2021, https://www.catholicleague.org/bidens-war-on-religious-liberty-spikes/.

243  Wesley J. Smith, "Infanticide Advocate Peter Singer Awarded $1 Million Philosophy Prize," *Epoch Times*, November 21, 2021, theepochtimes.com/infanticide-advocate-peter-singer-awarded-1-million-philosophy-prize_4116547.html.

Wendy Wang, in their research "The Marriage Divide: How and Why Working-Class Families Are More Fragile Today," found that elites live a split existence, valuing traditional marriage and the family in their own lives, while hawking more "progressive" values for everyone else.

In fact, their study led them to conclude that "when it comes to the structure and quality of marriage and family life, America is increasingly divided by class. Middle- and upper-class Americans are more likely to benefit from strong and stable marriages; by comparison, working-class and poor Americans increasingly face more fragile families."[244] One of the reasons for this disparity, they found, was the greater effects of the 1960s counterculture on those at the bottom of the income scale.

The sexual revolution and the decline in traditional moral norms hit the working class and the poor much harder than the affluent. Indeed, wealthier Americans "have rejected the most permissive dimensions of the counterculture for themselves and their children, even as poor and working-class Americans have adapted a more permissive orientation toward matters such as divorce and premarital sex."[245]

Hollywood has played a major role in challenging traditional moral norms. It promotes a libertine culture in which everything goes, showing nothing but contempt for moderation. Yet as Wilcox and Wang observed, "the actual neighborhood that stands at the center of historic Hollywood, the Whitley Heights neighborhood

---

[244] W. Bradford Wilcox and Wendy Wang, *The Marriage Divide: How and Why Working-Class Families Are More Fragile Today* (research brief, Opportunity America, AEI, and Brookings Working Class Group, 2017), 7, https://www.aei.org/wp-content/uploads/2017/09/The-Marriage-Divide.pdf.

[245] Ibid., 10.

just between the Hollywood sign and the Dolby Theatre where the Oscars are held, has virtually no single parents amid the hundreds of families who make their home there." Indeed, they are "dominated by two-parent families."[246]

The significance of this finding was not lost on these social scientists. "When it comes to family, California elites tend to 'talk left' but 'live right.'" Their duplicity is striking. "The vast majority of Californians (85 percent) with a college or graduate degree agree that family diversity, 'where kids grow up in different kinds of families today,' should be publicly celebrated, compared to 69 percent of Californians without a college education."[247] Yet most of the better educated, and more affluent, Californians live as if an intact family is important.

Timothy P. Carney learned that this phenomenon is not limited to Hollywood Californians. "The norm of marriage is dead not among our elites but among our working class. It's not the Wesleyan alumnae living in Greenwich, Connecticut, who are killing the norm as much as it is working-class men and women living in Middle America."[248] The members of the ruling class who live in the wealthiest neighborhoods, places like Chevy Chase, Maryland, Carney says, are not likely to live "amoral lives," despite their progressive views. "They tend to live family-focused lives tied up with community. And their communities are made up of people just like them."[249]

---

[246] W. Bradford Wilcox and Wendy Wang, "Happily Ever After—Even in Hollywood," *National Review*, January 17, 2020, https://www.nationalreview.com/2020/01/marriage-story-movie-real-life-brighter-than-hollywood-version/#slide-1.

[247] Ibid.

[248] Timothy P. Carney, *Alienated America: Why Some Places Thrive While Others Collapse* (New York: Harper, 2019), 69.

[249] Ibid., 240.

In the late 1990s, David Horowitz invited me to attend a huge conference in California—with actors, producers, and directors—that addressed various controversial issues that were brewing in Hollywood. After listening to many of the speakers, I got a chance to say a few words. After I spoke, the man sitting next to me on the platform turned to me and said, "They're going to have to get extra security to escort you out of here."

What did I say that was so controversial? I told the crowd that they were a bunch of phonies. One after another, I said, you came to the microphone to tell us that you don't allow your children to watch the television shows that you make. No, you said, your children watch Nickelodeon. I asked, "So whose children are your shows good for?" They knew exactly what I meant. There was dead silence.

One brave woman who was a writer for a major TV drama approached me afterward to say that she agreed with what I said. She also made a confession, of sorts. She said a female character in the show she wrote for, *Beverly Hills, 90210*, had long been portrayed as living a modest lifestyle but was now going to be portrayed as living a promiscuous one. Why was the writer doing this? She said she was following the orders of the producer, Aaron Spelling. To top things off, it was his own real-life daughter, Tori Spelling, who was now going to live a trashy lifestyle. Apparently in Hollywood, if it sells, it's okay even to exploit your daughter.

The cultural elites who live in Hollywood know very well the kinds of messages their sex-laden fare delivers. But they don't care whom it hurts, as long as there's good money in it. But when it comes to their families' real lives, that's a different story. Just as Wilcox and Wang discovered, they "talk left" but "live right."

It's not just the Hollywood elites who are at war with the nuclear family: those in the ruling class—particularly those who dominate the leading foundations—think the same way. Nothing seems to upset them more than to see minorities embrace the bourgeois family and the vital virtues it bequeaths to children. The elites really do appear to look down on minorities, as if they believe that they do not have what it takes to succeed. Or perhaps they suffer from a disturbed form of paternalism and believe that minority success must be achieved only according to their plan.

Take, for example, the Ford Foundation. It spent decades manipulating Mexicans, trying to convince them they should think of themselves as victims and forgo the traditional avenues of upward mobility. Quite frankly, the Ford Foundation practically invented the category "Hispanics."[250]

Before the 1970s, American citizens who hailed from Latin America did not think of themselves as Hispanic. Previously, their identity was grounded in their nationality. Indeed, it was the tenacity of Mexican Americans in refusing to see themselves as anything other than Mexicans that bothered the sages at the Ford Foundation.

What really seemed to have gotten the goat of the elites was the Mexican reliance on personal responsibility as a lever to upward mobility. The elites reasoned that it would be better if Mexicans adopted the politics of victimhood—perhaps so they could be aggregated with other immigrants into a political block. To do this, they reasoned, they had to craft norms and structures that facilitated the creation of a larger identity, one associated with victimhood. Thus the dawn of the Hispanic American. The manipulative policies of the ruling class don't get much more dramatic, and cynical, than that.

---

[250] Mike Gonzalez, "The Invention of Hispanics," *Claremont Review of Books* (Fall 2019).

## The Sexual Revolution's Effects on the Family

The sexual revolution may have started in the 1960s, but its effects are still with us. The wholesale questioning of traditional norms and the values governing marriage, family, and sexuality have wreaked havoc with the social order, generating psychological and physical trauma for generations of Americans. Those who laid the groundwork for this cultural crisis were intellectuals in Europe and the United States, most of whom worked at elite institutions.

In the first part of the nineteenth century, Robert Owen in England and Charles Fourier in France led the intellectual war on the family and traditional moral values. Owen hated both marriage and the family and saw in both of them the same kind of "irrational" elements that affected religion. He even went so far as to declare marriage "evil."[251] Fourier celebrated debauchery, praising orgies for their liberating effects. He spoke of "amorous freedom," a condition in which the liberated woman could have "as many lovers as she chooses."[252] Both Fourier and Owen equated liberty with libertinism, holding that true freedom could be realized only by throwing off the yoke of traditional moral norms and values. Sexual expression should have no bounds, they reasoned, thus setting the table for the likes of Karl Marx and Friedrich Engels, who also declared war on the family.

Marx made plain his interest in abolishing the family. He assailed the "bourgeois family," saying it was a generator of "domestic slavery." He predicted that "the bourgeois family will vanish as a

---

[251] Colin Wilson, "Sexuality and Capitalism," *International Socialist Review* 94, https://isreview.org/issue/94/sexuality-and-capitalism/.

[252] Ibid.

matter of course" and pledged to assist in its demise.[253] Unlike many modern elites, however, he did live by the code he promoted: he neglected his own family and refused to work to provide for his wife and children. He even wound up impregnating his maid and then failed to acknowledge his paternity.

On his deathbed, Engels told one of Marx's daughters, Elena, that the boy he had raised, Freddy Demuth, was fathered by her father; Engels had to protect Marx's reputation. This devastated Elena so much that three years later, she committed suicide. Marx's other daughter, Laura, also killed herself. But Engels himself was a rogue:[254] he had a penchant for mistresses and condemned monogamy.

In the twentieth century, it was the "cultural Marxists" associated with the Frankfurt School who led the attack on marriage and the family. It was elites such as Wilhelm Reich and Herbert Marcuse who were the intellectual godfathers of American radicals in the 1960s.

Reich learned a lot from his hero, Sigmund Freud, blending Freud's ideas with those of Marx. Reich envisioned a world in which individuals would enjoy sexual liberation and society would experience a social revolution. He certainly succeeded in liberating his own life: he became a sex maniac (he loved prostitutes) and a member of the Communist Party—and was widely known as the "Father of the Sexual Revolution."[255]

---

[253] Paul Kengor, *Takedown: From Communists to Progressives, How the Left Has Sabotaged Family and Marriage* (Washington, D.C.: WND Books, 2015), 21.

[254] Ralph Buultjens, "What Marx Did," *New York Times*, March 14, 1983, https://www.nytimes.com/1983/03/14/opinion/what-marx-hid.html.

[255] Kengor, *Takedown*, 107–114.

Marcuse drew financial support from the ruling class. The Rockefeller Foundation partially underwrote his book *Eros and Civilization*, which became sort of a New Left bible in the 1960s. Married three times, he never stopped railing against our Judeo-Christian heritage, which he considered to be the source of "sexual repression." What he proposed was a society in which the family was abolished and "polymorphous perverse" sexuality reigned. He even sought to undo "the taboo on perversions," a condition that, in many ways, he succeeded in realizing.[256]

According to Scott Yenor, feminism and sexual liberation define our sexual constitution. The independent woman, freed from the shackles of domestic life and sexual taboos, is what feminist intellectuals have long sought to achieve. Sexual liberationists want no boundaries, sexual or otherwise, for males and females of all ages. We are now at the point, Yenor says, of achieving what he calls the *rolling revolution*, "the seemingly unfinishable series of changes in marriage and family life toward the realization of individual autonomy." Getting to this stage, he says, means "stripping away the Christian or traditional aspects of marriage."[257] We have seen this played out in a declining marriage rate, an increase in cohabitation, declining birth rates, gay marriage, and gender fluidity. It is not a pretty sight.

In the 1960s, Betty Friedan was the archetype feminist who derided the housewife's dependence on her husband; she contended that women were living vicariously through their husbands and children. Women have become so used to their infantile, passive existence that it resembles a "comfortable concentration camp."

---

[256] Ibid., 115–126.

[257] Scott Yenor, *The Recovery of Family Life: Exposing the Limits of Modern Ideologies* (Waco, TX: Baylor University Press, 2020), 9.

The feminine mystique, she maintained, "has succeeded in burying millions of American women alive."[258]

Friedan, of course, lived an affluent lifestyle. She was bored and unhappy. But she was not representative of most women. Millions of suburban women found happiness in suburbia, and millions of working-class and poor women wanted to live in her "concentration camp." Interestingly, Friedan was not a sexual liberationist, at least not to the extent that other feminists were.

Shulamith Firestone maintained that "pregnancy is barbaric," arguing that it was unfair that "half the human race must bear and rear the children." She said that children should enjoy sexual relations and that the taboo against incest should be abolished.[259] Vivian Gornick contended that to be a housewife was to be in "an illegitimate profession."[260] Linda Gordon insisted that "the nuclear family must be destroyed,"[261] and Gloria Steinem pleaded that we have to "abolish and reform the institution of marriage."[262] Kate Millett, a bisexual who was inspired by Marcuse, said her goal was the creation of "a permissive single standard of sexual freedom" where all "traditional sexual inhibitions and taboos" would be abolished.[263] She spent many years in an asylum.

These are just some of the people who fostered the sexual revolution. The depth of their despair over the human condition is at the heart of their problem. They reject nature and God, believing

---

[258] Donohue, *The New Freedom*, 56.

[259] Ibid., 60.

[260] Thomas S. Garlinghouse, "The Left's War on the Family," *American Thinker*, February 24, 2004, https://www.americanthinker.com/articles/2004/02/the_lefts_war_on_the_family.html.

[261] Ibid.

[262] Ibid.

[263] Kengor, *Takedown*, 133.

that they can create a world that has no reference point in history. The world they envision is a fantasy, not reality. Nevertheless, their assault on marriage and the family has contributed to wrecking the real-world prospects of the American dream for millions of Americans, especially those with the hardest struggle to attain it.

It would be unfair to blame the ruling class entirely for creating the sexual revolution. They certainly had nothing to do with the baby boomers' coming of age in the 1960s and their proclivity to engage in sexual experimentation. The introduction of the birth control pill also clearly played a major role in triggering the sexual revolution. Similarly, times of economic prosperity are often associated with a relaxation of traditional norms and values, and again the ruling class did not orchestrate that effect.

There are, however, at least four contributing factors to the sexual revolution that were midwifed by the ruling class: the changes in schools and education; the role of social policy; the effects of the media and Hollywood; and the crafting of new norms and values that changed the way we think about sexuality.

In every instance, traditional sexual ethics such as those that Catholicism teaches — indeed, the very merit of sexual reticence — were thrown overboard. Instead of teaching students the virtue of chastity, teachers told students there were no moral absolutes, enticing them to experiment. Instead of devising social policies that put a premium on safeguarding the best interests of the family, administrators dismissed such concerns as irrelevant. Instead of offering good role models for young people, the media and Hollywood produced materials that were morally debased. Instead of promoting traditional moral values, the ruling class declared war on them.

Most kids who grew up in the 1950s went to public schools in which the day began with a prayer, usually a selection from

the Old Testament. It was a cultural statement, as much as a religious statement, setting a tone of reverence. Few complained or
felt oppressed. But in the 1960s, the Supreme Court prohibited
school prayer. While the abolition of prayer in the schools did
not play a direct role in the promotion of the sexual revolution,
it opened the door to "values clarification," a mode of instruction that was at a minimum skeptical of traditional norms and
values, if not overtly hostile to them. The elites in education and
cultural institutions supported, and in many cases created, this
new moral landscape. It was certainly felicitous to championing
new ideas about sexuality.

Changes in social policy, fostered by elites in government, had
a deleterious effect on the family, especially the black family. This
will be addressed in detail in the next chapter. But it is worth
mentioning here that government welfare programs allowed poor
women with children to enhance their economic condition if the
father abandoned his family. The ruling class devised these schemes
and institutionalized them. The results were catastrophic.

The media and the entertainment industry, run by elites,
started offering programs in the 1960s that became more and
more graphic and coarse. So guarded was the culture of traditional
norms and values that prior to the sixties, no one ever saw the
bedroom in TV sitcoms — not even on the most popular show,
*The Honeymooners*, starring Jackie Gleason. If a woman celebrity
showed too much cleavage on a TV game show, journalists wrote
critically about her the next day. Young men and women were
shown dating and dancing, but they never engaged in anything
beyond kissing.

Hollywood did not follow the culture into depravity. It led it.
The big studios decided to "push the envelope," as they like to
say, to see how far they could go in making movies with off-color

language and sexualized scripts. The corporate sponsors didn't object any more than TV advertisers to newly relaxed norms. The elites were not responding to changes demanded by average Americans. Rather, they were imposing their liberal vision of sexuality on them. The consequences are everywhere apparent.

Hollywood played a role in crafting new norms and values that changed the way we think about sexuality, but its role was actually secondary to the elites who tapped into the male libido prior to the sexual revolution of the 1960s.

## Playboy

Hugh Hefner, and the elites who supported *Playboy*, opened the door to Hollywood to exploit the new moral order. Hefner founded his magazine in 1953 and quickly succeeded in making it an important cultural marker. He rebelled against his conservative Protestant parents, whom he called "very repressed," and set out to rectify the problem of repression by targeting Christianity.

Hefner cleverly sought the support of the ruling class. He wanted to break new ground by creating a girly magazine that featured distinguished public figures, including those in government, law, education, finance, the arts, the media, music, entertainment, acting, sports, and the corporate world. By involving celebrities, business tycoons, and the literati, he made *Playboy* respectable. Indeed, his magazine was considered mainstream, having won the plaudits of elites in every quarter of the country.

As important as the magazine was, the importance of the Playboy Mansion to many All-Star members of the ruling class is often overlooked. It became the hottest ticket in town, the venue of high-scale parties that lasted until dawn. In 2000, presidential candidate Al Gore held a fundraising event there. Bill Cosby and Roman Polanski were regulars, as were others who would later be tainted by their own sexual scandals. After Hefner died in 2017 at age ninety-one, stories of what went on at his Mansion materialized, and a docuseries that aired on A&E in 2022 changed the way even some of his fans thought about him. The distribution of hard-core drugs was commonplace, as were orgies. Perhaps most startling was the behavior of Hefner himself.

Hefner was an equal-opportunity predator who had sex with men, women, and dogs.[264] He was accused of raping multiple women.[265] If he got a gal pregnant, he arranged for an abortion.[266] Like many men who are addicted to pornography and live a promiscuous lifestyle, Hefner was unable to get aroused without partaking in new experiences, some of which were sickening, to put it mildly. He provided girlfriends with drugs to endure constant orgies that he watched voyeuristically. Further, he engaged in acts of bestiality and forced others to do the same.[267]As revealing as all of this is, it was the advent of "The Playboy Philosophy" series in the December 1962 issue of the magazine that gave the sexual revolution its

[264] Libby Torres, "From Bestiality to Unprotected Group Sex, Here are the Biggest Bombshell Allegations Made about Hugh Hefner and Playboy Magazine on 'Secrets of Playboy,'" *Insider*, April 6, 2022, https://www.insider.com/secrets-of-playboy-hugh-hefner-girlfriends-allegations-sexual-misconduct-2022-4.

[265] Taryn Ryder, "Hugh Hefner Accused of Raping Multiple Women in 'Secrets of Playboy,'" Yahoo! Entertainment, March 21, 2022, yahoo.com/entertainment/hugh-hefner-rape-allegations-secrets-of-playboy-011034682.html.

[266] Lanford Beard, "Hugh Hefner's Ex Karissa Shannon Says She Aborted the 84-Year-Old's Baby, Claims Sex Was 'Like Rape,'" *People*, March 28, 2022.

[267] Asia Grace, "Playboy Bunnies Blast 'Predator' Hugh Hefner's Bestiality, 'Cult' Sex and Worse," *New York Post*, January 24, 2022, https://nypost.com/2022/01/24/playboy-bunnies-blast-predator-hugh-hefner-in-new-doc/.

ideological springboard; Hefner offered several installments of his work. It reached millions of men, an audience no cultural Marxist or feminist liberator could ever command.

"The Playboy Philosophy" was adamant in contending that the individual is "the all important element in society."[268] Those who hold to our Judeo-Christian heritage, of course, regard this as nonsense: it is the family, not the individual, that is "the all important element in society." But it would have been inconceivable for a man like Hefner to believe this. Indeed, he harbored a particular antipathy for Catholicism.

Similarly, "The Playboy Philosophy" maintained that "the primary goal of society should be individual happiness." Predictably, happiness was defined as pleasure. "Happiness and pleasure are mental and physical states of being and society should emphasize the positive aspects of both."[269] It would be hard to make a more anti-Christian philosophical statement.

Hefner rightly saw in Christianity, and especially in Catholicism, a sexual ethic that is the antithesis of "The Playboy Philosophy." He claimed that there was not enough separation of church and state and that freedom *from* religion was being neglected.[270] As usual, he was given to overstating reality. "Church-state legislation has made common criminals of us all." His proof? He cites Alfred Kinsey, the pervert who allowed children to be sexually abused for the sake of his research.[271]

Self-discipline, perseverance, and personal responsibility are virtues that Hefner disparaged. All require a measure of restraint,

[268] Hugh Hefner, "The Playboy Philosophy," *Playboy*, December 1962, 36.
[269] Ibid., 173.
[270] Ibid., 4.
[271] Ibid., 197.

a property "The Playboy Philosophy" abhorred. In fact, it treated selflessness as a sin. "We oppose the tendency to meaningless self-lessness in our present society"; he singled out self-sacrifice and self-denial for condemnation.[272]

Hefner's obsession with satisfying individual primordial appetites did not allow him to appreciate that selflessness is a virtue, one that is best expressed when we sacrifice for the good of others. Mother Teresa exemplified this virtue.

But for Hefner, nothing was more important than happiness defined as pleasure. Therefore, selflessness was seen as irrational. A more adolescent understanding of human nature would be hard to find. It seems never to have occurred to Hefner that it is the vital virtues (which his parents' Protestantism espoused) that are, in fact, the ultimate keys to happiness.

## Abortion

Aborting children remains the most vicious assault on the family in the world today. It would not have happened without the support of the ruling class.

Not surprisingly, the pro-abortion movement has a long and ugly record of anti-Catholicism. It is important to remember that the push to legalize abortion was based on a stew of lies about Catholicism, led by Dr. Bernard Nathanson and Lawrence Lader.[273] It is also important to remember that initially the Catholic Church stood practically alone in opposing *Roe v. Wade*. (Many evangelical Protestants initially supported this infamous decision, though within a decade many became pro-life.)

---

[272] Ibid., 173.
[273] Nathanson ultimately converted to Catholicism and became resolutely pro-life.

To understand the role of the ruling class in promoting the pro-abortion cause, it is important to understand the critical role played by the Rockefeller Foundation.[274]

On July 18, 1969, President Richard Nixon established an agency to examine the effects of population growth on America's future. He commissioned John D. Rockefeller III to chair the agency. On March 27, 1972, less than a year before *Roe v. Wade*, *The Rockefeller Commission Report on Population Growth and the American Future* was published and delivered to the president and the Congress.

The plea to legalize abortion was a foregone conclusion: the commission had been stacked with pro-abortion members. In fact, in 1967, Rockefeller himself was the recipient of Planned Parenthood's highest honor when he accepted the Margaret Sanger Award, an award named after the white-supremacist founder of Planned Parenthood.

John D. Rockefeller III followed in the footsteps of John D. Rockefeller Jr. ("Junior," as he was called), who had provided funding for eugenics. Some of his money was given to the Germans; some of it was put to use by the Nazis.

The commission's staff was headed by Dr. Charles F. Westoff. He was a member of the American Eugenics Society and Planned Parenthood's National Advisory Council. One of the special consultants was Daniel Callahan, a pro-abortion eugenicist who tried desperately to convince Catholics of the merits of abortion and eugenics. When he failed, he quit the Church.

In chapter 11, "Human Reproduction," the final report did not hide the pro-abortion sentiments of the commission. "A few

---

[274] Bill Donohue, "How the Rockefellers Teed Up *Roe v. Wade*," Catholic League for Religious and Civil Rights, January 19, 2022, https://www.catholicleague.org/how-the-rockefellers-teed-up-roe-v-wade/.

of the members of the Commission are opposed to abortion." It also said "the majority" were not.[275]

The number one population problem in the early 1970s, according to the commission, was "unwanted births." While only "one percent of first births were never wanted," the commission found that "nearly two-thirds of all sixth or higher order births" were unwanted.[276] Even if that is plausible, it seems hardly to constitute a crisis. How many women, even back then, had six or more kids?

It has been historically true that those who can least afford to have children tend to have the most, and vice versa. So it is not surprising that the commission would find that "unwanted fertility is highest among those whose levels of education and income are lowest." This, they argued, leads to psychological, economic, and health problems. "The Commission believes that all Americans, regardless of age, marital status, or income, should be enabled to avoid unwanted births."[277]

The solution to this alleged problem was to (a) allow minors to receive contraception information and services, (b) eliminate restrictions on sterilization, and (c) liberalize state abortion laws. Regarding the last, much of the reasoning was based on faulty information.

The commission maintained that there were between "200,000 and 1,200,000 illegal abortions per year in the United States." In fact, the Centers for Disease Control and Prevention estimated that in 1972, "130,000 women obtained illegal or self-induced procedures, 39 of whom died." In other words, the commission's estimates were dramatically inflated.[278]

275 Ibid.
276 Ibid.
277 Ibid.
278 Ibid.

The commission was also spectacularly wrong when it contended that "with the increasing availability of contraceptives and improvement in contraceptive technology, the need for abortion will diminish." We now know that following *Roe v. Wade*, both contraceptive use *and* abortion rates increased dramatically.

If there is one demographic segment of the population that the Rockefeller Commission believed was a problem, it was African Americans. The report said that "if blacks could have the number of children they want and no more, their fertility and that of the majority white population would be very similar." The goal could not have been plainer: get blacks to stop reproducing. What they need, the report said, was greater access to "the various means of fertility control."[279]

Some of the commission's members cited Planned Parenthood's efforts to meet this goal. The same thinking is evident today. It was reported in 2020 that Planned Parenthood locates 86 percent of its abortion clinics in or near minority neighborhoods. Though blacks are 13 percent of the population, they account for one-third of all abortions.[280]

This is so typical of the ruling class. Their solution to "the urban problem" has always been to rely on abortion. And the Rockefellers epitomized this WASP solution. Through its report, the commission had teed up the controversy that led to *Roe v. Wade* and helped the Supreme Court justices rationalize their abortion-on-demand ruling.

Thanks be to God, *Roe* was overturned in 2022. But the ruling class is still carrying the torch for abortionists—and it is no longer the Rockefellers who are the number-one funder of pro-abortion

[279] Ibid.
[280] Ibid.

activism in the world. That honor goes to one of the newer genera-
tion of billionaires, Warren Buffett. Between 2000 and 2018, the
Susan Thompson Buffett Foundation gave $4 billion to left-wing
groups that lobby for abortion policies. Of that money, the Buffett
Foundation paid $675 million to the Planned Parenthood Foun-
dation of America, the largest abortion provider in the nation.
It also shelled out more than $112 million to the Guttmacher
Institute, the think tank founded as the research arm of Planned
Parenthood. The National Abortion Federation picked up $239
million to continue its pro-abortion activism.[281]

## Same-Sex "Marriage"

"How does it affect you if two men get married?" I have been asked
that question by some defenders of same-sex "marriage." To be fair,
I am not directly affected. I am also not directly affected if a man
beats his wife. The relevant question is not whether I am directly
affected, but whether society has an interest in preserving the
institution of marriage as it has always been understood.

We have a number of special social and political accommodations for seniors and veterans. Our society makes them because we
believe that seniors and veterans are special people, in particular
ways. If we were to make those same special accommodations available to everyone, they would no longer be special, which would
undercut their raison d'être. So this is the important question:
Is marriage between one man and one woman special, and if so,
should it be treated specially in law? The sociological evidence is

---

[281] Hayden Ludwig, "Warren Buffett's Foundation Has Poured $4
Billion into Pro-Abortion Advocacy," Capital Research Center,
March 11, 2020, https://capitalresearch.org/article/warren
-buffetts-foundation-has-poured-4-billion-into-pro-abortion
-advocacy/.

unambiguous: the best way to rear children is in a home with a mother and a father. Therefore, for the benefit of children, who are special, the social arrangement that serves them best should be prioritized, and all rival social arrangements—single-parent families, cohabitation, gay "marriage," polygamy—should be discouraged.

Political philosophy aside, we must not forget that the idea of two men "marrying" is so bizarre that as recently as the presidency of Barack Obama, few supported it. Obama himself was opposed to it (before the political tide turned). His predecessor George W. Bush also opposed it, though, like many other WASP members of the ruling class, he was uncomfortably opposed.

In February 2004, about a week before President Bush announced his endorsement of a constitutional amendment that would restrict marriage to one man and one woman, a small group of Catholics met with him in the Roosevelt Room in the White House. I was part of this group. When Bush spoke about education and foreign policy, he showed great intensity. But when the subject turned to gay "marriage" and the need to secure a constitutional amendment defending marriage as a union between two people of the opposite sex, he seemed uneasy, though he reluctantly got on board. It was no surprise to learn that, in 2013, the *Boston Globe* reported that he offered to officiate at a lesbian wedding (though it seems he never did and claimed not to recall making the offer).[282]

Prior to the Supreme Court decision legalizing gay "marriage" in 2015, Americans were split on the issue, with a small majority favoring it. But the ruling class wasn't split, and they were not

---

[282] Stephanie Condon, "George W. Bush Reportedly Offered to Officiate Same-Sex Wedding," May 26, 2015, CBS News, https://www.cbsnews.com/news/george-w-bush-reportedly-offered-to-officiate-same-sex-wedding/.

content to be simply cheerleaders. In fact, 379 corporations and employer organizations implored the Supreme Court to recognize marriage between people of the same sex, filing friend-of-the-court briefs in support of it. The list included Coca-Cola, Goldman Sachs, Google, Morgan Stanley, the New England Patriots, the San Francisco Giants, and the Tampa Bay Rays.[283] Today, there is no bigger advocate of gay marriage than Big Tech. Silicon Valley companies are awash with money, and they lavishly fund gay-rights causes. Moreover, anyone who crosses them pays a price. In 2014, Mozilla CEO Brendan Eich, a Catholic, was pressured to resign after he opposed gay "marriage."[284]

However, without the backing of the ruling class, gay "marriage" may never have become a legal reality. In 2008, the elites on the California Supreme Court ruled that same-sex "marriage" was legal; but this didn't sit too well with most Californians. A few months later, they passed Proposition 8, the ballot initiative that limited marriage to a union between a man and a woman. California, of course, is home to some of the most liberal Americans in the nation, so if they rejected gay "marriage," it was doubtful that any state would approve it.

No racial or ethnic group was more supportive of Proposition 8 than African Americans: 70 percent backed traditional marriage. A majority of Hispanics voted the same way. Religious organizations that campaigned to get this measure passed included the Church

---

[283] Alexander C. Kaufman, "Here Are the 379 Companies Urging the Supreme Court to Support Same-Sex Marriage," *HuffPost*, March 5, 2015, huffpost.com/entry/marriage-equality-amicus_n_6808260.

[284] Peter Rex, "Silicon Valley's Secret Christians," *Wall Street Journal*, February 10, 2022, https://www.wsj.com/articles/silicon-valleys-closet-christians-religious-diversity-startup-culture-tech-faith-google-church-secular-beliefs-atheist-catholic-culture-war-11644510973.

of Jesus Christ of Latter-day Saints, the Union of Orthodox Jewish Congregations of America, and the Eastern Orthodox Church. Catholics and Protestants, especially Evangelicals, also worked to see Proposition 8 succeed.[285] All of these groups were met with vitriol and violence; no group was targeted more viciously than the Mormons.[286]

Within no time, the ruling class struck back, working tirelessly to overturn the express will of the people. The same elites who had for years screamed "Power to the people" from the bleachers got organized to silence the voice of the people.

Many people were surprised to learn that Theodore B. Olson and David Boies had teamed up to have Proposition 8 overturned by the courts. They shouldn't have been. Yes, it is true that these elite lawyers squared off against each other in *Bush v. Gore*, the Supreme Court decision that resolved the 2000 presidential election. It is also true, however, that the interests of the ruling class often allow for joint ventures on issues of mutual importance. In January 2010, when Olson and Boies were granted a hearing in a San Francisco court, the voters in thirty states had already taken up the issue of gay "marriage" and had voted 30–0 to affirm legal marriage as a union between a man and a woman.[287] When court challenges were filed in many states, however, matters

---

[285] "2008 California Proposition 8," Wikipedia, last edited December 29, 2022, https://en.wikipedia.org/wiki/2008_California_Proposition_8.

[286] Bill Donohue, "Gay Marriage Loses; Protests Turn Ugly," Catholic League for Religious and Civil Rights, December 24, 2008, https://www.catholicleague.org/gay-marriage-loses-protests-turn-ugly/.

[287] Bill Donohue, "Prop 8 Challenge Puts Religion on Trial," Catholic League for Religious and Civil Rights, January 21, 2010, https://www.catholicleague.org/prop-8-challenge-puts-religion-on-trial/.

quickly changed. Judges are typically members of the elite. By the time the U.S. Supreme Court voted to create same-sex "marriage" in 2015, judges in thirty-seven states had already voted to legalize it; in only three states was legalization accomplished by popular vote.[288] Thus, it was the ruling class that upended marriage. Their votes, amplified and camouflaged by the legal system, count more.

The case put forth by Olson and Boies was sociologically illiterate. During oral arguments, Olson maintained that marriage is a "personal right," not "society's right."[289] This is disingenuous. Societies do not have rights—only individuals do. But societies have interests, chief among them being the stability of marriage. Boies also argued that marriage, traditionally defined, has no rational basis but is based on "the residue of centuries of figurative and literal gay bashing."[290] This is absurd. Not only is the claim unsupported by historical evidence, it is self-evident that marriage, as originally conceived, is the recognition of the natural mating of men and women. Moreover, marriage exists for the purpose of supporting a stable and institutionalized setting for the creation of the family, the most important cell in society, and the rearing of children. The universality of this institution has absolutely nothing

---

[288] Bill Chappell, "Supreme Court Declares Same-Sex Marriage Legal in All 50 States," NPR, June 26, 2015, https://www.npr.org/sections/thetwo-way/2015/06/26/417717613/supreme-court-rules-all-states-must-allow-same-sex-marriages.

[289] Scott Shane, "Good Friends, Same Party but Legal Opponents," *New York Times*, March 26, 2013, https://www.nytimes.com/2013/03/27/us/politics/conservative-lawyers-are-opponents-on-gay-marriage.html.

[290] Edwin Meese III, "Stacking the Deck against Proposition 8," Heritage Foundation, January 11, 2010, https://www.heritage.org/marriage-and-family/commentary/stacking-the-deck-against-proposition-8.

to do with homosexuals, let alone "bashing" them; it has only to do with providing for the best interests of society.

## Transgenderism

Among many members of the ruling class, gender ideology is all the rage. But the fact is that we cannot change our sex. We are either male or female. We cannot change our chromosomes. While there is a very small minority of men who carry an XXY chromosome (anomalies in nature exist), most of us are either XX (female) or XY (male); there is no such thing as an XYZ person. We may imagine being a member of the opposite sex—or fantasize about flapping our arms and flying away—but nature is a stubborn fact of life. Nevertheless, we live in a time when the elites in almost all of our societal institutions have intimidated many into thinking that it is a mark of intolerance to criticize a male who says he has "transitioned" to a female and wants to compete against females in girls' and women's sports—or shower with them.

Ask the baby boomers, the post–World War II generation, if they had even heard of someone who considered himself to be someone of the opposite sex, and the answer will almost always be no. In fact, even today, only 0.1 percent of that generation say they are transgender. Yet 2.1 percent of those who belong to Generation Z, those born between 1997 and 2012, say they are transgender persons.[291] In other words, in recent times, there appears to have been a 2,000 percent explosion in transgender persons.

This sudden increase has nothing to do with nature: it has everything to do with culture. A concerted effort by LGBT activists,

[291] Jeffrey M. Jones, "LGBT Identification in U.S. Ticks Up to 7.1%," February 17, 2022, https://news.gallup.com/poll/389792/lgbt-identification-ticks-up.aspx.

lawyers, educators, and therapists to promote the notion that it is normal to question one's sex status and seek to change it has produced a profound effect on society.

This is not a medical reality; it is a fanatical ideology. Transgenderism, like all other "isms," is an idea, and in this case, it is laden with horrendous physical and psychological consequences. No wonder Pope Francis calls gender ideology "dangerous," even "demonic."[292]

Erica Anderson, a transgender person, is one of the few clinical transgender psychologists specializing in transgender youth. Noting the huge increase in young boys and girls attempting to switch their sex, Anderson says, "A fair number of kids are getting into it because it's trendy. I think in our haste to be supportive, we missed that element." In fact, the situation is so serious that Anderson has had enough of it. "This has gone too far. It's going to get worse. I don't want any part of it."[293]

According to Kara Dansky, a feminist writer who authored a book on this subject, the goal of the transgender movement is "the abolition of sex." By that she means the abolition of "the *legal, social* and *physical* category of human beings" (her italics).[294] While this is detrimental to everyone, it is women and girls who are hurt the most by it. The subtitle of her book is apt: "How the

---

[292] Bill Donohue, "Pope Brands Transgender Theory as Evil," Catholic League for Religious and Civil Rights, February 13, 2020, www.catholicleague.org/pope-brands-transgender-theory-as-evil/.

[293] Jenny Jarvie, "At the Center of a Culture War: Transgender Erica Anderson Has Helped Hundreds of Teens Transition. But She's Come to Believe That 'It's Gone too Far,'" *Los Angeles Times*, April 17, 2022, A1.

[294] Kara Dansky, *The Abolition of Sex: How the 'Transgender' Agenda Harms Women and Girls* (New York: Bombardier Books, 2021), 11.

'Transgender' Agenda Harms Women and Girls." She makes a compelling case that this movement has not only abridged the rights of women but has allowed men to be the big winners (e.g., they can compete in women's sports).

The ruling class is behind all of this. "What is actually happening is that there is a massively well-funded industry that is pushing this agenda." Dansky adds that it is strongly supported by the administration of President Biden, which has "literally told every federal agency that sex doesn't matter. That all that matters is gender identity."[295]

Transgenderism wouldn't succeed as an ideology if it weren't for the ruling-class efforts to rebel against reality and adopt the postmodern idea that truth is a fiction. That is the heart of the real danger. It used to be that only crackpot professors believed that there is no such thing as truth; but now elites in virtually every sector of society either believe it or are too weak to speak out against it. Hence, the triumph of transgenderism, complete with its new vocabulary and pronoun usage.

The ruling class has been devaluing the family for decades, but in recent times, the pace has quickened. The nurturing of self-discipline, perseverance, and personal responsibility depends on a cultural climate that supports fathers and mothers. Today it is manifestly apparent that the elites are intent on undercutting it. Their cause is not that of social harmony or families or children but only of radical individualism. And in a society without strong families, the weakest—always our children—suffer the most.

---

[295] Virginia Allen, "What You Need to Know About Real Agenda of 'Transgender' Movement," *Daily Signal*, January 5, 2022, https://www.dailysignal.com/2022/01/05/what-you-need-to-know-about-real-agenda-of-transgender-movement/.

# 5

# Giving Up on the Poor

## The Folly of Good Intentions

The greatest enemies of the poor are often, sadly, those who claim to champion their cause. This may sound counterintuitive, but it is a historical reality. From Karl Marx, whose ideas have impoverished millions in many parts of the world, to the latest welfare schemes in the West, the poor have suffered mightily at the hands of their purported allies.

Some of those who have taken up the cause of the poor have been well-meaning; others have used the poor to further a political objective. As to the former, it must be said that good intentions are not enough. God gave us each a head and a heart. Results matter. When programs that are designed to help the poor are based not on an accurate understanding of human nature but rather on mere empathy, they are bound to fail—at which point they inevitably devolve into opportunities for self-congratulatory grandstanding.

On May 25, 1986, six and a half million Americans participated in an event called Hands Across America to raise money for the homeless and the hungry. The nation's most celebrated pop stars sang "We Are the World." They were joined, across the country, by everyone from President Ronald Reagan and the White House staff to fans at baseball games, who formed human chains. Mickey

Mouse and Donald Duck at Disneyland chimed in. The media heralded it as a smashing success.

More than five months later, the poor had not received a dime. Most of the more than $32 million that was raised went to pay for the event's expenses, and no one knows how much actually reached the target population.[296] But a good time was had by all—all who were already well-off, that is—and at least the backslapping didn't harm the poor, as many anti-poverty campaigns have.

The only historically proven way to help the able-bodied poor is to imbue in them the vital virtues. All the money in the world cannot do for the poor what the poor must, in the end, learn to do for themselves. Yes, they can be provided with increased opportunity. But America is already brimming with opportunity for those who know how to take advantage of it. Without personal responsibility, self-discipline, and perseverance, economic mobility cannot be achieved.

"There is an expiry date on blaming your parents for steering you in the wrong direction; the moment you are old enough to take the wheel, responsibility lies with you": This astute statement attributed to J. K. Rowling is shared by Dr. Alan Zimmerman, an expert business consultant who has studied what makes for winners and losers on the job. He cites personal responsibility as the key to success: "Losers believe they are entitled to success, wealth, happiness, and position. So they wait for it to fall into their laps rather than doing something (or lots of things) to make it happen." On the other hand, Zimmerman says, winners "seldom think

---

[296] Dennis McDougal, "Hands Across America, May 25, 1986: Hands' Bills Paid in Full, but Homeless Still Waiting," *Los Angeles Times*, November 2, 1986, https://www.latimes.com/archives/la-xpm-1986-11-02-ca-15476-story.html.

about being entitled to the prizes in life ... without working for them. Winners adhere to Winston Churchill's admonition, that '*the price of greatness is responsibility*.' "[297]

As we shall see, the problem with most welfare programs is that they induce a sense of entitlement in the recipients, and that makes it *more* difficult for them to improve their condition. Paternalism deprives the poor of the virtues that make for success, so it should be condemned, not commended.

## The Poor Laws

Throughout most of the history of Western civilization, the vast majority of people were poor. The only help they could access was from family members and local churches. Eventually, local government agencies provided food, clothing, and shelter. But there was no overarching government effort to deal with the indigent until England instituted the Speenhamland system (named after the town of origin) in 1795. The Speenhamland system offered an allowance to those whose earnings were insufficient to pay for basic goods, thereby setting the table for more expansive initiatives.

In 1834, the New Poor Law, as it was called, created a formal legal right to public assistance, locking in the most contentious aspects of Speenhamland. It made a distinction between the "impotent"—those who could not provide for themselves, such as the sick, the aged, and widows with small children—and the able-bodied. The "impotent" were not expected to support themselves. But the able-bodied were expected to move on and eventually wean themselves off public relief.

[297] Alan Zimmerman, "Personal Responsibility Is Vital to Success," Dr. Alan Zimmerman, CSP, https://www.drzimmerman.com/tuesdaytip/personal-responsibility-success.

Alexis de Tocqueville, the brilliant Frenchman known for his classic book *Democracy in America*, assessed these programs in England and was distraught by what he found. He compared the conditions of the poor in Portugal and Spain with those in England in 1833. There were many more poor persons in Portugal and Spain than in England, but what was noticeably absent in those countries was a sizable pauper population. Working-class poor were not regarded as paupers, only those who were able-bodied and were nonetheless on public relief (typically because of some behavioral problem). In England, there were many more persons whom we would call today the underclass—namely, thieves, prostitutes, beggars, and the like. The Portuguese and the Spaniards may have been an "ignorant and coarse population"—they were certainly "ill-fed [and] ill-clothed"—but unlike the English poor, they were not paupers.[298]

Rich countries such as England, Tocqueville reasoned, were ironically not likely to rid themselves of paupers. The sharp divide between the affluent and the poor in rich countries would encourage the development of relief programs for the less fortunate; however, because these programs did not take human nature into account, they were bound to fail. "Man, like all socially organised beings," the Frenchman said, "has a natural passion for idleness."[299]

We have seen in our own time much evidence proving Tocqueville's legendary prescience to be correct. It is one thing to have private charitable giving, such as that provided by churches. Private giving establishes a relationship between the donor class and recipients and is easily monitored by the donors. On the other

---

[298] Alexis de Tocqueville, "Memoir on Pauperism," translated in 1968 by Seymour Drescher (Great Britain: Civitas, 1997), 17.
[299] Ibid., 27.

hand, once the administrative state takes over and establishes "legal charity on a permanent basis," it "creates an idle and lazy class, living at the expense of the industrial and working class."[300] In fact, Tocqueville warned us that "any permanent, regular, administrative system whose aim will be to provide for the needs of the poor, will breed more miseries than it can cure, will deprave the population that it wants to help and comfort,"[301] resulting in serious economic harm to everyone. We didn't listen.

### America Helps the Poor

In the nineteenth and early twentieth centuries, the poor were assisted by a myriad of Catholic, Protestant, and Jewish agencies. Local government relief was available, but its delivery was spotty, and it mostly supplemented aid to private charitable agencies so that orphans, the sick, and the truly needy could be helped. These anti-poverty initiatives worked well because those who manned them believed in, and nourished, the much-maligned bourgeois virtues.

Howard Husock has studied this chapter in American history as thoroughly as anyone. It is his conclusion that such virtues as self-respect and self-control must operate in any initiatives that hope to combat poverty.[302] The application of those virtues pays great social dividends.

"Bourgeois norms—from education to temperance and so much more—are the ethical soil in which individuals and their communities can thrive," writes Husock.[303] He was not speaking about

---

[300] Ibid., 30.
[301] Ibid., 37.
[302] Husock, *Who Killed Civil Society?*, 4.
[303] Ibid., 142.

the culture of the affluent, which mostly observed these values; rather, he was speaking about the initiatives of nineteenth-century social reformers. They knew it was their job to impart these virtues to the dispossessed whom they served. They were not shy about doing so. Indeed, this was the very stuff that characterized the settlement houses.

The most famous of the settlement-house pioneers was Jane Addams, who founded Hull House in Chicago in 1889. She was a realist who relied on her religious upbringing to inform her approach to social work. She recruited well-educated young women to live with and to instruct the poor, thus providing them with exemplary role-model support. She never discounted, disparaged, or diminished the moral dimension of uplifting the poor. She knew full well that poverty of spirit had to be attended to as well as material poverty. It was her hope that the inculcation of bourgeois virtues would enable those at the bottom of the income scale to progress. She was not disappointed with her results. Neither were her benefactors.

Unfortunately, she was so successful that she attained almost rock-star status—she was enamored by the ruling class—which had a coarsening effect on Addams. After she received her inheritance, she abandoned her faith and became critical of the very virtues that had allowed so many of the poor she had served to progress. No longer a moral reformer, she lost her special charism and became comfortably secularist and cynical about her earlier beliefs.[304]

By contrast, Charles Loring Brace never renounced his Christian roots—and his ameliorative efforts among the marginalized did not falter. He worked with prisoners and delinquents in New York, giving selflessly of himself. According to Husock, "Brace was a missionary of bourgeois norms: education, thrift, marriage, and

[304] Ibid., 10, 55.

honesty."[305] In 1881, he recounted his record before an audience at Harvard, drawing on New York City police statistics to demonstrate his success in curbing vagrancy among girls and women. His flagship project, the Children's Aid Society, improved the lot of his young clients precisely because he respected the role that bourgeois values played in reforming their lives.[306]

Mary Ellen Richmond was another crusader for the poor. Raised poor herself, she put virtue into action in her approach to social work. "Richmond was resolute in her belief that the question of character and values should never be neglected," writes Husock, "even as efforts were made to improve social conditions."[307] She did as much as anyone to bring a moral foundation to social work. Unless the recipients of aid were capable of reforming themselves, she realized, self-improvement was unlikely to follow. When she died in 1927, it was already apparent that her faith-based approach to government-run programs for the needy was giving way to a more secular variant.

Dorothy Day secured her place in history by establishing the Catholic Worker Movement. Her yeoman's work with the poor, done in collaboration with Peter Maurin, a French immigrant and former Christian Brother, is a tribute to her deep Catholic faith. An enigma in her own time—even more so today—she defied all political labels. She was opposed to racial segregation, nuclear warfare, and the draft, while also opposing birth control, eugenics, abortion, and the welfare state.[308]

---

[305] Ibid., 28.

[306] Ibid., 8.

[307] Ibid., 69.

[308] Casey Cep, "Dorothy Day's Radical Faith," *New Yorker*, April 6, 2020, https://www.newyorker.com/magazine/2020/04/13/dorothy-days-radical-faith.

"When it comes to labor and politics," Day said, "I am inclined to be sympathetic to the left, but when it comes to the Catholic Church, then I am far to the right." As for population control, she declared that "birth control and abortion are genocide." She implored everyone to "make room for children, don't do away with them."[309] She was just as insistent on not shunning the "non-deserving poor." Prostitutes, drug addicts, and alcoholics should be tended to the same way as others in need.

Day was relentless in promoting personal responsibility among the downtrodden. According to sociologist Harry Murray, her newspaper, the *Catholic Worker*, "always advocated personal responsibility rather than government programs as the way for Catholics to share their resources with poor neighbors."[310] This could be done, she understood, only by respecting the integrity of the family, the most important element in society. She wanted those who worked with the poor to have some skin in the game, to personally provide for the needy. "It is not the function of the state to enter into these realms," she said, allowing exceptions only for the victims of natural disasters.[311]

While she supported some aspects of the New Deal, Day was strongly opposed to Social Security. "We believe that social security legislation, now hailed as a great victory for the poor and the worker," she said, "is a great defeat for Christianity."[312] It was her Catholic belief in the necessity of being "my brother's keeper" that explained her thinking.

[309] "50 Quotes from the Revolutionary Activist," Everyday Power, April 16, 2021, https://everydaypower.com/dorothy-day-quotes/.

[310] Harry Murray, "Dorothy Day, Welfare Reform, and Personal Responsibility," *St. John's Law Review* 73, no. 3 (Summer 1999): 789.

[311] Ibid., 790.

[312] Ibid., 798.

In hindsight, we can see that poverty among the elderly has been significantly reduced since the introduction of Social Security. Perhaps because the system required contributions—or perhaps because of the long-delay before withdrawal—Day's fear that it might encourage dependency did not materialize for most recipients. Nonetheless, her concerns reflect her conviction that we cannot help those in the lower-income bracket without recognizing and giving top priority to the role that virtue plays in improving their condition.

Day's response to the poor was quintessentially Catholic. In fact, in 1986, six years after she died, the U.S. bishops issued a document, *Economic Justice for All*, that would have made her proud. "The responsibility for alleviating the plight of the poor falls upon all members of society. As individuals, all citizens have a duty to assist the poor through acts of charity and personal commitment," wrote the bishops. Furthermore, our job, the bishops said, was to "empower the poor," not patronize them.[313] The bishops also took aim at modern public policy makers, saying "Self-help efforts among the poor should be fostered by programs and policies in both the private and public sectors."[314]

President Franklin Delano Roosevelt launched his New Deal programs to address economic conditions caused by the Depression. When he was elected, one-third of the workforce was unemployed, and this, he said, necessitated public-works programs. In 1935, as part of the Social Security Act, Aid to Dependent Children (ADC) was the first federal welfare program established to help widows and orphans. Roosevelt was not unaware of the problems that such programs might

---

[313] United States Catholic Bishops, *Economic Justice for All: Pastoral Letter on Catholic Social Teaching and the U.S. Economy* (1986), no. 189, https://www.usccb.org/upload/economic_justice_for_all.pdf.

[314] Ibid., no. 200.

create. Indeed, he sounded very much like Tocqueville. "Continued dependence upon relief induces a spiritual and moral disintegration fundamentally destructive to the national fiber."[315]

Roosevelt was right to warn of the corrosive moral effects of welfare. Fortunately, his worst fears did not materialize in the 1930s because the bourgeois virtues were still widespread and a culture of dependency did not yet exist. Significantly, there was no "welfare rights movement" in the 1930s; the justification for assistance was still solely economic.

After that decade, however, the kind of problems envisioned by Tocqueville—and Roosevelt himself—began to emerge. As many of the New Deal programs expired after World War II, ADC continued to grow. In 1950, it was renamed Aid to Families with Dependent Children (AFDC) to include mothers. In the late 1940s and 1950s, poverty declined, but the AFDC welfare rolls continued to tick up. By today's standards, welfare's most notorious effects were still then in check. But that was about to change, and no segment of society was harder hit than African Americans.

## The Black Family

The black family in America got off to a profoundly rocky start. Slave masters had more use for men than women in the New World, which generated a skewed sex ratio. Historically, whenever this imbalance occurs, trouble ensues. For example, soldiers throughout history have been inclined toward self-destructive behaviors such as alcoholism, drug abuse, and gambling. Prostitution increases, often accompanied by sexual disease. Family life suffers.

Of course, even in America, there were so-called free blacks who were not enslaved. For them, the sex ratio was close to normal. Not

---

[315] Charen, *Do-Gooders*, 89.

only did their communities not experience the loose sexual relations that marked the black slave experience, but rather their family stability helped ensure their economic success. In fact, the first "black bourgeoisie," or middle class, are traceable to the families of free blacks.

How much damage slavery did to the black family is still a matter of debate. Daniel Patrick Moynihan, who was a New York State senator and a Harvard professor, is well known for chronicling the devastating effects of welfare on the black family. He also argued that the black family's instability is a consequence of slavery. "It was by destroying the Negro family under slavery that white America broke the will of the Negro people."[316]

But others disagree. Herbert Gutman is considered one of the most important scholars on the history of the black family. He maintains that deep family problems now present in the black community are a relatively recent phenomenon and that, right up until the Depression, most black families were intact. For example, his research found that in three-fourths of nineteenth-century slave families, children had the same father and mother.[317] As recently as the 1950s, most black families were intact.[318] It was reported in 2021, that as of 2019, 37 percent of black children were living in a home headed by their own two biological parents, and 48 percent were living in a home headed by a single parent.[319]

[316] Daniel Patrick Moynihan, *The Negro Family: The Case for National Action* (1965), 19.

[317] Robert Cherry, "Responses to Adversity," in Woodson, *Red, White, and Black*, 56.

[318] Bill Donohue, *Common Sense Catholicism: How to Resolve Our Cultural Crisis* (San Francisco: Ignatius Press, 2019), 150–151.

[319] W. Bradford Wilcox, Wendy Wang, and Ian Rowe, "Less Poverty, Less Prison, More College: What Two Parents Mean for Black and White Children," American Enterprise Institute, June 17, 2021, https://aei.org/research-products/report/

Economist Thomas Sowell, the most influential black social scientist in American history, examined conditions among slaves in the West Indies and in America. Slaves were treated much more harshly in the West Indies, but they had one advantage denied to American slaves: they were allowed to keep what they earned from their labor. American slaves were given food by their masters; but in the West Indies, slaves were given land and allowed to raise their own food. They could then sell it in the market and use the proceeds to buy other goods. "In short," Sowell writes, "West Indian Negroes had centuries of experience in taking care of themselves in a significant part of their lives, even under slavery, as well as experience with buying and selling."[320]

This fact cannot be overstated: blacks, like everyone else, succeed by practicing the vital virtues, but when the opportunity to practice these virtues is denied, the effects are traumatic and long-lasting.

If it is true that Moynihan overstated the negative impact of slavery on the black family, he was spot-on in his analysis of what happened to it under the welfare state. Indeed, he was the first social scientist to sound the alarm; he did so by analyzing statistics in his capacity as assistant secretary of labor. In 1965, he released the report *The Negro Family: The Case for National Action*, informally known as the "Moynihan Report."

What Moynihan saw in the 1960s was an increase in welfare at a time when unemployment rates were declining. Typically, welfare rolls paralleled economic conditions: when times were tough, the rolls expanded, and vice versa. But no longer. At that time, the

---

less-poverty-less-prison-more-college-what-two-parents-mean-for-black-and-white-children/.

[320] Thomas Sowell, *Ethnic America: A History* (New York: Basic Books, 1981), 218.

unemployment rate was 3.5 percent nationwide, and only slightly higher (4 percent) for blacks. And yet more women and children were applying for AFDC.

Moynihan's primary concern was the state of the family. He rightly understood that without intact families, economic progress was doomed. Although Moynihan was scurrilously attacked for criticizing women (who typically headed broken families), that was never his intent. In fact, he was championing their cause: he understood that the burden of broken families fell nearly as heavily on women as it did on children. He warned that it is folly to think that broken families—and they are broken if the father or the mother is absent—are without educational and economic consequences, regardless of the racial, ethnic, or religious affiliation of the families. It is simply a sociological fact of life that broken families produce broken people.

Moynihan was convinced that "the Negro family in the urban ghettos is crumbling," and this meant "the cycle of poverty and disadvantage will continue to repeat itself."[321] Even in his time, nearly a quarter of black women never married or were divorced or separated. The number of absent husbands was even higher, creating additional economic and social disadvantages. Out-of-wedlock births were also increasing. Today the percentage of black women who never marry or are divorced, separated, or widowed tops 70 percent (almost half never marry).[322]

One of the factors driving these conditions was increasing reliance on AFDC. It was indeed generating the dependency that

---

[321] Moynihan, *The Negro Family*, 2.

[322] RoseM, "Why Are There So Many Single Black Women?," May 29, 2018, https://medium.com/@AngelaRMCrane/why-are-there -so-many-single-black-women-c8462d500690.

Tocqueville feared it would. "The steady expansion of this welfare program, as of public assistance programs in general," Moynihan observed, "can be taken as a measure of the steady disintegration of the Negro family structure over the past generation in the United States."[323]

Moynihan's prescience was born out by the figures. Matters got worse, just as he predicted. By 1980, fifteen years after the "Moynihan Report" was issued, the out-of-wedlock birthrate among blacks had more than doubled; the majority of black children born had no father in the home. In New York City, two-thirds of black children had no dad in their lives. Teenage black girls were giving birth at a record pace. The fact that there was no stigma attached to the fathers or the mothers (which there had been prior to the 1960s) made it all too easy for them to live with the consequences of their decisions.

Government elites, following the advice of academic elites, created these programs. When the out-of-wedlock birthrate increased, they called for the distribution of birth control pills. When that didn't work, they asked for more pills. Then the elites pushed for an expansion of sex education in the schools. When that didn't work, they asked that it be more "progressive" and start in the early grades. By 1990, the situation was out of control. Kay S. Hymowitz looked at the data and was alarmed. "About 80 percent of those young girls who became mothers were single, and the vast majority would be poor," she said.[324] Family disorganization creates many problems, and one of the biggest is the erosion of the vital virtues.

---

[323] Moynihan, *The Negro Family*, 10.
[324] Kay S. Hymowitz, "The Black Family: 40 Years of Lies," *City Journal*, Summer 2005, https://www.city-journal.org/html/black-family-40-years-lies-12872.html.

There are many reasons for racial inequality today, but racism and discrimination—which are so often cited now—are no longer determinative. If they were, blacks from Nigeria and the West Indies should fare about as well as African Americans. But that is not the case. In fact, they do much better than African Americans on virtually every measure. The number-one reason for racial inequality today is simple: the absence of fathers in most black homes. The absence of fathers matters a lot for girls, but it matters even more for boys. Boys and young men need positive male role models—and certainly not the negative models provided by the media and Hollywood. Across all racial and ethnic lines, males are more inclined to self-destructive behaviors than females. When there is no father to check young boys, trouble predictably follows.

Furthermore, it is not sufficient simply to have any male figure around. Live-in boyfriends will not do. Our society is fixed on supposed inequality between females and males. But the limited attention that boys receive is a national disgrace.

Raj Chetty, who is one of the leading scholars on the subject of social mobility, has found that having fathers in the neighborhood—not just in the home—is one of the most important factors affecting income mobility. In neighborhoods where fathers are commonplace, a social structure is maintained that benefits everyone in the community, providing the kind of social support that is particularly important to boys.[325] This is obviously true for black boys as well. Research shows that black boys who grow up in

---

[325] Willis Krumholz, "Family Breakdown and America's Welfare System," Institute for Family Studies, October 7, 2019, https://ifstudies.org/blog/family-breakdown-and-americas-welfare-system.

neighborhoods where there is a high rate of fathers in the home do much better in terms of wages and employment.[326]

Young black men used to have male role models to emulate. From 1890 to 1950, black women married at a higher rate than white women, and as recently as 1950, just 9 percent of black families were fatherless.[327] Today the figure is an astonishing 70 percent.

Thomas Sowell understands the direct line between fatherless homes and poverty: "The most dramatic reduction in poverty among blacks occurred between 1940 and 1960, when the black poverty rate was cut almost in half, without any major government programs of the Great Society kind that began in the 1960s."[328] Kay James, the former president of the Heritage Foundation, understands the connection as well. Here is what she said about the corrosion of the black family in the 1960s: "The welfare state substitute[d] a check for a father, a social worker for a caring mother or grandmother, and a slew of civil rights organizations for the neighborhood church."[329]

Our elites still don't get it.

### The Ruling Class Punishes the Poor

The expansion of the welfare state and its deleterious effects on the black family did not occur by happenstance. Nor did it happen for economic reasons. It happened because the ruling class decided that it knew what was in the best interests of African Americans and that it was their job to do for them what they believed blacks were incapable of doing for themselves. It was a patronizing and

---

[326] Chris Wellisz, "Data Evangelist," *People in Economics* 55, no. 3 (September 2018): 37.

[327] Krumholz, "Family Breakdown."

[328] Sowell, *Ethnic America*, 118.

[329] Brush, *Racism and Anti-Racism*, 69.

condescending ruling-class mindset that drove them to act. (Worse, some elites cynically exploited blacks, deliberately using them to further their own political agenda.) They called themselves enlightened and their opponents racists; yet what they have done to blacks is astronomically worse than what white supremacists have ever done.

No city epitomized the disastrous effects of the welfare state more than New York City. Mayor John Lindsay wound up bankrupting the city and himself, so profligate was he with the taxpayers' money and his own.

Lindsay came from an affluent family, attended elite private schools, and graduated from Yale. Yet he had no common sense. A simple man, he listened to the advice of political and educational elites and made "reforms" that only exacerbated matters for the poor. He took over as mayor on January 1, 1966. Halfway through the year, welfare rolls were more than doubled. Then they almost doubled again. Five years after task-force recommendations were implemented, the welfare rolls had gone from 531,000 to 1,165,000. The dependency that Tocqueville had warned about had become rampant.

How did this happen? For one thing, the elites whom Lindsay turned to for advice did not all share the Catholic view that blacks and whites were equal: many saw them as unlikely to make it on their own. They argued that it was demeaning to ask blacks to prove their poverty as a condition of welfare (it would stigmatize them), and so they told the mayor that no means test should be required. All one had to do was apply for welfare, and, bingo, the request was granted.

Lindsay followed the advice of Mitchell Ginsberg, a social-work professor at Columbia University. He banned welfare caseworkers from checking to see if a woman on the dole was living with a man. Most importantly, he implored caseworkers to find everyone who was remotely eligible for public assistance and make sure they got welfare. This caused the welfare rolls to balloon. But by the time Lindsay was forced to reverse his policy, the damage had been done.

Ginsberg and Lindsay were following the advice of two other Columbia University professors, Frances Fox Piven and Richard Cloward, who were married to each other. They used blacks as a means to their end: the creation of a socialist state.

In "A Strategy to End Poverty," an influential article they wrote for the *Nation*—a left-wing magazine that supported Stalin—they informed Ginsberg, who, in turn, advised Lindsay, to find everyone who might qualify for welfare and get them on the rolls as fast as possible. In doing so, they intentionally politicized social workers, turning them into left-wing activists. The professors believed that this would bankrupt New York City, forcing the federal government to step in and adopt socialism. They did not succeed in creating socialism, though the policies they recommended did bankrupt the city in the 1970s. But they succeeded in devastating the black community.

These members of the ruling class were more interested in furthering their own political agenda than they were in furthering the well-being of the black poor. Piven and Cloward remain unapologetic about their work.

In 2010, they revisited the thesis of their 1966 piece in the *Nation*. They bragged about how they inspired "the minority poor and their allies" to "create sufficient disturbances to force reforms in the American income support programs." Their goal was not to help blacks become upwardly mobile. No, their goal was to create "a political crisis" that would "lead to legislation for a guaranteed annual income." The strategy they proposed was "a massive drive to recruit the poor *onto* the welfare rolls" (their italics).[330]

Piven and Cloward, like so many elites, believe that the exercise of the vital virtues—which has worked well for everyone else—will not work for blacks. "A federal program of income redistribution has become necessary to elevate the poor en masse from poverty," they said. They provided no evidence for this remarkable conclusion. "Compared to other groups, then, many of today's poor cannot secure a redistribution of income by organizing within the institution of private enterprise."[331]

This is exactly what George Fitzhugh said about blacks: they were not capable of competing in a market economy and should therefore remain slaves. Piven and Cloward were not as blunt, but their thinking was analogous. Unlike every other racial, ethnic, and religious group that experienced adversity and had to work their way up the economic ladder, blacks could not do it on their own. They could only escape poverty if other people's money were transferred to them through welfare programs. The racist overtones are palpable. It doesn't get more condescending than that.

It would be a mistake to think that Piven and Cloward were simply naïve and didn't understand how their policy recommendations would undermine the work ethic of poor blacks. They knew exactly what would happen; it was part of their plan:

> "Why work?" The danger thus arises that swelling numbers of the working poor will choose to go on relief.... For all practical purposes, the relief check becomes a surrogate for

---

[330] Frances Fox Piven and Richard Cloward, "The Weight of the Poor: A Strategy to End Poverty," *Nation*, March 8, 2010, www.thenation/article/archive/weight-poor-strategey-end-poverty/.

[331] Ibid.

the male breadwinner. The resulting family breakdown and loss of control over the young is usually signified by the spread of certain forms of disorder—for example, school failure, crime, and addiction.[332]

In other words, those who created the welfare state knew what to expect and didn't care. They wanted to disrupt the political order and crush the market economy; they wanted to use blacks as their political weapon. But the worst aspect of welfare dependency is the destruction of the vital virtues because it ensures that one generation after another will be stuck in neutral, unable to advance.

Myron Magnet has studied economic mobility as much as anyone. "American culture underwent a revolution in the 1960s, which transformed some of its most basic beliefs and values," he writes, the results of which "downplayed the personal responsibility, self-control and deferral of gratification that it takes to succeed." The vital virtues. Magnet further noted that a new culture arose that celebrated self-indulgence. It proved to be a disaster for blacks in particular.[333]

Charles Murray, the author of the most influential book on the welfare state, argues that between 1964 and 1967, public policy underwent a radical change. It was during this "reform period," as he calls it, that the ethic of entitlement was born. Social policy makers told black Americans the dominant new mantra of the ghetto: "It's not your fault."[334] Welfare had become a right, not the privilege it had previously been.

Gertrude Himmelfarb noted that the older "work ethic" meant "responsibility, prudence, self-discipline." These vital virtues,

---

[332] Ken Auletta, *The Underclass* (New York: Vintage Books, 1983), 43.
[333] Myron Magnet, *The Dream and the Nightmare: The Sixties' Legacy to the Underclass* (San Francisco: Encounter Books, 1993), 1.
[334] Donohue, *The New Freedom*, 158.

however, did not survive a "culture of dependency," largely because dependency demoralizes "not only the individual but also the family." The ethic of entitlement yields bad fruit. "As the state becomes the chief provider," she writes, "the father is reduced to the role of procreator, the husband becomes dispensable, and the family, often reduced to one parent, becomes impoverished and unstable."[335]

For the vital virtues to work, there must be a willingness and desire to progress. But if a sense of powerlessness has overwhelmed the individual, progress is no longer desired. Lawrence Mead, another social scientist who studied this issue, explains how this happens. "At the core of the culture of poverty is the conviction that one is not responsible for one's fate, what psychologists call inefficacy."[336]

None of this has anything to do with race. "You cannot take any people, of any color," says Sowell, "and exempt them from the requirements of civilization—including work, behavioral standards, personal responsibility and all the other basic things that the clever intelligentsia disdain—without ruinous consequences to them and to society at large."[337] In short, when there is no demand to exercise the vital virtues, our virtue muscles atrophy—and our future withers.

### Welfare Reforms and Their Undoing

By the mid-1990s, there was enough evidence to convince all but the most blind activists that welfare dependency had done

---

[335] Himmelfarb, *One Nation*, 71.
[336] Donohue, *The New Freedom*, 160.
[337] "Thomas Sowell Destroys the Welfare State in One Sentence," *The Federalist Papers*, September 22, 2017, https://thefederalist-papers.org/us/thomas-sowell-destroys-welfare-state-one-sentence.

incredible harm. Republicans had taken control of the Congress, and they labored hard to get President Bill Clinton to endorse welfare reforms. They advocated time limits for those on the dole, a work requirement for the able-bodied, and other reforms. Left-wing activists went into orbit, shrieking that the reforms would do irreparable harm. Even Moynihan was pessimistic. "In five years' time," he said, "you'll find appearing on your streets abandoned children—helpless, hostile, angry, awful—in numbers we have no idea."[338]

None of these doom-and-gloom predictions came true. In fact, the welfare reforms of 1996 led to a decline in poverty and the welfare rolls. Women found jobs, which engendered a sense of accomplishment. African American children did not wind up on the streets; rather, poverty among African America children hit an all-time low. With lifetime limits on eligibility for welfare, recipients were motivated to be virtuous, developing a sense of personal responsibility. Indeed, they persevered, much to the surprise (in some cases, it seemed, the chagrin) of those who said they couldn't make it on their own.

The evidence that the 1996 welfare legislation pushed by Republicans and signed by President Clinton worked is indisputable. Even so, those who were opposed to it would not change their tune. The welfare establishment is huge, involving lobbyists, government personnel, education elites, foundations, lawyers, and activists. They waited for the right moment to revisit their policies; they found it in the administration of President Joe Biden.

Midway through 2021, the huge amount of government spending prompted by the Covid-19 pandemic was said to have cut poverty nearly in half from prepandemic levels. The *New York Times*

---

[338] Charen, *Do-Gooders*, 113.

celebrated by noting that the Biden policies were set to "push the share of Americans in poverty to the lowest level on record." It also said this came "at extraordinary cost, with annual spending on major programs projected to rise fourfold to more than $1 trillion."[339]

There is little doubt that the Biden response helped people like Kathryn Goodwin, a single mother of five in Saint Charles, Missouri. She managed a trailer park before the pandemic eliminated her job. She said she would be homeless without the government money she received. But she knows plenty of others who ripped off the system, people who bought big TVs or drugs, like her former boyfriend. "All this free money enabled him to be a worse addict than he already was," she said. "Why should taxpayers pay for that?"[340]

Similarly, John Asher of Indianapolis was grateful for the money he received to help tide him over. But he was not sanguine about the future. He said of poor people, "If you want to change your life, you have to get up and do something—not sit home and get free money."[341]

Of course, there is no such thing as "free money." Someone had to earn it. But the way the Biden administration spent money on this program sure made it seem as if it grew on trees.

Under the Biden administration, $300 a month was allotted for every child under six; $250 for each older child. The families that received these grants did not have to work, or even look for work, to qualify. The recipients no longer had to go to a welfare

---

[339] Jason DeParle, "Temporary Pandemic Safety Net Drives Poverty to a Record Low," *New York Times*, July 29, 2021, A1.

[340] Ibid.

[341] Ibid.

office and ask for help, nor did they have to listen to government workers who had previously encouraged them to find a job. Thus, these new programs effectively undid the 1996 welfare reforms. The workfare requirement was gone, and with it went the virtue-building effects that stemmed from it.

Daniel Henninger is a commonsensical columnist for the *Wall Street Journal*. He raises the right questions about the Biden family policy: "Is the traditional American idea of upward mobility still important? If so, how should upward mobility happen—through Washington or individual effort? Indeed, should the habit of individual striving give way to a presumably more important goal of nationalized paternalism?" He accused the Democrats of "killing the American dream."[342]

Henninger treats poor people with respect. He is not patronizing. He knows that if any demographic group is to become upwardly mobile, it must be through individual effort, which means putting the vital virtues into practice. The idea that Washington can do this is not only flawed; it is demeaning.

The Catholic approach to helping the poor mirrors what Henninger has written. St. John Paul II was wary of the welfare state. He said that "the principle of subsidiarity must be respected," and he maintained that "needs are best understood and satisfied by people who are closest to them and who act as neighbors to those in need."[343] Similarly, Pope Benedict said that subsidiarity is "the most effective antidote against any form of all-encompassing

---

[342] Daniel Henninger, "Democrats Are Killing the American Dream," *Wall Street Journal*, May 5, 2021, https://www.wsj.com/articles/democrats-are-killing-the-american-dream-11620251334.

[343] Bill Donohue, *Why Catholicism Matters: How Catholic Virtues Can Reshape Society in the 21st Century* (New York: Image, 2012), 110–111.

welfare state."[344] But this practical, commonsense way of helping the poor is resisted, indeed rejected, by much of the ruling class.

Bill de Blasio, the former mayor of New York City, does not believe in individuals. He believes in government. He says that "our mission is to redistribute wealth."[345] His detractors point out that there is only so much money to go around (though de Blasio snorts: "There's plenty of money in the world. There's plenty of money in the city—it's just in the wrong hands"[346]). But the more serious objection is de Blasio's assumption that some classes of people are incapable of moving forward on their own.

The ruling class has given up on the poor, especially the black poor. They have adopted the Fitzhugh mindset: blacks need to be supported by the government because they cannot make it on their own.

If there is one ruling-class organization that has long fostered dependency on government welfare programs, it is the Kellogg Foundation. The W. K. Kellogg Foundation was established in 1930 for uncontroversial good causes, such as providing aid to vulnerable children. It has evolved, however, into a mammoth benefactor to activists and organizations that are often closely aligned with socialist policies.

Michael Volpe is a student of philanthropies, and his writings for the Capital Research Center on the history of the Kellogg

[344] Ibid., 111.

[345] Tyler O'Neil, "Bill de Blasio Doubles Down: 'Our Mission Is to Redistribute Wealth,'" PJ Media, December 23, 2020, https://pjmedia.com/news-and-politics/tyler-o-neil/2020/12/23/bill-de-blasio-doubles-down-our-mission-is-to-redistribute-wealth-n1227512.

[346] Seth Barron, "Mayor Gimme," *City Journal*, January 15, 2019, https://www.city-journal.org/de-blasio-new-york-wealth.

Foundation are revealing. The foundation now lavishly funds "left-wing causes like open-borders groups, liberal think tanks, and projects supported by billionaire leftist George Soros." Indeed, since 1930 "it has given billions of dollars to causes and projects that encourage dependency on government." Volpe further concludes that "it supports trendy, left-wing causes that contend America is a hopelessly racist country, along with groups that wage war on the free markets that the great capitalist [W. K.] Kellogg championed while alive."[347]

It is not just the big foundations that have adopted these causes. Hayden Ludwig, another Capital Research Center writer who tracks philanthropies, found that "community foundations," or entities that are supposed to aid their local communities, now "serve as funnels for liberal billionaires." In fact, "America's community foundations are some of the biggest conduits for activist groups." Yet they receive almost no media coverage. Ludwig shows how "our country's generous nonprofit sector has been hijacked by the Left. Charity has been weaponized." The evidence suggests that humanitarian giving "is more political than charitable and utterly disconnected from its roots in Christianity's love for one's fellow man."[348]

No one understood this point better than Mother Teresa. When Prime Minister Margaret Thatcher boasted to her that Britain

---

[347] Michael Volpe, "The W. K. Kellogg Foundation's Radical Leftward Drift," Capital Research Center, September 13, 2017, https://capitalresearch.org/article/kellogg-foundation-radical-leftward-drift/.

[348] Hayden Ludwig, "Philanthropy for 'Citizens of the World': Community Foundations," Capital Research Center, September 20, 2021, https://capitalresearch.org/article/philanthropy-for-citizens-of-the-world-part-1/.

had a fine welfare system, the saintly nun replied, "But do you have love?"[349] For Mother Teresa, helping the poor was a personal exchange, an ongoing relationship between the two parties; it was not a "program."

The Christian idea of charity has always meant that those who serve the poor, in whatever capacity, should have some "skin in the game." Not everyone can be a Mother Teresa. But those who are truly interested in helping the poor must give of themselves, either in their service to the needy—as a volunteer or a paid worker—or directly as a donor. There is surely some role for government, especially for those who are unable to provide for themselves (or especially, as Dorothy Day believed, after natural disasters). But what cannot be tolerated are low expectations for the able-bodied poor. It is demeaning, and damaging, to treat an entire class of people as helpless victims, when they are not.

The latest policy iteration of the Fitzhugh mentality is universal basic income. The ruling class of Silicon Valley can be credited for promoting it. They, too, seem to harbor a deep-seated belief that blacks cannot make it on their own. Facebook's Mark Zuckerberg and his rich friends have endorsed the idea that monthly government stipends should be made available for those in need.[350] Nothing in what they propose demands anything from able-bodied persons. In fact, their policy proposal would eviscerate the need to practice the vital virtues.

---

[349] Bill Donohue, *Unmasking Mother Teresa's Critics* (Manchester, NH: Sophia Institute Press, 2016), 78.

[350] Patrick Gillespie, "Mark Zuckerberg Supports Universal Basic Income," CNN Business, May 26, 2017, https://money.cnn.com/2017/05/26/news/economy/mark-zuckerberg-universal-basic-income/index-html.

In 2022, a "Reparations Task Force" in California explored a wide-ranging plan to compensate blacks for past wrongdoings.[351] It revealed, once again, how the ruling class has given up on blacks. It also showed how they continue to wage war on virtue in the black community. Here are some of its proposals:

- Black deadbeat dads will no longer be held accountable for their behavior. The panel recommends that the state "eliminate past-due child support owed to the government for non-custodial parents." What about collecting interest on child support that is past due? It has been eliminated. A big win for irresponsible black men; a big loss for black women.

- All blacks in California should be allowed to send their children to any college they choose, free of charge. If more black males are being cited for disciplinary problems, that is going to end. Racial equity means "racially equitable disciplinary practices." This is a win for black Hollywood actors and professional athletes—their kids can go to college free of charge. It's a big loss for well-behaved black students.

- Putting more cops in high-crime neighborhoods is discriminatory. That is the obvious takeaway from the proposal, which seeks to "eliminate the over-policing of predominantly Black communities." The winners here are the criminals, and the big losers are the vast majority of law-abiding black Americans.

[351] See "California Reparations Task Force Releases Interim Report Detailing Harms of Slavery and Systemic Discrimination on African Americans," press release, Rob Bonta, June 1, 2022, https:// oag.ca.gov/news/press-releases/california-reparations-task-force -releases-interim-report-detailing-harms.

- Blacks are entitled to free health care, regardless of how much money they make. Moreover, it must be cost-free high-quality care. The big winners are the hospitals that will be reimbursed by the government, and the big losers are the taxpayers.
- Reparations must be offered in the form of cash payments to close the racial wealth gap. Among the big winners are blacks whose ancestors owned slaves, and the big losers are immigrants who arrived after slavery ended.

This is the happy face of condescending, white supremacy today.

It is also a classic example of Charles Murray's "custodial democracy." In effect, the ruling class would become the new custodians, promoting policies for the poor that would make their lives easier but at the expense of their integrity. Exercising the virtues of self-discipline, personal responsibility, and perseverance would not be required—and as history shows, this will make it nearly impossible for them ultimately to lift themselves up.

The goal of the ruling class is to provide low-income Americans with virtually every amenity that those in higher income brackets enjoy. But they won't have to do anything to earn it. "Transit equity" programs in cities such as Boston provide free transportation service; New York City has a host of subsidized programs covering a wide range of other services. Illegal aliens, of course, are welcome to apply. Food, clothing, shelter, schooling, health care, transportation—almost everything will be underwritten by government. This is what happens when the ruling class gives up on the poor.

If elites weren't so patronizing, if they were truly committed to treating blacks as equals, they would never embrace these policies. Instead, they would focus their attention on helping those in the lower class who are able-bodied to reject the values that account for their condition in favor of the vital virtues, the proven path to the American dream.

One of the first things that must be changed is the time horizon of the lower class. Political scientist Edward Banfield noted years ago that middle-class people are future-oriented: they plan for the future and take the steps that are necessary to achieve their goals. "At the present-oriented end of the scale," he writes, "the lower-class individual lives from moment to moment."[352] That's because the lower-class individual lacks the self-discipline and perseverance that mark a future-driven orientation. "Impulse governs his behavior, either because he cannot discipline himself to sacrifice a present for a future satisfaction or because he has no sense of the future. He is therefore radically improvident: whatever he cannot use immediately he considers valueless."[353]

Ken Auletta spent a lot of time with the underclass, those at the lowest end of the lower class. Unlike those who believe that poverty "is primarily a lack of money," he recognizes that "the underclass suffers from *behavioral* as well as income deficiencies" (his italics).[354] Such simple things as owning an alarm clock and being responsible enough to use it are uncommon among the underclass. Saying "thank you" was another trait that was conspicuously missing.[355] These are the kinds of things that most of us take for granted. But adults who do not know these things—and who want to improve themselves—have to be taught them.

One of the persons whom Auletta interviewed was honest enough to know why he was immobilized and why he is now moving

---

[352] Edward C. Banfield, *The Unheavenly City Revisited* (Boston: Little Brown, 1974), 54.

[353] Ibid., 61.

[354] Auletta, *The Underclass*, 28.

[355] Ibid., 47–48.

forward. Howard Smith, a black man, was understandably bitter about some of the racist aspects of American history. But he also realized that he had to deal in a mature fashion with the cards he was dealt. "You can't get away from individual responsibility," he said. He used to see himself as a victim, but he learned that if he was to succeed, he had to stop the self-pitying. He came to believe that "man is responsible for his actions."[356]

It is tragic that so many of those who work with the able-bodied poor do not help them to rid themselves of their debilitating values and behavioral patterns. Husock rightly observes that "the profession of social work no longer promotes the idea that the right attitudes and habits can help the poor and working-class to succeed. Today's social workers believe that only structural changes in the economy will prevent the problems associated with poverty."[357] Such thinking is one important reason why so little progress has been made, despite massive expenditures and decades of work. Nothing is demanded, or expected, of social workers' charges.

We know what works. Ron Haskins and Isabell Sawhill, two scholars at the Brookings Institute, concluded a decade ago that there is no secret to "curing" poverty: finish high school, get a full-time job, and get married before you have babies. These outcomes have since been dubbed the "success sequence."[358] Wendy Wang and Brad Wilcox picked up on this insight and found how true it is. They found that 97 percent of those who followed this

---

[356] Ibid., pp. 152-53, 156.

[357] Husock, *Who Killed Civil Society?*, p. 12.

[358] Bryan Caplan, "What Does the Success Sequence Mean?," Econlib, February 22, 2021, https://econlib.org/the-meaning-of-the-success-sequence/.

sequence "are not poor by the time they reach their prime young adult years (ages 28–34)."[359]

But even more fundamentally: the ability to stay in school, obtain a job, and get married before having a family are all dependent on personal responsibility, self-control, and perseverance. As a society, we need to commit ourselves, once again, to these vital virtues and do everything we can in the home, in schools, and in community programs to cultivate them. That is the real, proven way to achieve the "success sequence."

[359] Ibid.

6

# Sabotaging Education

## Success Depends on the Vital Virtues

Members of the ruling class frequently attend the best elementary and secondary schools, often private ones, and, of course, the best colleges and universities. They know what it takes to succeed: they have to take personal responsibility for their academic achievement; they have to be disciplined in their study habits; they have to know how to persevere when faced with daunting challenges. Hard work requires all three of the vital virtues. To its credit, the ruling class is a living embodiment of these qualities. To their shame, members of the ruling class seem determined to undermine these keys to success for everyone else, particularly those at the very bottom. It is a scandal.

We have known for a long time what it takes to succeed in school. In the 1960s, a major research undertaking was conducted by renowned sociologist James S. Coleman. *Equality of Educational Opportunity*, informally known as "The Coleman Report," found that money, teacher credentials, quality of learning facilities, and student-teacher ratio, though important, were not the key variables explaining academic achievement. In fact, what matters most is not even what happens in the classroom—it is what happens in the family. In other words, it is the resources that a child takes to school that matter most.[360] Other researchers, including those who have very different perspectives, have come to the same conclusion.

The Coleman Report found that the number one determinant of academic achievement was self-responsibility.[361] Students who took responsibility for their performance, although more burdened than those who did not, were the most successful in school. Not surprisingly, schools that actively sought to develop self-responsibility had a better record than those that did not.

Twenty years later, the Department of Education issued the study *What Works: Research about Teaching and Learning*. It underscored Coleman's emphasis on the family and went even further: it was not even the income level of the family that mattered most; it was what parents did to help their children academically that was most significant. However, schools mattered too: according to the report, schools that did best had a safe and orderly environment, stressed daily homework, had high expectations of students, and held them to rigorous standards of accountability.[362]

Importantly, a sequel to this report studied disadvantaged students and concluded, not surprisingly, that building character and instilling the values of hard work, self-discipline, and self-responsibility were essential to academic achievement. The vital virtues again. They are every teacher's business. By doing simple things such as giving students responsibilities and insisting on daily homework, the study found, teachers were helping students develop persistence and self-control, thus enabling them to succeed.[363] Accountability is also critical. When students are trained

---

[360] Donohue, *The New Freedom*, 168.
[361] Ibid.
[362] Ibid., 168–169.
[363] Ibid., 169.

to assess the future consequences of their behavior, such problems as teenage pregnancy, drugs, and dropping out of school are significantly reduced.

Ian Rowe is a black scholar at the American Enterprise Institute who has written extensively about education. He understands why those reports that emphasize the critical role of the family and the vital virtues are just as relevant today as they were then. "Today," he says, "we have a mountain of irrefutable evidence that children raised in stable, married, two-parent households (regardless of gender) have, on average, far superior life outcomes, not only in education but also in virtually every other category of healthy human development."[364] This has particular significance for blacks: family instability is a prime reason why black academic achievement lags behind other racial and ethnic groups.

Economist Ron Haskins is convinced that nothing is more important than personal responsibility in accounting for academic success. "Hard work is a must because the single most accurate predictor of college performance is high school grade point average, probably because grades reflect both capacity and hard work."[365]

Neuroscientists Sandra Aamodt and Sam Wang have found that self-control "predicts success in education, career and marriage. Indeed, childhood self-control is twice as important as intelligence in predicting academic achievement." This explains why Asian students succeed, they say—because "they show good self-control

---

[364] Ian Rowe, "Measure What Matters," in Petrilli and Finn, *How to Educate an American*, 211.

[365] Ron Haskins, "The Sequence of Personal Responsibility," July 31, 2009, Brookings, https://www.brookings.edu/articles/the -sequence-of-personal-responsibility/.

from an early age."[366] The work of psychologist Angela Duckworth confirms this thesis. Studies done on students in the United States and in New Zealand found that nothing was more important than self-control in accounting for academic excellence.[367]

Homework is also a very important aspect of academic success and an excellent tool to help students learn self-control, self-responsibility, and perseverance. Michael Hansen and Diana Quintero, two Brookings scholars, analyzed data from the American Time Use Survey to see how homework patterns varied by racial, ethnic, and income groups. In a sample of 2,575 full-time high school students between ages fifteen and eighteen, they found that Asian students spent the most time on homework (nearly two hours a day), followed by whites, Hispanics, and blacks. Students from low-income families spent considerably less time on homework than those in the upper brackets.[368] Duckworth observes that nothing distracts young people from doing homework more than cell phones and social media, and that is why, in her home, there are strict usage rules for her children.[369]

---

[366] Sandra Aamodt and Sam Wang, "Building Self-Control, the American Way," *New York Times*, February 17, 2012, https://www.nytimes.com/2012/02/19/opinion/sunday/building-self-control-the-american-way.html.

[367] "Self-Control May Lie at the Heart of Student Success," APS, December 21, 2017, https://www.psychologicalscience.org/publications/observer/obsonline/self-control-may-lie-at-the-heart-of-student-success.html.

[368] Michael Hansen and Diana Quintero, "Analyzing 'The Homework Gap' among High School Students," Brookings, August 10, 2017, https://www.brookings.edu/blog/brown-center-chalkboard/2017/08/10/analyzing-the-homework-gap-among-high-school-students/.

[369] Duckworth, *Grit*, 288.

The prevalence, or absence, of the vital virtues is what accounts for racial and ethnic differences in educational outcomes. In 2019, 21 percent of black students were proficient in math, compared with 54 percent of white students and 74 percent of Asian students. Their respective scores on English proficiency were 33 percent, 65 percent, and 77 percent. Just 24 percent of graduating black high school students were prepared for secondary education, compared with 54 percent of whites and 74 percent of Asians.[370] The average black math score on the SAT in 2020 was 454, compared with 547 for whites and 632 for Asians. Only 21 percent of blacks met the math benchmark of 530, compared with 59 percent of whites and 80 percent of Asians.[371]

## The Role of Money and Teachers

Some educators, such as Richard H. de Lone, look at test scores, observe that they are correlated with income levels—those in the higher income brackets do better in school than those in the lower brackets—and conclude that social inequality explains why some students do better than others.[372] This suggests that income redistribution would improve the scores of those at the bottom. But money can no more buy academic achievement than it can

[370] Walter Myers III, "The Rise in Black Unemployment Is about More Than Race," *National Review*, September 15, 2021, https://www. nationalreview.com/2021/09/the-rise-in-black-unemployment -is-about-more-than-race/.

[371] Heather Mac Donald, "The NIH's Diversity Obsession Subverts Science," *Wall Street Journal*, June 30, 2021, https://www.wsj .com/articles/the-nihs-diversity-obsession-subverts-science-11625090811?mod=opinion_lead_pos5.

[372] Richard de Lone, *Small Futures: Children, Inequality, and the Limits of Liberal Reform* (New York: Harcourt Brace Jovanovich, 1979), 101–102.

buy happiness. Students from affluent families do not do better in school than students from poor families because their parents have more money; they do better because affluent families are more likely to be intact, two-parent families. It is family stability, not income, that explains educational outcomes.

Thomas Sowell has sized up neatly the argument that income drives educational achievement. "Poverty might cause low educational outcomes—or parents' low educational outcomes might be a cause of family poverty, when a lack of basic skills prevents parents from getting well-paying jobs. In such cases, their children's low educational outcomes could be a result of behavior patterns similar to that of their parents." He aptly notes that social scientists have little interest in examining these issues.[373]

It would be heartening to learn that the more money we spend on education, the better the outcomes. After all, we are a rich country, and if all that mattered were spending more money, the solution to academic underperformance by the underclass would be simple. But such is not the case. Ask yourself why Catholic schools excel, especially with minorities? It certainly isn't because they are flush with cash.

Each year, the amount of money spent per pupil in the District of Columbia exceeds that of most, if not all, of the fifty states, yet D.C. is dead last in test scores. In fact, states such as North Dakota and South Dakota spend relatively little on education, yet they are consistently near the top on measures of educational outcomes.[374] Of the hundred largest public-school systems based on enrollment, New York City spent the most per

---

[373] Thomas Sowell, *Charter Schools and Their Enemies* (New York: Basic Books, 2020), 87.

[374] Donohue, *Common Sense Catholicism*, 167–168.

pupil in fiscal year 2019. Yet only 10 percent of black eighth-grade students were proficient in math, and only 14 percent were proficient in English. At least this was better than in Detroit, where only 4 percent and 5 percent were proficient in math and reading, respectively.[375]

If money bought academic achievement, New York City would have the best results in the nation. It spent approximately $38 billion on schools in fiscal year 2021; that amounts to $42,700 per student, an astonishing amount.[376] Yet as we have seen, it posts abysmal scores. To make matters worse, consider that under Mayor Michael Bloomberg, failing public schools were shut down and replaced with smaller ones, and under his successor, Bill de Blasio, failing schools were awarded *more money*: in 2014, de Blasio gave $839 million exclusively to these New York City schools to make improvements. To complete his sabotage of the public schools, de Blasio did not let any of the bad teachers go—instead, he gave them more money for professional training.[377]

After my twenty years of teaching—four in an elementary school and sixteen as a professor—I am convinced that one of the best

[375] William McGurn, "The Real Structural Racism," *Wall Street Journal*, September 6, 2021, https://www.wsj.com/articles/systemic-structural-racism-naep-report-card-harvard-law-suit-supreme-court-affirmative-action-black-educational-achievement-11630956788.

[376] "Spending over $42K Per Kid, NYC Department of Education Has No Excuse for Reopening Chaos," *New York Post*, September 12, 2021, https://nypost.com/2021/09/12/the-city-department-of-education-has-no-excuse-if-reopening-brings-chaos/.

[377] Bill Donohue, "De Blasio Suffers from Leadership Problems," NewsMax, December 29, 2014, https://www.newsmax.com/BillDonohue/Mayor-Bill-de-Blasio-Michael-Bloomberg-New-York-City-Al-Sharpton/2014/12/29/id/615441/.

ways to increase academic proficiency is to *spend less money* on education. If school budgets were cut, it would force administrators to concentrate on basic skills—and that doesn't take a lot of money. It might also lead to fewer administrators. Most government schools are top heavy with men and women seeking to justify their jobs by coming up with new, untested programs and projects. The amount of time wasted on paperwork is hard to conceive for those who have not experienced it.

The ruling class in education, of which the teachers' unions are an important part, is aided and abetted by the political ruling class, most of whom are Democrats. Their prime interest is job security, not student achievement. This misalignment of incentives helps explain why academic achievement is given so little attention. If the teachers' unions would just do their jobs and concentrate on giving students what we know works, we could save money and boost test scores.

Barbara Lerner, who has a keen eye for what works in school, said it all boils down to "the hard work variable." After examining the research literature on school performance, she cited four factors: amount of homework; amount of time spent directly on relevant schoolwork; frequency of class attendance; and textbook demand level. None of these take a lot of money, nor do they require a roster of administrators to implement.[378]

Administrators might be as much a problem as part of the solution, but the same is not true of teachers. Though they cannot make up for what is done in the home, they can make a big difference in students' lives. Eva Moskowitz is a pioneer educator who has seen firsthand how much teachers matter. "In a classroom

---

[378] Donohue, *The New Freedom*, 170.

with an excellent teacher," she says, "the whole class may make a year and a half's progress in nine months."[379] I know firsthand that she is right.

When I taught at a Catholic elementary school in Spanish Harlem in the 1970s, my seventh-grade students made a year and a half's progress in nine months, according to their standardized test scores. Their success was clearly not due to money: the cost of their tuition was a pittance compared with what is spent on public school students. Their success was not because of my teacher credentials—I had none: I have never taken even one education course. Their success was a result of the demands I placed on them. I gave them lots of homework, and I had high expectations for them.

Having low expectations for minority students (my students were all Puerto Rican and black) is a very serious problem among educators. In my experience, it was those teachers who voiced the most liberal and sympathetic views about minorities who were themselves the biggest problem. This may sound strange to some. But think about it. Those teachers were most often convinced that non-white students from the ghetto were so badly disadvantaged that they simply could not be expected to do well in school. Those teachers were quick to blame racism and discrimination for their students' plight. Naturally, this lowered their expectations. When teachers expect little, they demand little—and that is why they get so little in return. It's a vicious, self-fulfilling process.

I taught at St. Lucy's School, and remedial teachers were sent there from the public schools to assist students having difficulty in

---

[379] Eva Moskowitz and Arin Lavinia, *Mission Possible: How the Secrets of the Success Academies Can Work in Any School* (New York: Jossey-Bass, 2012), 16.

some subjects. One of them criticized me for rejecting a homework assignment from a student because it was ripped sloppily from a spiral notebook. She told me that I should understand that the student came from a bad neighborhood and could not be expected to do otherwise. She was aghast when I told her that she was the problem. "You would never allow white middle-class students to get away with turning in such trash," I told her.

The Knowledge Is Power Program (KIPP) schools serve elementary and secondary students across the country. The vast majority of their students are from low-income families. The schools have high expectations for their students and demand much from them. Almost all of the students graduate from high school, and more than 80 percent go to college. Teachers are told not to tell students such things as "Maybe this isn't your strength. Don't worry, you have other things to contribute." Instead, teachers are encouraged to say, "I have high standards. I'm holding you to them because I know we can reach them together."[380]

These techniques pay off in more ways than one. Economist Raj Chetty worked with some fellow economists on a study of 2.5 million New York City students. They found that dismissing the least effective teachers not only improves educational outcomes but also vastly improves students' earnings in adulthood. Chetty even developed a way known as "value added" to evaluate teachers. But guess what? The teachers' unions gave his metric a chilly reception.[381]

---

[380] Duckworth, *Grit*, 181–182.

[381] Chris Wellisz, "Data Evangelist: Chris Wellisz Profiles Raj Chetty, Who Is Reshaping the Study of Social Mobility with Big Data," *People in Economics* 55, no. 3 (September 2018), International Monetary Fund, https://www.imf.org/en/Publications/fandd/issues/2018/09/harvard-economist-raj-chetty-profile-people.

## The Attack on Merit

If the American dream is to become a reality for those at the bottom of the socioeconomic scale, the ruling class will have to stop assaulting merit, particularly for blacks. The phrase "people of color" encompasses blacks, Hispanics, Asians, and other minorities. It is typically used to describe those who are in a disadvantaged position; but it is a meaningless term with respect to education. Asians, for example, are one of the best-educated racial and ethnic groups in the country, and their income puts them in the top tier. So when it comes to giving preferential treatment to "people of color," it makes no sense to include Asians. (The University of Maryland recognized this fact and invented new racial categories—"Students of Color, minus Asians" and "White or Asian Students."[382] Look for more of these racial games to be played in the future.)

Even worse than the elites' patronizing attitude toward black students is the elites' patronizing attitude toward black professors. A cadre of left-wing professors at Princeton demanded that the university provide special accommodations for certain "favored" colleagues: "Reward the invisible work done by faculty of color with course relief and summer salary"; "Faculty of color hired at the junior level should be guaranteed one additional semester of sabbatical"; "Provide additional human resources for the support of junior faculty of color."[383]

---

[382] Luke Gentile, "University of Maryland Distinguishes Asian Students from Students of Color," *Washington Examiner*, November 11, 2021, https://www.washingtonexaminer.com/news/university-of-maryland-distinguishes-asian-students-from-students-of-color.

[383] Rod Dreher, "Persecution & Propaganda at Princeton," *American Conservative*, August 31, 2021, https://www.theamericanconservative.com/dreher/persecution-propaganda-princeton-joshua-katz-racism/.

Though these demands may have been well meant, they are actually deeply racist and even dehumanizing. Naturally, they could apply equally to Asians—but Asians are so successful that Princeton was sued for discriminating against them. (Though Princeton was not found guilty, it admitted to using national origin and race as criteria for admission, measures that make it harder for Asians to be treated on the basis of merit.)

In 2021, Princeton's ruling class authorized one of its faculty members, Dan-el Padilla Peralta, to prepare a required video for freshman that asked them to participate in "tearing down" the university. They were told that free speech is not a right but a "privilege." Padilla Peralta instructed the students to extol "free speech and intellectual discourse that is [sic] flexed to one specific aim, and that aim is the promotion of social justice, and an anti-racial social justice at that."[384] In other words, for speech to be protected, the content must further the left-wing agenda.

It's not just in colleges and universities where merit is under attack but also in the nation's elite public and private high schools. New York City has eight elite public schools, the top three of which are Stuyvesant, Bronx Science, and Brooklyn Tech. Many of the best students in the city attend these schools, and many go on to the top colleges or universities and then the most prized professions. In the past, the schools were disproportionately Jewish; now they are disproportionately Asian. But the ruling class is uncomfortable with those demographics. Mayor de Blasio and his schools chancellor, Richard Carranza, argued that school screening

---

[384] John Londregan and Sergiu Klainerman, "Profs: Princeton Diversity Office's 'Nihilistic' Attack on University's History and Anti-Woke Dissidents," *New York Post*, September 1, 2021, https://nypost.com/2021/09/01/profs-princeton-diversity-offices-attack-on-universitys-history-and-the-anti-woke/.

was racist. "Why are we segregating kids based on test scores?"[385] School administrators, in an effort to admit more black and Hispanic students, dutifully eliminated entrance criteria. Why didn't they work harder at educating black and Hispanic students so they could satisfy the criteria?

Carranza's comments also undermined excellence at the best elementary schools. It is true that about 70 percent of the student body in New York City is black or Hispanic, and that roughly 75 percent of those in the gifted elementary program are white or Asian.[386] But these demographics reflect achievement scores on standardized tests. Should we punish those who do well or help those who do not do as well to improve?

In de Blasio's last year in office, he proposed eliminating merit-based entrance criteria for the elite public schools. He also declared war on honor rolls, grades, and class rank, maintaining that it would be better to consider "contributions to the school or wider community, and demonstrations of social justice and integrity." Worse, he said that staff should "eliminate practices that penalize students who have been marginalized based on their race, culture, language and/or ability."[387] When struggling students are told that their poor grades are a reflection of a system that penalizes them

---

[385] Seth Barron, "Diversity, Not Merit," *City Journal*, June 4, 2018, https://www.city-journal.org/html/diversity-not-merit-15948.html.

[386] Eliza Shapiro, "De Blasio to Phase Out N.Y.C. Gifted and Talented Program," *New York Times*, October 8, 2021, https://www.nytimes.com/2021/10/08/nyregion/gifted-talented-nyc-schools.html.

[387] "De Blasio's DOE Takes Its War on Learning to a New Extreme with 'No Honor Roll' Push," *New York Post*, September 1, 2021, https://nypost.com/2021/09/01/de-blasios-doe-takes-its-war-on-learning-to-a-new-extreme-with-no-honor-roll-push/.

rather than a measure of their own performance, it makes it harder to teach them to excel.

The fight against excellence has been going on for years. Fortunately, Asian parents are pushing back and blocking (for now) some of the most discriminatory new entrance rules. These parents realize that gifted students need to be challenged and that watering down standards undermines parents' efforts to demand excellence from their children. Ethicist and author Aaron Ross Powell explains: "My wife has been a gifted education specialist for 20 years, so I know a bit about this, and gifted kids need specialized attention, just like special education kids. Without it, they fail out, have social problems, and just don't thrive."[388]

The assault on merit reached new heights in Oregon in 2021 when Gov. Kate Brown signed a bill that eliminated a high school graduation requirement that students demonstrate proficiency in reading, writing, and math. Parents, including non-white moms and dads, did not demand the bar be lowered—the ruling class demanded it. Why? A reporter at *Fox News* got it right: "Supporters of the bill insist that considering math and reading essential skills has been an unfair challenge for students who do not test well."[389]

[388] Hans Bader, "NYT Attacks 'Segregated' Gifted and Talented Courses, but They're More Diverse Than the NYT," CNSNews, October 11, 2021, https://www.cnsnews.com/commentary/hans-bader/nyt-attacks-segregated-gifted-and-talented-courses-theyre-more-diverse-nyt.

[389] Edmund DeMarche, "Oregon Governor Signs Bill Suspending Math, Reading Proficiency Requirements for HS Graduates," Fox News, August 10, 2021,https://www.foxnews.com/us/oregon-governor-signs-bill-suspending-math-reading-proficiency-requirements-for-hs-graduates.

But we don't say that those who cannot make the varsity basketball and baseball teams are being treated unfairly because their athletic skills are insufficient. It is condescending to hear Gov. Brown's communications office declare that doing away with proficiency requirements will help "students of color." It will do nothing of the kind. What it will do is show them that the governor has given up on them.

What really makes this war on merit so disastrous is that the achievement levels of Oregon's students were already slipping. In 2017, it was reported that "Oregon students lost ground in reading, writing and math over the past year." In fact, "roughly 60 percent of Oregon public school students fell short in mathematics as did 45 percent in reading and writing. It was the worst showing yet by Oregon schools, particularly in the language arts." The elementary grades were the hardest hit, where "fewer students achieved proficiency on end-of-year exams designed to show whether they are on track to be ready for college and the world of work." Instead of addressing these problems, Gov. Brown decided to kill the messenger—namely, the test results.[390]

But Oregon is hardly unique. Honors programs all across the country are under attack. "Equity educators" campaign to cancel advanced-placement courses. They say this will make schools more inclusive for black and Hispanic students. In fact, it will do nothing of the kind. It is simply another means to placate those who have given up on blacks. Ten times as many black students take AP tests today as they did twenty years ago. But because their 32 percent

[390] Betsy Hammond, "Oregon Reading, Writing, Math Scores Decline Across the Board," *Oregonian*, September 14, 2017, https://www.oregonlive.com/education/2017/09/oregon_reading_writing_math_sc.html.

pass rate trails Asians (72 percent), whites (65 percent), and His-panics (44 percent), the ruling class wants the courses stopped.[391]

The National School Boards Association (NSBA), led by former district administrator Joe Feldman, has told school administra-tors and teachers across the country that traditional grading sys-tems—those that assign grades on the basis of performance—are racist. Feldman, the author of *Grading for Equity*, further notes that teachers who consider a student's "participation" in assigning grades must be biased against "African-American, Latino, low-income, and special education students."[392]

In the 2022–2023 school year, the Oak Park and River Forest High School in Chicago implemented Feldman's ideas by develop-ing what they called "equitable grading." Gone were penalties for failing to turn in homework assignments on time: such penalties were considered racist because "underprivileged students may not be able to master those skills."[393]

Shelby Steele is one of the most influential black scholars in the United States. He takes great umbrage at the ruling class for the way it looks down on blacks. He deplores the elimination of the SAT requirement for University of California admission, branding

---

[391] Betsy McCaughey, "Racial-Equity Warriors Are Hurting the Dis-advantaged by Dumbing Down Schools," *New York Post*, March 11, 2022, https://nypost.com/2022/03/10/racial-equity-warriors-are-actually-hurting-the-disadvantaged/.

[392] "Accurate and Equitable Grading: Your District's Grading System Could Be Perpetuating Inequities," National School Boards As-sociation, February 3, 2020, https://www.nsba.org/ASBJ/2020/February/Accurate-Equitable-Grading.

[393] Ben Kelley, "Some Public Schools Implementing 'Equitable Grading' to Eliminate Alleged Bias in Grading," June 6, 2022, https://www.cnsnews.com/article/national/ben-kelley/some-public-schools-implementing-equitable-grading-eliminate-alleged.

it simply another one of the "victimization" games being played. He warns that "a society that keeps responding this way is going to destroy itself, going to eat [itself] up. My argument is that if you come from a group, as I do, that had four centuries of oppression, you don't need people to lower standards for you, you need people now to raise them. Ask us to perform at the same level or higher than everybody else."[394]

That is the commentary of a distinguished man who does not want to be patronized by the ruling class. Steele is obviously not oblivious to the historical wrongs that blacks endured. But he knows that the only way that blacks will improve their condition is if excellence is demanded of them. The curse of low expectations and the pernicious attack on merit are further burdens blacks must bear and yet more stumbling blocks on the long, hard road of upward mobility.

### The Politics of Progressive Education

Progressives took over the education establishment in the 1960s. At that time, students were doing well on standardized tests and improving year by year. Instead of building on the success of traditional teaching techniques, progressives attacked them. They complained about too much emphasis placed on homework, too much time spent on disciplining students, and not enough time for creative thinking. Of course, thinking creatively presupposes a mastery of the basics, something that these educators took for granted.

But today's progressives are far worse. They are consumed not with educational techniques but with race and social engineering. Never has education been more politicized than it is

---

[394] Klein, "Shelby Steele and Eli Steele on *What Killed Michael Brown?*"

today; indeed, progressives are presiding over the most dramatic transformation in education the nation has ever seen. Gone is the idea that students need to be creative. The emphasis is not on critical thinking skills or the amount of homework. What matters is getting students to *think the right way*. Thought control is the name of the game.

Education specialist Sol Stern noted this trend two decades ago. But in recent times, it has shifted into high gear. "Social justice teaching is a frivolous waste of precious school hours," he writes, "grievously harmful to poor children, who start out with a disadvantage. School is the only place where they are likely to obtain the academic knowledge that could make up for the educational deprivation they suffer in their homes. The last thing they need is a wild-eyed experiment in education through social action." Why, then, do progressive educators persist? "Either because the professors are stupid (possible), or (more likely) they care more about their own anti-American, anticapitalist agendas than they do about the actual education of children."[395]

The assault on the vital virtues is the most dangerous aspect of modern progressive education. In New York City, and in other cities across the nation, almost every attribute that catalyzes success has now been branded as racist. Take, for example, what the New York City Department of Education teaches school administrators about our "White Supremacist Culture." Here are five of their ten teachings:[396]

---

[395] Sol Stern, "The Ed's Schools' Latest—and Worst—Humbug," *City Journal*, Summer 2006, https://www.city-journal.org/html/ed-schools%E2%80%99-latest%E2%80%94and-worst%E2%80%94humbug-12948.html.

[396] Susan Edelman, Selim Algar, and Aaron Feis, "Richard Carranza Held 'White-Supremacy Culture' Training for School Admins,"

- *Perfectionism.* Administrators are told that there is too much emphasis on academic "shortcomings"—that is, doing poorly on tests. They are told that telling a student he has made a mistake is equivalent to telling him that he *is* a mistake. No evidence is provided to support this absurd statement.

- *Quantity over quality.* It is wrong to be "results oriented" and to insist on "measurable results." Can you imagine if the same reasoning were applied to the school's basketball team—if athletes were told that winning doesn't matter and that even keeping score is suspect?

- *Worship of the written word.* "This idea prioritizes documentation and writing skills, rather than the 'ability to relate to others.'" In other words, as long as illiterates have good street smarts, that's all that matters.

- *Individualism.* This characteristic is considered antithetical to being a team player. Tell that to any star athlete—that he hurts the team by developing his own skills.

- *Objectivity.* This "can lead to the belief that there is an ultimate truth and that alternative viewpoints or emotions are bad." But if there is no ultimate truth, perhaps administrators should not abide by any of this nonsense. Wouldn't their refusal to accept these marching orders reflect their "alternative viewpoint"?

Not only are these directives a frontal assault on the vital virtues; they are patently racist. Worse, by attributing to "white supremacists" virtues required to succeed, the implication is that racial and

*New York Post*, May 20, 2019, https://nypost.com/2019/05/20/richard-carranza-held-doe-white-supremacy-culture-training/.

ethnic minorities should studiously avoid their exercise—which will inevitably result in failure.

On the West Coast, progressive educators in California have declared war on math. Why? Asians do better than everyone else in this subject. Why some "people of color" do so much better than other "people of color" is confusing to these elite savants. So their answer is to punish the former, rather than to assist the latter. The new curricula give short shrift to calculus, emphasizing instead social justice and applying math to topics such as immigration and inequality.[397]

Even private schools have adopted a woke curriculum. The top-ranked independent high school in California is the College Preparatory School in Oakland. Teaching critical race theory—essentially telling white kids they are racists—is central to that school's new initiative. The school has also gotten rid of Shakespeare and now offers courses on "the intersection of monstrosity and race/racism." Every subject has been politicized. But some courses are more skewed than others. Students can take classes in "Conscious vs. Unconscious Racism," "Privilege, Power, Racism Hierarchies," "Internalized and Interpersonal Racism," and so forth.[398] Aside from satisfying the immense self-regard of those who teach this nonsense, it is not certain what else is accomplished.

Perhaps the most extreme curriculum ever proposed by progressive educators was the one developed by the Evanston-Skokie School District in Illinois. It was so radical that President Trump's

[397] Jacey Fortin, "California Tries to Close the Gap in Math, but Sets Off a Backlash," *New York Times*, November 4, 2021, https://www.nytimes.com/2021/11/04/us/california-math-curriculum-guidelines.html.

[398] John D. Sailer, "A Woke Education," *City Journal*, August 5, 2021, https://www.city-journal.org/california-top-private-school-embraces-diversity-equity-and-inclusion.

Department of Education notified school officials that it would commence an investigation. A teacher in the district, Stacy Deemar, filed a lawsuit claiming the school's anti-racism curriculum would treat teachers and students in racially disparate ways, thus violating the equal protection provisions of the Fourteenth Amendment and Title VI of the 1964 Civil Rights Act.[399] Deemar charged that the school district "pitted different racial groups against each other." Teachers were told that they need to realize that white people are "loud, authoritative ... [and] controlling." They are also racists—all of them. "White identity is inherently racist," and nothing is worse than "white privilege."

This racist programming was thought suitable for pre-K. Kids are taught that "white people have a very, very serious problem and they should start thinking about what they should do about it." When white people say we should treat everyone equally, no one should be fooled: that is a "color blind message" and "color blindness helps racism."

The most direct assault on the vital virtues is the program's injunction to undermine the nuclear family: "It [is] important to disrupt the Western nuclear family dynamics as the best/proper way to have a family." One way to do this is to discredit the idea that there is such a thing as a "normal" family: "There is the belief that a 'normal' family consists of a mom, dad, son, daughter, and pet. We've learned that this isn't true."

There is also a racial element to the thinking of these progressives that is eerily reminiscent of the 1930s in Germany. The school

---

[399] All of the quotes that follow are taken from the lawsuit. See "In the United States District Court for the Northern District of Illinois Eastern Division," *Stacy Deemar v. Board of Education of the City of Evanston/Skokie.* It was filed on June 29, 2021.

district's mandatory Beyond Diversity training defines privilege as "the amount of melanin in a person's skin, hair and eyes." Similarly, teachers are taught that "White privilege … refers to the advantages that White people receive simply by virtue of their appearance." There is nothing nuanced about their approach—it is a summary indictment of all white people.

The letter sent by the Trump administration to the school district notifying officials of its investigation was made at the end of the Trump term, in early January 2021. Biden administration elites killed it in two days.[400]

Even if the progressive curricula somehow raised student test scores, its blatantly racist methodology would be reason enough to junk it. But as it is, it is an academic disaster.

Seattle is one of the most left-wing cities in the nation. Not surprisingly, it has had one of the most radical "equity education" programs for decades. Under the leadership of Tracy Castro-Gill, the Seattle public schools replaced math courses with classes on "power and oppression." Not surprisingly, math scores dropped dramatically.

This self-described "radical atheist" and "far-left anarchist" was given a district-wide position in Seattle. She instituted "math ethnic studies," and in order for students to pass, they had to explain how math is "used to oppress and marginalize people and communities of color." They also had to "explain how math dictates economic oppression."[401]

---

[400] Houston Keene, "Biden Admin Suspends Probe into School Allegedly Segregating Students by Race; Rep. Owens Blasts Decision," Fox News, March 11, 2021, https://www.foxnews.com/politics/biden-admin-education-department-racial-segregation-burgess-owens.

[401] Luke Rosiak, "Meet the Seattle Schools Woke Indoctrination Czar Who Married a Child Molester," Daily Wire, January 19,

This "math ethnic studies" program was piloted in six schools in the spring of 2018. "On the next state math exam," a news story reported, "the performance of black students at those schools plummeted." In one of the schools, "black achievement had been rising steadily every year, but all those gains and more were wiped out, with the black passing rate dropping from 28% to under 18% the next school year." The scores of white students also plunged.[402]

When confronted with the data, Castro-Gill said she never had any intention of improving math scores. School officials agreed with her and even went so far as to "prioritize ethnic studies."[403] It did not matter to any of these officials that the students were incompetent in math.

There is some good news. The backlash has been significant—and it appears to be lasting. At the end of 2021, hundreds of America's top quantitative scientists issued a public statement warning about the assault on math in the schools. "We write to express our alarm over recent trends in K-12 mathematics education in the United States." An editorial in the *Wall Street Journal* observed that "The social-justice wave of 2020 accelerated efforts to eliminate standardized testing and lower standards in math to give the appearance that achievement gaps don't exist."[404]

Asians are among the most vociferous critics of progressive education. Xi Van Fleet is a Chinese woman from Virginia who

---

2022, http://dailywire.com/news/meet-the-seattle-schools-woke-indoctrination-czar-who-married-a-child-molester.

[402] Ibid.

[403] Ibid.

[404] "Squaring Up to Defend Mathematics," *Wall Street Journal*, December 5, 2021, https://www.wsj.com/articles/defending-mathematics-science-stem-equity-education-california-k12-math-matters-11638728196.

has witnessed this kind of politically correct curriculum before. "When I was in China," she said, "I spent my entire school year in the Chinese Cultural Revolution, so I'm very, very familiar with the communist tactics of how to divide people, how they canceled the Chinese traditional culture and destroyed our heritage." She added, "All this is happening here in America."[405] She was referring to accusations that parents who were questioning school boards about extremist curricula were labeled "domestic terrorists" by the National School Boards Association.

In 2022, San Francisco parents who were fed up with thought control disguised as education succeeded in ousting three progressive members of the board of education. This revolt against the ruling class was supported by more than 70 percent of voters in the recall election. "It's the people rising up in San Francisco and saying it's unacceptable to abandon your responsibility to educate our children," said Siva Raj, a parent who was one of those responsible for the recall.[406]

But none of this should ever have happened. We have known for a very long time both what works best in the schools and that social-justice education is a stunning failure. Sol Stern said it best in 2006:

As E.D. Hirsch has exhaustively shown, the scientific evidence about which classroom methods produce the

405 "Parent: School Board Association, DOJ Use Same 'Communist Tactics' I Saw Growing Up in Maoist China," Breitbart, October 14, 2021, https://www.breitbart.com/education/2021/10/13/mother-who-survived-maoist-revolution-doj-using-communist-tactics/.

406 Leah Barkoukis, "San Francisco Voters Succeed in Ousting Three Progressive School Board Members," Townhall, February 16, 2022, http://townhall.com/tipsheet/leahbarkoukis/2022/02/16/san-francisco-voters-oust-three-members-of-board-of-ed-n2603362.

best results for poor children point conclusively to the very methods that the critical pedagogy and social justice theorists denounce as oppressive and racist. By contrast, not one shred of hard evidence suggests that the pedagogy behind teaching for social justice works to lift the academic achievement of poor and minority students.[407]

None of this has stopped the ruling class—or dissuaded the Ford, Kellogg, MacArthur, and other foundations—from funding radical "racial equity" policies and curricula.[408] The harm they are doing to all students, especially minorities, cannot be exaggerated. They are killing their chance to realize the American dream.

## School Discipline

Students who are not taught self-control are a menace to themselves and to others. Yet too many teachers and administrators seem oblivious to the fact that without discipline in the classroom, academic proficiency cannot be achieved.

As a society, we talk a lot about students' "rights." But before children can be given rights, they should be expected to master their responsibilities. If they don't, they will inevitably abuse their rights by acting irresponsibly. This is a lose-lose situation: the child fails to develop character, and those with whom he interacts suffer the abridgement of their own rights.

The courts have played a leading role in creating this society-wide problem. In 1969, the Supreme Court found that a principal

---

407 Stern, "The Ed Schools' Latest—and Worst—Humbug."
408 Luke Rosiak, "Foundations Destroying American Public Education: The Hydra," Capital Research Center, May 20, 2022, https://capitalresearch.org/article/foundations-destroying -american-public-education-part-1/.

had violated the free-speech rights of students who wore black armbands to protest the Vietnam War. Perhaps the principal overreacted. Perhaps not. But the fallout of this ruling has been profound: students now feel empowered by judges and lawyers to resist efforts by their teachers to discipline them. When lawyers threaten school officials, the officials understandably look to protect their own short-term interests—and stop disciplining unruly students—rather than look after the long-term interests of their students.

A more controversial decision was rendered in 1975 in a case that concerned students suspended for brawling in the school lunchroom. Although the principal had witnessed the fight, the Supreme Court pondered the question of whether the students' "due-process rights" were violated. The high court sided with the students and said the principal failed to give the brawlers an adequate hearing.

Manhattan Institute scholar Kay S. Hymowitz understands the issue of student discipline well. She notes that those responsible for these decisions saw themselves as "progressive reformers, designing fairer, more responsive schools." What they failed to see was "how they were radically destabilizing traditional relations between adults and children and thus eroding school discipline."[409]

The ACLU measures students' rights by calculating the number of students disciplined for disorderly conduct. The New York Civil Liberties Union was highly critical of New York mayor Michael Bloomberg because he had a zero-tolerance policy for unruly students. It did not matter to these rights-defenders that his policies

---

[409] Kay S. Hymowitz, "Who Killed School Discipline?," City Journal, Spring 2000, https://www.city-journal.org/html/who-killed-school-discipline-11749.html.

enabled students to learn; they were not interested in defending the right to an education. What mattered was the soaring suspension rates, a result of rampant disorder in the classroom. Naturally, the civil libertarians found racism involved in the suspensions: more black students were disciplined than whites. They did not consider whether blacks were acting out more than whites.[410]

In a classic study on school discipline, Abigail Thernstrom and Stephan Thernstrom found that black students were "two-and-a-half times as likely to be disciplined as whites and five times as likely as Asians." They also found that whites were disciplined at a rate twice that of Asians. (Thomas Sowell raises an interesting question: "Was that racism against whites? If not, then why was it automatically racism when blacks were disciplined two and a half times as often as whites?")[411]

The Thernstroms found that the key variable that explains school discipline rates was not race: it was the family. Students from one-parent families were the most likely to misbehave.[412] As we have seen, intact families do a better job of imparting the vital virtues. So it is no surprise that black students—who typically come from one-parent families—are less likely to practice self-discipline. The absence of the father is the key.

More recently, a study released in 2019 by the Institute for Family Studies found that black students who were raised in intact families had suspension rates half as high as other blacks. In fact, their suspension rate was even less than that of white

---

[410] Jake Martinez, "De Blasio's Education Legacy," NYCLU, August 10, 2021, https://www.nyclu.org/en/news/de-blasios-education -legacy.

[411] Sowell, *Charter Schools and Their Enemies*, 105–110.

[412] Ibid.

students who came from one-parent families.[413] So much for racism.

The fact is that black students self-report being in fights at school at over twice the rate of white students. Another Manhattan Institute scholar, Heather Mac Donald, notes that given the high rate of suspensions for black kids—which she also traces to their family status—it is even more important to have "strict school discipline and high expectations for behavior," or their social situation will only deteriorate further. "Self-control is essential for functioning in modern society. If it hasn't been learned at home," she writes, "schools must be all the more insistent in demanding it in the classroom."[414]

Amitai Etzioni, a prominent sociologist, secured access to the computer tapes of the Coleman study discussed earlier in this chapter. After careful analysis, he concluded that self-discipline was the variable that most accounted for academic success. (As previously noted, Coleman named another vital virtue, personal responsibility, as the most important attribute, thus suggesting that being accountable for one's performance was even more important than exercising self-control.) It was the internal attitudes and motivations of students, he said, that best explained school performance. That is why he recommended that more homework be given to students: it nurtured self-discipline.[415]

---

[413] Jason L. Riley, "Classroom Chaos in the Name of Racial Equity Is a Bad Lesson Plan," *Wall Street Journal*, May 11, 2021, https://www.wsj.com/articles/classroom-chaos-in-the-name-of-racial-equity-is-a-bad-lesson-plan-11620771445?mod=searchresults_pos1&page=1.

[414] Heather Mac Donald, "Race, Discipline, and Education," in Petrilli and Finn, *How to Educate an American*, 94–95.

[415] Donohue, *The New Freedom*, 170.

### Charter Schools

The greatest threat to the public schools' dominance in education is not coming from homeschooling, private schools, or parochial schools—it is coming from charter schools, which are actually a subset of public schools. Charter schools allow administrators far more autonomy than other public schools; they depend heavily on parental involvement; and they are publicly funded but privately run. Most important, they deliver. Their success rate, measured by standardized testing and graduation rates, especially in poor neighborhoods, is astounding. No wonder all "people of color"—African Americans, Asians, and Hispanics—want more of these schools. But the ruling class, made up largely of Democratic politicians, and the teachers' unions (almost all of whom donate to Democrats), stand in the way.

Critics of charter schools complain that charter schools threaten the status quo. Perhaps they do. But the status quo, particularly in poor neighborhoods, is often abysmal. In New York City, the majority of students in standard public schools are not proficient in math or English; a majority of students in charter schools are. Moreover, black and Hispanic charter school students in New York City do better than white students statewide on math and English. "In a realm where educational failure has long been the norm—schools in low-income minority neighborhoods—this is a success, a remarkable success."[416] That was how Sowell put it in his influential book *Charter Schools and Their Enemies*.

If Sowell is the charter school's top intellectual defender, Eva Moskowitz is the nation's top charter school educator and activist. Her work promoting academic excellence at Success Academy in Harlem is legendary. Why do charter schools work? "Every member

---

[416] Sowell, *Charter Schools and Their Enemies*, 49–52.

of our community takes ownership of ensuring that our schools are upholding the highest possible standards at everything they do."[417] By "standards" she means the vital virtue of personal responsibility.

Unlike those who have given up on blacks, people such as Moskowitz know that high expectations are essential. "We pride ourselves on the rigor of Success Academy," she says, "but the atmosphere and the ethos are the opposite of Camp Lejeune." The school may have the rigor of boot camp, but it also has the joy of Macy's at Christmastime, she says. The teachers and the students are happy to be there. "Simply by raising the bar and accelerating the expectations," she advises, "you can make a revolutionary change in schooling."[418]

In 2022, a case study of the Success Academy charter network was released by Harvard Business School. The results were spectacular. The study traced Moskowitz's initiative, which began in 2005, to transform the public schools. She opened forty-seven charter schools, winning the plaudits of many minority parents. During Covid, in 2020, students struggled nationwide. But at Success Academy, 100 percent of the senior class was accepted to college. The fact that almost all of those students were from low-income families made this outcome all the more startling. Parents in neighborhoods with low-performing district schools took notice and lined up to enroll their children. Unfortunately, they could not all be accommodated: there were six applicants for every available seat.[419]

---

[417] Moskowitz and Lavinia, *Mission Possible*, 21.

[418] Ibid., 77.

[419] "Harvard Study Can Teach NY Officials the Secrets of Success Academy's ... Success," *New York Post*, March 26, 2022, https://nypost.com/2022/03/26/harvard-study-can-teach-ny-officials-the-secrets-of-success-academys-success/.

The study also showed that 93 percent of Success Academy eighth graders did exceptionally well in the end-of-year 2022 New York State Regents Exams. A *New York Post* editorial exclaimed, "These kids are predominantly poor and black or Hispanic, and they were stuck in remote learning for more than a year. But they're outperforming students in the regular public schools who are three or four years older."[420]

Wai Wah Chin is the founding president of the Chinese American Citizens Alliance of Greater New York and an avid proponent of charter schools. She notes that Randi Weingarten, president of the American Federation of Teachers, has worked tirelessly to kill charter schools in cities across the county. In the District of Columbia, black mayor Adrian Fenty and Korean immigrant Michelle Rhee teamed up to promote charter schools—but Weingarten would have none of it. She used her considerable resources to crush their progress and help prevent Fenty's reelection bid, and she forced Rhee to resign as the head of the D.C. public school system.[421] This scorched earth attack on the American dream for minorities is typical of the American ruling class.

Blacks and other minorities want more charter schools. But Democratic politicians and teachers' unions work against them. So does Black Lives Matter, which is funded by the ruling class. The disdain that Black Lives Matter shows for the vital virtues and for charter schools is toxic. It got so bad in 2016 that Rashad

[420] "Success Academy Shows Again That Public Schools Can Excel," *New York Post*, July 18, 2022, https://nypost.com/2022/07/18/success-academy-shows-again-that-public-schools-can-excel/.

[421] Wai Wah Chin, "Asian Parents—Fed Up with Public Education—Want More Charter Schools," *New York Post*, March 19, 2022, https://nypost.com/2022/03/19/asian-parents-want-more-charter-schools-available-to-their-kids.

Anthony Turner, one of the leaders of this organization in St. Paul, Minnesota, quit. "Being that I am all for charter schools and ed reform, and as someone who is seeking educational justice for students and families," he exclaimed, "I could no longer be under the banner of Black Lives Matter. Black Lives Matter has been co-opted. The movement's been hijacked."[422] But ruling-class money pays the piper, and so ruling-class opinions call the tune.

Charles Barron is a black politician and activist from New York City. He claims to represent blacks, but, like Black Lives Matter, he makes it harder for blacks to move ahead. His bigoted comments about whites and Jews, and his regard for former Libyan president Muammar Gaddafi, a known terrorist, put him on the fringes. But he still exercises clout: in 2021, he succeeded in getting a statue of Thomas Jefferson removed from City Hall. He hates charter schools and has opposed raising academic standards at the City University of New York. Like so many others, he seems to believe that blacks cannot compete with whites. In 2011, when twelve failing public schools were slated to close, he showed up at a hearing to protest the decision to *shut them down!*[423]

Former New York City mayor Bill de Blasio is another advocate for the downtrodden whose policy prescriptions invariably keep blacks down. Over and over again, he has sought to undermine charter schools. But never once has he offered evidence that they don't work. In 2014, busloads of inner-city African Americans and Hispanics showed up in Albany to protest the mayor's decision to

---

[422] Bill Donohue, "The Truth about Black Lives Matter," Catholic League for Religious and Civil Rights, September 21, 2020, https://www.catholicleague.org/the-truth-about-black-lives-matter/.

[423] Bill Donohue, "Jefferson Statue Removed from NYC Office," Catholic League for Religious and Civil Rights, October 19, 2021, www.catholicleague.org/jefferson-statue-removed-from-nyc-office/.

kill three charter schools that had been approved by the previous administration. The mayor had a thousand supporters of his own, mostly union teachers. But Eva Moskowitz drew eleven thousand parents, students, and mostly nonunion teachers.[424]

In 2021, de Blasio and Moskowitz squared off again, this time over de Blasio's decision to stop furnishing space for students by reducing enrollment in charter schools. Parents in the mostly black neighborhood of Hollis, Queens, were up in arms, pointing out that the city's traditional public schools had a 4 percent decline in enrollment in the year before while the charter population climbed by ten thousand.[425]

The problem extends beyond New York City to the state legislature in Albany. In 2022, lawmakers, mostly Democrats, refused to lift a cap on creating new charter schools. They said charters harmed the traditional public schools and diverted funds from those schools' students.[426] As Sowell points out, this argument is seriously flawed.

Charter schools do not "siphon" money from traditional public schools—parents exercising parental choice are responsible for the transfer of money. Moreover, this does not result in a decline in per-pupil funding: it simply means the money is transferred

[424] Bill Donohue, "Why Is de Blasio Punishing the Poor?," Catholic League for Religious and Civil Rights, April 22, 2014, www. catholicleague.org/de-blasio-punishing-poor/.

[425] Selim Algar, "Success Academy Boss Slams de Blasio for Blocking Low-Income NYers' School Choice," *New York Post*, March 10, 2021, https://nypost.com/2021/03/10/success-academy-head -slams-de-blasio-for-blocking-school-choices/.

[426] Ray Domanico, "Albany's Ridiculous Reluctance to Lift the Charter Cap Is Based on Fiction," *New York Post*, April 11, 2022, https://nypost.com/2022/04/11/albanys-reluctance-to-lift-the -charter-cap-is-based-on-fiction/.

*with the students* who leave to go to a charter school. Sowell rightly contends that those who make these specious arguments "seldom mention that per-pupil expenditures provided by local, state and federal government sources for children in charter schools are, on average, *less* than per-pupil expenditures on traditional public schools nearby."[427]

The data support Sowell's observation. A fiscal analysis of 40 school-choice programs from their inception through fiscal year 2018 found that these initiatives saved taxpayers up to $28.3 billion. This came out to a savings of $7,500 per student, meaning that for every dollar spent on school-choice programs, taxpayers saved about $2.80.[428]

The Biden administration has done more to kill charter schools than any prior presidential administration. In its first appropriations bill, in 2021, House Democrats did the president's bidding and proposed a $40 million cut in federal funding for charter schools. They even sought to stop funds to "any charter school that contracts with a for-profit entity to operate, oversee or manage the activities of the school."[429]

In 2022, the Biden administration offered new rules designed to discourage all federal support for charter schools. (Congress rejected that proposal and provided level funding for charter schools.) One of the rules declared that long waiting lists to attend a charter

[427] Sowell, *Charter Schools and Their Enemies*, 80–81.
[428] Martin F. Lueken, "School Choice Saves Money and Helps Kids," *Wall Street Journal*, December 12, 2021, https://www.wsj.com/articles/school-choice-saves-money-and-helps-kids-education-charter-in-person-learning-remote-covid-11639340381.
[429] James Cross, "The Corrupt Charter Myth," *City Journal*, August 13, 2021, https://www.city-journal.org/myth-of-the-corrupt-charter-school.

school were no longer satisfactory criteria to justify the start of a new charter school.[430] The expressed concern was that school districts experiencing declining enrollments in traditional public schools should not be open to new charter schools because they would suffer even larger declines; this, of course, only punishes parents seeking to have their children escape the failing neighborhood school.

Another rule says that charter schools would have to show "plans to establish and maintain racially and socio-economically diverse student and staff populations."[431] But this is a cynical ruse: charter schools have a demonstrated record of success in minority neighborhoods!

## Catholic Schools

In the early 1980s, the redoubtable James S. Coleman concluded that Catholic schools did a better job educating the same children that public schools serve.[432] He upset many members of the ruling-class educational establishment. But I found out firsthand why he was right.

After serving four years in the air force and receiving my B.A. degree from New York University, I enrolled at the New School for Social Research for my master's in sociology. (I would later return to NYU for my PhD.) When I had only a few courses left for my master's, I took a job at St. Lucy's in Spanish Harlem. I turned down a good-paying job as an accountant—the skill I learned in

---

[430] "A Case of Charter School Sabotage," *Wall Street Journal*, March 27, 2022, https://www.wsj.com/articles/charter-school-sabotage-biden-teachers-union-public-school-achievement-gap-hispanic-black-students-charter-schools-program-rules-11648224610.

[431] Ibid.

[432] Moskowitz and Lavinia, *Mission Possible*, 14.

the air force—and took a much lower-paying job in a dangerous inner-city neighborhood. I never regretted it.

My students were Puerto Rican and African American. Their mothers (the fathers were usually absent) sent their children to St. Lucy's for four reasons: safety, discipline, academic excellence, and religious instruction. It is hard for middle-class white people to appreciate the physical conditions in low-income neighborhoods, particularly the necessary emphasis on physical safety. In a high-crime area, it means a great deal to parents to feel confident that their children will be safe, and unharmed, when they come to pick them up. Indeed, I had my share of run-ins with dangerous men and gangs and was fortunate enough to be big enough to protect my students.

The school was committed to the vital virtues. Discipline in the classroom was never compromised, and students were expected to practice self-control. Copious homework helped them to exercise self-discipline as well as perseverance. High expectations were the norm. Moreover, the students all knew they were personally responsible for their grades.

Don't believe the canard that Catholic schools in the ghetto are self-selective, choosing only students who are less likely to be a problem. When I worked at St. Lucy's, just the opposite was true: recalcitrant public school students were often "dumped" on Catholic schools. We did our best with them—and it was invariably better than what the public schools did with them.

In 1993, New York archbishop Cardinal John O'Connor made an offer to New York City public schools. Send me your lowest-performing 5 percent of students, he said, and we'll put them in Catholic schools where they will succeed. City officials never responded. That same year, the New York State Department of Education issued a report that compared academic achievement in the public schools and Catholic schools. The difference was huge: Catholic students significantly outperformed public school students.[433]

Does religion play a role in the academic success of Catholic school students? In a word, yes. A study by a University of Chicago professor, William H. Jeynes, found that "very religious black and Hispanic students outperformed less religious students in academic achievement."[434] This shows that while charter schools do an excellent job, Catholic schools do even better.

The most authoritative study showing the importance of the vital virtues in Catholic education was released in 2018 by the Thomas B. Fordham Institute. Students in Catholic schools were less likely to be disruptive than their peers in other private schools or in public schools. They exhibited more self-control and were more likely to control their temper, respect others' property, accept their fellow students' ideas, and handle peer pressure. In fact, self-discipline was a hallmark of Catholic schools. As with other studies, this one demonstrated the value of religious instruction in academic success.[435]

In March 2000, best-selling author Tom Wolfe spoke at a conference of the Children's Scholarship Fund foundation. He noted the tremendous success of Catholic schools, making the point that the inculcation of bourgeois virtues in Catholic students is badly needed in public school students. His list of moral imperatives that lead to success in school highlighted the vital virtues. Calling himself a "lapsed Presbyterian," he said, "I'm not Catholic, but I

---

[433] Bill Donohue, "Blacks Excel in Catholic Schools," Catholic League for Religious and Civil Rights, March 18, 2021, www.catholicleague.org/blacks-excel-in-catholic-schools.

[434] Ibid.

[435] Ibid.

have eyes." He observed that "the Catholic system has kids from the same demographic as the public school system—and teaches 10% of all the students in [New York] city. The difference in the results is very striking."[436]

Wolfe concluded his remarks saying, "The obvious lesson of all this is that [New York City] should hand the whole thing over to the Catholic Church—and do it tomorrow."[437] Interestingly, I said the same thing in the same month of the same year in a debate I had with Christopher Hitchens in the same city.

### Elites Opt for Private Schools

Education is the focus of Harvard professor Paul E. Peterson's work. He wryly notes that "a fifth of all school teachers with school-age children has placed a child in a private school, and nearly three out of ten have used one or more of the main alternatives to the traditional public school—private school, charter school, and homeschooling." In fact, "school teachers are much more likely to use a private school than are other parents."[438]

If teachers like school choice, why does our educational establishment resist school-choice initiatives for minority students from low-income families?

Rev. Jesse Jackson opposes school choice. But he sent his own children to the best private schools. Senator Ted Kennedy was

[436] John Burger, "Tom Wolfe: Catholic Schools Are the Right Stuff," *National Catholic Register*, March 19, 2000, https://www.ncregister.com/news/tom-wolfe-catholic-schools-are-the-right-stuff.

[437] Ibid.

[438] Paul E. Peterson, "Teachers More Likely to Use Private Schools for their Own Kids," Education Next, January 11, 2016, https://www.educationnext.org/teachers-more-likely-to-use-private-schools-for-their-own-kids/.

ready to conduct a filibuster over a bill that would have given D.C. parents school choice. He sent his children to private schools. Hillary Clinton is an ardent foe of school choice. She made sure her daughter went to the prestigious Sidwell Friends School in D.C., where President Obama, another anti-school-choice politician, sent his daughters. President Biden sent his children to private schools. But he opposes school choice for others. Vice President Kamala Harris, an enemy of school choice, sent her stepchildren to private schools. House Speaker Nancy Pelosi spent a small fortune sending her children to the most expensive private schools. But she argues that "private school vouchers are a bad idea."[439]

Bill de Blasio went so far as to say, "I'm going to be blunt with you, I am angry about the state of public education in America. I am angry at the privatizers. I am sick and tired of these efforts to privatize a precious thing we need—public education." He concluded, "I hate the privatizers and I want to stop them."[440] Guess what? His daughter went to Beacon School, one of New York's most elite high schools, and then attended Santa Clara University, a Jesuit school. His son attended Brooklyn Tech, one of the most prestigious and selective high schools, and then went to Yale.

San Francisco has earned a reputation as a left-wing city. Though the city is 48 percent white, only 15 percent of white children go to public schools. "For all the city's vaunted progressivism,"

[439] Jessica Chasmar, "Biden, Pelosi, Other Dems Sent Kids to Private School but Oppose School Choice," Fox News, June 16, 2022, https://www.foxnews.com/politics/biden-pelosi-top-dems-sent-kids-private-school-oppose-choice.

[440] Jack Crowe, "De Blasio Considering Eliminating Gifted Programs to Achieve Racial Parity in NYC Schools," Yahoo! News, August 27, 2019, https://news.yahoo.com/blasio-considering-eliminating-gifted-programs-122150593.html.

the *New York Times* says, "it has some of the highest private school enrollment numbers in the country—and many of those private schools have remained open."[441]

One of the most hypocritical elites is Rep. Jamaal Bowman, a black radical from New York who was elected to Congress in 2020. He is highly critical of suspending and expelling students for their conduct. He is opposed to the "test-and-punish regime that stigmatizes, labels, and ranks students, teachers and schools." He hates the Core Curriculum. He wants to ban private colleges and universities and make higher education free. Of course he wants to ban charter schools. But Bowman himself not only attended a charter school; he became the principal of the one he started before running for office.[442]

The ruling class has one set of rules for itself and another for its subjects. It is chasing the American dream for itself and its children—and it is killing the dream for everyone else.

---

[441] "California Is Making Liberals Squirm," *New York Times*, February 11, 2021, https://www.nytimes.com/2021/02/11/opinion/california-san-francisco-schools.html.

[442] "A New Deal for Education," JBBowmanNY16, https://bowman-forcongress.com/issues/a-new-deal-for-education/.

7

# Rewarding Incivility

## Family and Religion Provide for Civility

The prerequisite for academic success—indeed, success in almost any area of life—is civility. But when self-discipline breaks down, the incidence of criminal behavior increases. When personal responsibility is eschewed, crime follows. When young men, in particular, fail to develop the virtue of perseverance, attempts at rehabilitation invariably fail—resulting in more crime. When all three virtues are under attack, it is nearly impossible to achieve civility.

Throughout much of the nineteenth century, both in Britain and in the United States, there was a mass migration from the countryside to cities. In the United States, there was also a large infusion of immigrants. According to some sociological models, these changes are typically associated with an increase in crime. But that didn't happen. In fact, crime rates decreased. Why? Bourgeois virtues were central to the Victorian ethos.

Francis Fukuyama explains that, since then, "the essential change that took place was a matter of values rather than institutions. At the core of Victorian morality was the inculcation of impulse control in young people," resulting in a decrease in casual sex, alcohol, and gambling. "Victorians sought to create respectable personal habits in societies where the vast majority of inhabitants can be described only as crude."[443] Not anymore.

Young men are hardwired to reject the virtue of "impulse control" (testosterone is linked to aggressive behavior), so unless they learn to bridle their impulses, aberrant behavior is bound to result. Regrettably, as a society, we are doing a poor job of instilling self-discipline in everyone, not simply in young men. This is true across racial, ethnic, and class lines. While there is plenty of blame to go around, the ruling class has helped to create a culture of nonresponsibility in the younger generation. Older generations always carp about the young. But never before have judges, elected officials, and socially prominent elites excused young people's failure to take responsibility for their behavior. If anything, prominent elites are encouraging misbehavior by cultivating a culture of victimology.

Robert Nisbet was one of America's most brilliant sociologists. He observed that victimology is a

> form of thinking that allows victims for any given crime and no victimizer or criminal. The individual robbed, raped, or slain is certainly a victim, but so is the robber, rapist, and murderer a victim—of circumstances, of poverty, of broken family, in sum, of society. Few things please the liberal heart more than a victim, especially that of society, and when a choice has to be made between the rights of the victim who was robbed and the victim of society who did the robbing, the right-thinking humanitarian almost tropistically sides with the latter.[444]

---

[443] Fukuyama, *The Great Disruption*, 268, 270.

[444] Robert Nisbet, *Prejudices: A Philosophical Notebook* (Cambridge, MA: Harvard University Press, 1982), pp. 304–305.

A woman I know told me the story of her encounter with a robber at Sunday Mass that gives credence to Nisbet's reflection. She was standing at the back of the church when a man grabbed her purse and fled. When he was caught and brought back to the church, a priest who knew the robber said he was sorry to see that he had offended again. He showed compassion for the robber—but none toward the woman who was victimized. In the priest's mind, the robber was the victim of society; what happened to the woman was merely unfortunate.

James Ward Jr. is a black pastor and author who grew up in Tuscaloosa, Alabama. He wrote a book about victimology explaining that victim thinking is like wearing a set of dark lenses indoors and blaming others for not turning the lights up. "That's how victim thinking works," he said. "It's like people wearing lenses, and they literally read victimization into every situation in life, into every relationship, into everything that happens.... And there's nothing you can do to change that person's perspective until the lenses change." He adds that victim thinking will continue until people break with the "it's not my fault" mentality.[445]

In the latter half of the twentieth century, social scientists generally embraced the notion that there was no one who could not be rehabilitated. Parents were told that their most unruly children could change; teachers were instructed that their most recalcitrant students could change; social workers were taught that their most misbehaving clients could change; prison wardens were informed that their most violent inmates could change.

In truth, some did. But most did not. Attempts to rehabilitate them largely failed because these people never learned to persevere, to stick it out, to work relentlessly to change their

---

[445] Gerald Korson, "Victimhood," *Legatus* (May 2022): 18.

thinking and their behavior. They just didn't have the grit to stay the course.

The Moynihan Report detailed the findings of prominent social scientists who studied delinquency and criminal behavior. They all agreed on one thing: boys who come from fatherless families are the most likely to end up in trouble. They fail miserably at impulse control and find it almost impossible to defer gratification.[446] When they want something, they try to get it without considering the consequences of their actions.

Nothing has changed since Moynihan wrote his report. More recently, corrections expert Steve Martin put it this way: "Family is the solution—and the work ethic. You show me people with intact families, and those folks work—their chances of ending up in prison are zero."[447]

As I previously noted, I know firsthand what it is like to grow up in a fatherless home. That became an asset when I taught at St. Lucy's in Spanish Harlem in the 1970s. I could relate to the students because most of them came from fatherless homes too. I understood that it was a rough neighborhood. For the sake of the students, I confronted gangs and neighborhood criminals and even had to escort some students home. I also had to confront men who entered the school without permission (most of the teachers were women, and I was the biggest male teacher). But despite their surroundings, the boys knew not to misbehave in the classroom.

In my third year at St. Lucy's, having taught third and seventh grades, I began teaching eighth grade. On the first day of class, I

---

[446] Moynihan, *The Negro Family*, 26–27.
[447] Heather Mac Donald, "The Decriminalization Delusion," *City Journal* (Autumn 2015), https://www.city-journal.org/html /decriminalization-delusion-14037.html.

asked the biggest boy in the room to come to the front of the class. I picked him up by the waist, turned his feet to the ceiling and sat him down. He had not done anything wrong—I was just making a point. Everyone got the message.

If boys do not have fathers, they need father figures who make it clear that misconduct will not be tolerated. Father figures cannot replace fathers; but it is better to have some discipline than none.

Religion can also be a source of discipline. All three of the most influential sociologists in history—Marx, Weber, and Émile Durkheim—understood the stabilizing effect that religion plays in society. Durkheim, in particular, was adamant in his conviction that religiosity—measures of religious beliefs and practices—was central to maintaining social control. Studies done by sociologists in more recent times have confirmed Durkheim's thesis many times over. There is indeed an inverse relationship between religiosity and crime.[448] To put it differently, the vital virtues that Christianity champions encourage civility.

One of the reasons why my students at St. Lucy's rarely misbehaved is that they came from religious homes. Religion was further reinforced in school. Students learned right from wrong—and they learned that morality is outlined by the Ten Commandments and developed by Catholic moral teachings. They understood the necessity of being virtuous.

One does not have to be Catholic to appreciate the great work of Catholic schools in the inner city. In 1993, President Bill Clinton told religion reporters that it was not possible to solve urban social problems "without drawing on the immense reservoir of our spiritual heritage." Specifically, he cited his appreciation for "the whole Catholic concept of the social mission of the Church,"

---

[448] Donohue, *The Catholic Advantage*, 40–45.

noting that Catholic churches, schools, and programs in the inner city offer a viable alternative to drugs, gangs, and guns.[449]

## Incivility Reigns

After decades of relatively modest rates of crime, "the United States experienced its biggest one-year increase on record in homicides in 2020, according to new figures released ... by the F.B.I., with some cities hitting record highs."[450] That was how the *New York Times* put it in the fall of 2021. No group was more impacted than blacks. The *New York Post* reported that black New Yorkers are about 24 percent of the city's population, but they made up 65 percent of those murdered in 2020, and 74 percent of the shooting victims.[451]

It is not hard to figure out what happened. The ruling class had not only refused to enforce the law but had created a culture of lawlessness: what came to be known as "the Ferguson effect" explains it all.

Michael Brown was a huge, eighteen-year-old black man from Ferguson, Missouri. He was six foot four and weighed nearly three hundred pounds. On August 9, 2014, he manhandled a small Asian shopkeeper and stole some cigars, which were used to smoke marijuana. When it was reported that he was unarmed and was shot dead by a white police officer, the media declared that it was a racist incident. Some news stories said Brown was shot multiple

---

[449] Ibid., 41.

[450] Neil MacFarquhar, "Murders Spike at Record Rate across the U.S.," *New York Times*, September 27, 2021, https://www.nytimes.com/2021/09/27/us/fbi-murders-2020-cities.html.

[451] "Just How Backwards Can Criticism of Eric Adams' Return to 'Broken Windows' Policing Get?," *New York Post*, March 31, 2022, https://nypost.com/2022/03/31/eric-adams-facing-pushback-for-return-to-broken-windows-policing/.

times with his hands up over his head after the police had stopped him for walking in the middle of the street. Riots ensued.

The shocking violence and massive property loss that occurred were the direct result of the statements of reporters, politicians, and activists who had no idea what they were talking about.

An investigation by the Obama Department of Justice found that Ferguson policeman Darren Wilson was responding to the robbery at the convenience store when he and another officer encountered Brown and a friend of his walking in the middle of the street. From their car, the cops told them to move to the sidewalk. They refused. When Officer Wilson began to get out of his car, Brown slammed the door shut and attacked him, punching him twice in the face. Brown then reached for the officer's gun. During the altercation, Wilson fired two shots, one of which grazed Brown's hand. Wilson got out of his car and chased Brown down the street. Brown turned around and ran right at the police officer. Wilson shot at Brown in self-defense while stumbling backward. He ordered Brown to stop. Brown refused. That is when Brown was hit with a fatal bullet. The forensic evidence showed that Brown had his head down and was charging toward Wilson when the final shot killed him.[452]

Noted black scholar Shelby Steele and his son Eli released an important movie in 2020: *What Killed Michael Brown?* They are convinced that the ruling class deliberately hoodwinked America. The lies that were told became the conventional thinking in elite institutions. As Eli put it, "The false narrative became the dominant narrative of the shooting. And eventually, it became accepted by almost all the major institutions in America, through colleges, through corporations."[453]

---

[452] Horowitz, *I Can't Breathe*, 78–80.
[453] Klein, "Shelby Steele and Eli Steele on *What Killed Michael Brown?*"

Shelby offers a more searing observation. He blames political liberalism, as far back as the 1960s. The success of the civil rights movement led the white ruling class to push for government reforms across the board. He notes that "welfare expanded, the war on poverty came, Great Society, affirmative action, public housing, school busing, you name it." This was done, he says, so that white America could "win back its moral authority." It worked—but at an enormous cost. "It did absolutely nothing for blacks. It gave them public housing and then destroyed the black family in America. It gave them school busing. It tore up the entire American education system. It gave them welfare that did nothing more than breed dependency."[454]

Michael Brown was a product of these liberal policies. He had gone to four public schools in four years. According to Steele, Brown's death was "indirectly caused by the breakdown in black America that was the result of this liberalism that destroyed our family life, destroyed our value system, and created a black underclass. Michael was a part of that."[455]

What Steele describes is nothing less than the war on virtue and the assault on the American dream that is being waged by the ruling class. This culture of lawlessness reached a new level with the killing of George Floyd.

On May 25, 2020, George Floyd was arrested for passing a counterfeit bill in a Minneapolis store. After two police officers, one white and one black, collared him, another cop, Derek Chauvin, had to subdue him. In doing so, he put his knee on Floyd's neck for about nine and a half minutes. Floyd had nearly four times the lethal dose of fentanyl in his system. But while there were no

---

[454] Ibid.
[455] Ibid.

signs of asphyxiation resulting from what Chauvin did to Floyd, the officer was found guilty of murdering him.

Many cops and ex-cops understood that Chauvin had to subdue Floyd, but they believed it was unnecessary for him to have continued kneeling on Floyd once he was taken down. Still, Floyd was not your typical black male. He was a career criminal who had spent his twenties and thirties in and out of prison. He served nine jail sentences for crimes ranging from crashing into the apartment of a pregnant black woman and robbing her at gunpoint, to theft, firearm robbery, and possession of cocaine.

Immediately, the media portrayed this incident as another example of white racism. Riots exploded across the nation as tens of millions took to the streets, whipped up into a frenzy by Black Lives Matter. During the first 103 days of unrest following the death of Floyd in 2020, there were 633 violent protests in approximately 220 locations across the nation, including almost all of the country's 50 largest cities. Black Lives Matter was involved in 95 percent of those incidents. The riots were responsible for an estimated two billion dollars in insured property damage and untold more in uninsured property damage. There were twenty-four deaths and countless others who were injured, including many cops.

## Ruling Class Response to the Riots

When I was in the air force in the late 1960s, I was stationed in northern California. I took a sociology course on the base. One day, we went on a field trip to Folsom Prison, a maximum-security facility made famous by singer Johnny Cash. We had a chance to interview the inmates. I was only nineteen at the time, and I asked a question appropriate only to someone that age. I asked an inmate if he felt sorry for what he did. I will never forget his chilling answer: "The only thing I'm sorry about is that I got caught."

While my juvenile innocence can be attributed to youth, the refusal of the ruling class to understand that evil is evil and must be contended with cannot be so easily forgiven. The policies adopted during and after the riots were directly responsible for the subsequent crime spree. Common sense should tell us that when laws are not enforced, crime is bound to increase. Yet this is exactly the course chosen by those who command our elite institutions.

In 2014, California voters passed Proposition 47, reclassifying many drug and property felonies as misdemeanors. As such, many would-be criminals were neither incarcerated nor put on probation. Cops saw no reason to waste their time busting people for drugs and property crimes. This ballot initiative was sold to the public as a way of removing the stigma from felons and reducing the jail and prison population. But the wind was sown, and the whirlwind was reaped: crime soared.[456]

As we have seen, when the vital virtues are not taught, they are not observed. Lawmakers and prosecutors are supposed to hold criminals accountable for their behavior—personal responsibility is one of the three vital virtues. When they fail to do so, they are aiding and abetting the very behaviors they are sworn to hold in check.

Since 2014, the list of destructive policies has only grown: doing away with bail for most crimes, including serious ones; ignoring all sorts of smaller crimes; getting rid of undercover cops; putting an end to stop and frisk; prohibiting the police from mounting horses during demonstrations; emptying jails and prisons because of Covid; calling for the abolition of prisons; defunding the police; and telling cops to stand down. Of course these policies have caused crime to spike. A middle schooler could have told you

---

[456] Mac Donald, *The Decriminalization Delusion*.

they would. But middle schoolers don't make these policies. The ruling class does.

Here's one more example of the "Ferguson effect." Around Thanksgiving in 2021, a middle-aged black man in Waukesha, Wisconsin, stepped on the gas of his Ford Escape and plowed into a Christmas parade of children and older women. Five were killed, and forty-eight were injured. Just six days earlier, the driver, Darrell E. Brooks, had been freed on $1,000 bail after the mother of his child accused him of punching her in the face and then trying to run her over with the same car. The Milwaukee native had a long rap sheet, having been charged and convicted for crimes including battery, domestic violence, cocaine possession, and resisting arrest.

What happened to him? He was sent to jail on two occasions and spent years on probation and court-mandated work-release and anger-management programs.[457]

This is what happens in a culture of lawlessness. It doesn't happen by accident. It happens because elites make it happen.

### Cities Reel from Lawlessness

Homicides spiked in almost all major American cities in 2020 and 2021. The following cities broke their all-time high in 2021: Portland, Indianapolis, Toledo, St. Paul, Rochester, Tucson, Louisville, Philadelphia, Albuquerque, Baton Rouge, Columbus, and Austin.

---

[457] Dan Simmons, Serge F. Kovaleski, and Glenn Thrush, "Here Is What We Know about the Suspect in the Parade Tragedy," *New York Times*, November 22, 2021, https://www.nytimes.com/2021/11/22/us/driver-parade-crash-suspect.html. See also Ben Shapiro, "Ben Shapiro: Waukesha Proves Idiocy of 'Racial Equity' Incarceration Policies," CNSNews, November 24, 2021, https://cnsnews.com/commentary/ben-shapiro/ben-shapiro-waukesha-proves-idiocy-racial-equity-incarceration-policies.

Robert Boyce, retired chief of detectives for the New York Police Department, explained why. "Nobody's getting arrested anymore. People are getting picked up for gun possession and they're just let out over and over again."[458] He did not exaggerate.

In every one of these cities, prosecutors and lawmakers instituted reforms that handcuffed the police while also destroying their morale. They were told to stand down, and they dutifully complied. But seventy-three police officers were killed in 2021, a twenty-year high.

I work in New York City, across the street from Penn Station. Starting in 2020, I began to see countless numbers of obviously deranged men, and some women, passed out or hanging out on the corner by the station. I arrive in the city early, around 7:15 a.m. I began to see people who had a very strange look in their eyes. Some were violent. They had been up all night taking drugs—and there were many more of them strung out in the morning than in the late afternoon and evening when I was going home. But the cops were following orders. They did nothing.

In a matter of just a few weeks, from May 29 to June 9, 2020, an estimated 450 businesses were looted or destroyed in New York City by rioters. On the corner across the street from the Catholic League's office was a huge Foot Locker store; it has been empty for years. During one of the riots, thieves broke the glass and cleaned the place out. One of the security guards in my building caught the action on tape. It showed the rioters driving away in a Mercedes.

[458] Craig Bannister, "12 Major Cities Set Homicide Records—'Nobody's Getting Arrested Anymore,' Retired NY Chief of Detectives Says," CNSNews, December 13, 2021, cnsnews.com/blog/craig-bannister/12-major-cities-set-homicide-records-nobodys-getting-arrested-anymore-retired.

Nothing changed in 2021. Major crime—murder, rape, robbery, felony assault, burglary, grand larceny, and auto theft—topped one hundred thousand cases for the first time since 2016.

The *New York Post* got it right when it said, "Right now, anyone arrested for looting gets rapidly released, with no need to post bail to avoid jail until trial."[459] It got so absurd that if someone threw a brick through a window, and no one was on the other side, the brick was not considered a weapon (as it would normally have been) and no bail or jail time was warranted.

Statistics are useful, but they are bloodless and can get in the way of understanding a real-life crisis. In 2022, Frank Abrokwa, thirty-seven, spread his own feces all over a woman who was waiting for a subway train. He had a rap sheet dating back to 1999 and had been arrested nearly two dozen times. He was charged with reckless endangerment, assault, menacing, harassment, and disorderly conduct. He was immediately released on bail. Two days later, he was arrested on hate-crime charges and released again.[460]

In the summer of 2022, a forty-year-old woman got into an altercation with a twenty-three-year-old McDonald's worker in Brooklyn. She was upset that the french fries she had ordered were cold and was FaceTiming her twenty-year-old son during the argument. Her dutiful son quickly stormed the fast-food joint and shot the worker. His victim died a few days later. The killer had been arrested several times before and had confessed to murder in 2020. When his mother was questioned about what happened, she said, "My son is just saying that he gotta do what he gotta do."

---

[459] Horowitz, *I Can't Breathe*, 25.

[460] Steven Vago and Mark Lungariello, "Poop Attack Perp Bragged on Facebook about Getting Out without Bail," *New York Post*, March 3, 2022, https://nypost.com/2022/03/03/poop-attack-perp-bragged-on-facebook-about-getting-out-without-bail/.

A witness who owns a local business said, "I feel like crying. You shot someone over french fries?"[461]

In 2021, John Chappell, sixty-four, pushed a sixty-five-year-old Asian woman down a flight of subway stairs a block from my office. He had had seventy-seven prior arrests. What happened to him? He was issued a desk appearance ticket for assault and let go.[462]

All of this happens because the ruling class allows it to happen. "Obviously, the people in power don't really care," says a seasoned New York law-enforcement agent. "Everyone is carrying a gun because there are no repercussions. It's like the Wild West out there—except you have young kids who aren't old enough to drive shooting people on bikes and scooters instead of horses."[463]

Blacks kill blacks in Chicago on such a regular basis—especially on weekends—that it no longer triggers outrage. The city is run by Democrats. It has a black mayor. Their lack of response has become a national disgrace. In 2021, there were almost eight

---

[461] Angela Cavallier and James Gordon, " Career Criminal, 20, Who Shot NYC McDonald's Worker, 23, in the Face over His Mom's Cold Fries Is Perp-Walked After CONFESSING to 2020 Murder Where He Gunned Down a Man Six Blocks Away," *Daily Mail*, August 4, 2022, https://www.dailymail.co.uk/news/article-11079139/Man-shot-McDonalds-worker-cold-fries-does-perp-walk-confessed-murder-2020-killing.html; "Mc Donald's Worker Reportedly Shot over Cold French Fries Has Died, Police Say," Fox Business, August 5, 2022, https://www.foxbusiness.com/lifestyle/nyc-mcdonalds-worker-shot-over-cold-french-fries-died-police-say.

[462] Amanda Woods, "Criminal with Dozens of Prior Arrests Busted in NYC Subway Attack—Again," *New York Post*, June 1, 2021, https://nypost.com/2021/06/01/criminal-with-dozens-of-priors-busted-in-nyc-subway-attack-again/.

[463] Tina Moore, Larry Celona, and Bruce Golding, " 'Heed the Warning' of the 75th," New York Post, July 29, 2022, https://nypost.pressreader.com/article/281651078857447.

hundred murders. What precipitated this slaughter? Chicago cut its police budget by $63 million between 2020 and 2021. But even if they had more police, it wouldn't make much difference: cops are told to stand down.

It was reported in 2022 that the Chicago police arrested the fewest number of suspects in at least twenty years amid a big spike in crime. The cops were acting rationally by backing off. "In the past," said a decorated officer, "I might see a guy with a gun in his waistband, and I'd jump out and chase him. No way I'd do that now."[464]

The members of the ruling class—not blacks—made cops the enemy. The criminals get it. The cops get it. And so do the undertakers.

In 2020, Portland city commissioners voted to slash the police budget by nearly $16 million. Over the next few months homicides nearly tripled. In Seattle, they almost abolished the entire police department in 2020 and settled for drastic cuts. The city council forced its black police chief to flee the city, and more than two hundred of his fellow police officers followed. Though the voters did not want to cut the police budget again, in 2021 the ruling class overruled them and cut it. The result? There was a 20 percent surge in violent crime, which reached the highest level in fourteen years. As one writer put it at the end of 2021, Portland is now a "ghost town, except for zombies."[465]

---

[464] Emma Colton, "Arrests in Chicago Plummet to Historic Lows as Crime Rises and Police Admittedly Pull Back: 'No Way,'" Fox News, July 19, 2022, https://www.foxnews.com/us/arrests-chicago-plummet-historic-lows-crime-rises-police-admittedly-pull-back-no-way.

[465] Nate Hochman, "The Tragedy of Portland: 'It's a Ghost Town, Except for Zombies,'" *National Review*, December 17, 2021, www.nationalreview.com/2021/12/the-tragedy-of-portland-its-a-ghost-town-except-for-zombies/.

During this same period in San Francisco and Los Angeles, "smash and grab" thugs broke into high-end stores, looting them clean. This led to an exodus of more than a hundred thousand residents of San Francisco from 2020 to 2021. But it didn't lead to a decrease in crime—the numbers jumped. The editorial board of the *San Francisco Chronicle* asked residents to tolerate burglaries, so debased had they become.[466] Even the police department in Los Angeles chimed in, advising city residents to "cooperate and comply" when being robbed.[467]

## The Ruling Class Funds the Crime Wave

There is hardly a morally corrupt cause that George Soros has not funded. He epitomizes the worst of the ruling class.

Many corrupt district attorneys—those who refuse to prosecute dangerous criminals—got their job with the help of Soros. He gave Alvin Bragg $1 million when he was running for DA in Manhattan in 2021; he gave George Gascón nearly $3 million when he ran for DA of Los Angeles in 2020. In 2022, it was reported that he gave $40 million to elect seventy-five "social justice" prosecutors. The one thing they didn't deliver was justice, especially for crime victims.

Between 2016 and 2022, Soros gave more than $29 million to a personal network of political action committees specifically

---

[466] Matthew Miller, "*San Francisco Chronicle* Blasted for Asking If Residents Should 'Tolerate Burglaries,'" *Washington Examiner*, November 7, 2021, https://www.washingtonexaminer.com /restoring-america/fairness-justice/san-francisco-chronicle -blasted-for-asking-if-residents-should-tolerate-burglaries.

[467] AWR Hawkins, "LAPD Advises City Residents to 'Cooperate and Comply' with Robbers," Breitbart, November 10, 2021, https://www.breitbart.com/politics/2021/11/10/lapd-advises -cooperate-comply-robbers/.

established to back radical DA candidates. By mid-2022, one in five Americans, or seventy million people, were living in a jurisdiction overseen by a Soros-backed prosecutor. Soros DAs were running New York, Chicago, Saint Louis, New Orleans, Philadelphia, and Los Angeles as well as many smaller cities and towns. Soros also received help from his prized client, Black Lives Matter, to lead the charge to defund the police and abolish prisons.

The ruling class made sure that Black Lives Matter was treated well. After the 2020 riots, corporate America went to bat for them. Ten million dollars was instantly contributed. Shelby Steele asked, "What for? Who gets that money? What is it? Well, it's white guilt money, because Amazon wants to say, 'We're not racist, and $10 million is nothing to us.'" Black Lives Matter, he says, turned out to be master of the shakedown, exploiting race as a means of power.[468]

Black Lives Matter turned out to be a huge scam. It wasn't even registered with the IRS as a charity, yet tens of millions flowed into its coffers after Floyd's death. No one knows where all the money went. But it raised more than $90 million in 2020.[469]

Cofounder Patrisse Cullors turned out to be another Marxist millionaire. She left the organization in 2021 after reports that she purchased millions of dollars of real estate. In her role as executive director of Black Lives Matter Global Network Foundation, she paid a company run by the father of her young son $969,459 for "live production, design and media"; the company sold $145 sweatshirts and solicited donations for "the movement." She also

---

[468] Klein, "Shelby Steele and Eli Steele on *What Killed Michael Brown?*"

[469] Zoe Christen Jones, "Black Lives Matter Foundation Raised $90 Million in 2020," CBS News, February 24, 2021, https://www. cbsnews.com/news/black-lives-matter-raises-90-million-2020/.

availed herself of private jet service. Shalomyah Bowers, a board member of the foundation, received more than $2 million for her consulting services.[470]

Cullors passed the baton to two women. They later released a statement saying they were not able to come to an agreement about their role, and so they quit as well. According to the executive director of CharityWatch, Laurie Styron, the organization is "a giant ghost ship full of treasure drifting in the night with no captain, no discernible crew, and no clear intention."[471]

Not only was Black Lives Matter an organization of rip-off Marxists; it also made life worse for blacks. Jason Riley said black communities were "worse off" as a result of "overemphasizing the role of police; they've changed police behavior for the worse." The cops, he said, are "less likely to get out of their cars and engage with people in the community," which allows "criminals [to] have the run of the place." Because Black Lives Matter is "over-focused" on the police, it does not take into account that "97, 98% [of Black homicides] do not involve police at all." Dr. Carol Swain, a black political scientist, went even further, saying that "an intelligent observer would be hard-pressed to identify any area in American society where BLM's activism had benefited the Black community."[472]

---

[470] Isabel Vincent and Dana Kennedy, "BLM Paid Co-Founder's Baby Daddy Nearly 5 Times More Than Trayvon Martin Foundation," *New York Post*, May 17, 2022, https://nypost.com/2022/05/17/blm-paid-co-founders-baby-daddy-far-more-than-trayvon-martin-group/.

[471] "The Black Lives Matter Scam," *Washington Examiner*, January 31, 2022, https://www.washingtonexaminer.com/restoring-america/equality-not-elitism/the-black-lives-matter-scam.

[472] Emma Colton, "BLM Has Left Black Americans Worse Off Since the Movement Began, Experts Say," Fox News, May 12, 2022,

## Police Interactions with Blacks

Everyone knows there are bad cops. There are also bad lawyers, bad teachers, bad truck drivers, and bad nurses. But there are few professions in which bad apples are more demonized than the police force. The ruling class—politicians, the media, nonprofit activist groups, lawyers, philanthropists—has been leading the charge against them.

If it is reported that a black man was unfairly killed by the police, that fact becomes so embedded in the public mind that subsequent evidence to the contrary matters little. The ruling class sees to that. For example, after Jacob Blake was shot by police in Kenosha, Wisconsin, on August 23, 2020, widespread rioting took place. Few bothered to find out why Blake had been shot. In fact, he was a convicted domestic abuser, and the woman who accused him of sexual assault called the police because he had violated a court order by showing up at her home. The police tried to arrest him, but he reached for a knife. The shooting was eventually ruled "reasonable and justified." But the public's mind had been poisoned with lies, and it was almost impossible to change it—and the damage done by riots could not be undone.

Most Republicans tend to see sporadic killings of black Americans by the police as tragic, isolated instances. Most Democrats disagree. But the data simply do not support the idea that there is a pattern.

Michael Tonry, a researcher whom no one would consider a conservative, came to a surprising conclusion in his book *Malign Neglect*: "Racial differences in patterns of offending, not racial bias by police and other officials, are the principal reason that such

---

https://www.foxnews.com/us/black-lives-matter-black-america
-worse-off-police-murders-violence.

greater proportions of blacks than whites are arrested, prosecuted, convicted, and imprisoned."[473]

Robert Sampson and Janet Lauritsen, who have sterling liberal credentials, found that "large racial differences in criminal offending," not racism, explained why more blacks were in prison proportionately than whites for longer terms.

In 2016, Harvard professor Roland G. Fryer Jr. led a team of researchers to study the issue. They examined more than a thousand police shootings in ten major police departments in three states. "On the most extreme use of force—officer-involved shootings—we find no racial differences in either the raw data or when contextual factors are taken into account." The black economist admitted, "It is the most surprising result of my career."[474]

In 2019, social scientists from Michigan State University and Arizona State University reported on the results of their two-year study: "When adjusting for crime, we find no systemic evidence of anti-Black disparities in fatal shootings, fatal shootings of unarmed citizens, or fatal shootings involving misidentification of harmless objects."[475]

Glenn Loury, a Brown University professor, says:

We need to put the police killings in perspective. There are about a thousand fatal shootings of people by police in the United States each year, according to a carefully documented database kept by the *Washington Post*. Roughly three hundred (about one-fourth) of those killed are African

[473] Bill Donohue, "The Scourge of White Liberal Racism," Catholic League for Religious and Civil Rights, July 28, 2020, https://www.catholicleague.org/the-scourge-of-white-liberal-racism/.
[474] Ibid.
[475] Ibid.

Americans, while blacks represent about 13 percent of the American population. Black people are overrepresented among these fatalities, though they still make up far less than a majority. (Twice as many whites as blacks are killed by police in this country every year. You wouldn't know that from the activists' rhetoric.)[476]

A related myth is that blacks must be fearful of straying outside for fear of being killed by the cops. "The idea that I, as a black person," Loury says, "dare not leave my house for fear that the police will round me up, gun me down, or bludgeon me to death because of my race is ridiculous." The reality is much different. "For every black person killed by the police," he says, "more than twenty-five others meet their ends because of homicides committed by other blacks."[477]

Given the cacophony of vile accusations directed at the police by the media, it is hard to get the truth out. The education establishment has no interest in doing so. If anything, the ruling class has dug its heels in. But black cops—and there are many—know better.

### Defunding the Police: Second Thoughts

Chris Palmer is a former ESPN reporter who switched to covering basketball. When protesters set a Minneapolis building on fire in 2020, he cheered them, tweeting, "Burn it all down." But a few days later, when a mob tried to storm his California community—gated, of course—he went mad. He called them "animals," screaming, "Tear up your own ****."[478]

---

[476] Loury, "The Case for Black Patriotism," 45–46.
[477] Ibid., 46.
[478] Bill Donohue, "The Bane of Self-Righteousness," Catholic League for Religious and Civil Rights, July 31, 2020, https://www.catholicleague.org/the-bane-of-self-righteousness/.

It seems even cop haters want the police to show up when their lives and property are endangered. It is no surprise that the proponents of this movement are hypocrites: Rep. Cori Bush pushed hard to defund the police—yet she spent $400,000 of taxpayer's money for her own private security.

An adolescent would know that if we defunded the police, and there were fewer cops on patrol, crime would increase. The ruling class knows it too. But that didn't stop them. Defunding the police was only one part of the war on cops: when district attorneys put those arrested for serious crimes back on the streets, the demoralization of the police force spiked.

In June 2020, after calls to defund the police were at their height, white liberals were congratulating themselves for standing up for black Americans. Virtue-signaling signs sprouted up on manicured lawns across the country. But most blacks didn't want this kind of help: 61 percent said they wanted policing to remain the same; 79 percent of those who said they had had an interaction with the police in the past year said they wanted the police to spend the same amount of time—or more time—in their neighborhood. On the other hand, self-described liberals supported defunding the police by a thirteen-point margin. They stood up for blacks by stepping on them.

When the left-wing mayor of Austin, Texas, together with the city council, slashed the police budget by a third, or $150 million, homicides increased by 44 percent from 2020 to 2021—and 200 percent compared with five years earlier. Police retirements increased by 65 percent; resignations by 63 percent. All of this was predictable. All of it was preventable. But in November 2021, a ballot initiative to hire more police officers was defeated, largely thanks to $500,000 from George Soros. Some people never learn.

But some do. Burlington, Vermont, is a very liberal city, so it was not surprising that it defunded the police in 2020. A year later, the city was paying cops to stay on the job. Atlanta planned to defund the police budget by $70 million, but it reversed course and increased funding instead. Portland, Oregon, defunded the police in 2020. A year later, three-fourths of the residents said they wanted to put the brakes on their failed experiment. The cop haters in Seattle got whipped so badly in November 2021 that the *Seattle Times* dubbed the election "Fright night for Seattle progressives."[479]

Minneapolis crushed the police budget in 2020, put drastic restrictions on the ability of the police to apprehend criminals, and increased sanctions against them for misconduct. As a result, crime spiked, especially homicides. Cops quit the force in record numbers, and scores of police officers filed disability claims for post-traumatic stress disorder. In November 2021, the voters overwhelmingly rejected a ballot initiative to dismantle the police department and replace it with social workers.

Long Island voters in Nassau and Suffolk counties jettisoned the most left-wing district-attorney candidates. San Francisco mayor London Breed, who had led the movement to defund the police in 2020, said in 2021 that "the fact is things have gotten worse over time." Her honesty was welcome. "It's time that the reign of criminals who are destroying our city—it is time for it to come to an end," she said.[480] Across the bay, Oakland officials reversed plans to cut the city's police budget.

[479] Jim Brunner and David Gutman, "Progressives on the Ropes? 5 Takeaways from Seattle's Election Night Returns," *Seattle Times*, November 3, 2021, https://www.seattletimes.com/seattle-news /politics/progressives-on-the-ropes-five-takeaways-from-seattles -election-night-returns/.

[480] "Refunding the San Francisco Police," *Wall Street Journal*, December 16, 2021, https://www.wsj.com/articles/refunding-the-san -francisco-police-london-breed-crime-11639696468?mod=opinion _lead_pos2,

One big city that bucked the "defund the police" movement was Dallas. Mayor Eric Johnson, a moderate Democrat, said he was proud to have a strong police chief and a budget to support the police force. It paid off. While cities run by progressives were exploding with violence, the crime rate in Dallas decreased.

What happened in Dallas was unique in 2020 and 2021, but not historically so. We know from New York City's experience in the 1990s that good policing and crime reduction go hand in hand. The crime rate fell by more than 40 percent in that decade, due largely to more aggressive, yet fair-minded, police practices. Bill Bratton, who was the police commissioner for a period during that time, later co-wrote an article explaining what happened and accurately reported that "the decline in homicides and other violent crimes between 1990 and 2000 constitutes one of the great achievements in the history of urban America."[481]

New York mayor Rudy Giuliani instituted policies that worked. He enforced quality-of-life laws (e.g., laws against fare beating and public urination), checked minor offenders for guns, used decoys on the subways and streets, and launched a no-nonsense approach to serious crimes. In the next decade, under Mayor Michael Bloomberg and Police Commissioner Ray Kelly, the progress continued. "Stop and frisk" tactics, allowing the police to act when they have reasonable suspicion, not only saved lives, but in 2012, the number of civilian complaints was the lowest it had been in the previous five years. All those accomplishments were quickly undone, however, by Mayor Bill de Blasio, who undermined the police while failing to deal seriously with violent crime.

---

[481] William J. Bratton and Rafael A. Mangual, "Forgotten Lessons of the War on Crime," *National Review*, October 4, 2021, 14.

## Drugs

Abortion, pornography, prostitution, narcotics, homosexuality, and gambling used to be called "victimless crimes," though, in most cases, it's pretty easy to determine who the victims are, particularly when these behaviors become widespread. Society has an interest in maintaining order. If people in a free society will not police themselves, police must do the job for them. But policing ourselves means practicing the vital virtues.

Drug use poses an existential threat to the United States. It is exacerbated by ruling class laws legalizing usage. "Drug legalization is just the latest in a series of public policies that actively undermine the values forming the basis for a healthy economy and, even more important, for a fulfilling life—what economic historian Deirdre McCloskey unflinchingly terms 'bourgeois values,'" writes Howard Husock. He adds that "more and more, government is actively undermining bourgeois values."[482]

For decades, parents, teachers, the clergy, health professionals, and public officials warned against drug use. But opposition to drugs has waned, though fortunately the U.S. bishops still adamantly speak against lowering the bar. Nevertheless, more and more cities and states have legalized marijuana, and in a few cases, they have dropped penalties related to small amounts of more dangerous drugs. But we now have the evidence that relaxing restrictions yields devastating consequences.

In the 1980s, Harlem congressman Charles Rangel supported the War on Drugs. He said that "a lot of the drug-related bleeding was staunched." He also made an insightful comment about the

[482] Howard Husock, "Government against Bourgeois Values," *City Journal*, April 8, 2021, https://www.city-journal.org/marijuana -legalization-new-york.

reason the white ruling class wants to legalize drugs. Speaking about "white America," Rangel said, it seems that many are saying, "let's legalize drugs because we can't deal with the problem."[483] He was not naïve in understanding who pays the biggest price for this policy.

Let's face it. There is big money involved. An entire industry is waiting to cash in on drug legalization, and it has no plans on stopping after marijuana is legalized. The ruling class will see to it that it continues. The American dream will become an American nightmare for countless citizens.

It was reported in 2022 that drug overdoses now kill more than a hundred thousand Americans annually — more than those who die in car accidents or from gunshots combined. It is also almost twice the number of Americans who died in the Vietnam War between 1954 and 1975.

Doctors have been warning us for decades about the harm that smoking cigarettes does to our bodies, especially our lungs. They have also been telling us about the serious respiratory problems cause by Covid. Why, then, is the campaign to legalize a substance that causes more respiratory problems being pursued at this time?

Kenneth L. Davis is the president and chief executive of the Mount Sinai Health System, and Mary Jeanne Kreek is the head of the Laboratory of the Biology of Addictive Diseases at Rockefeller University. Their review of the medical literature led them to conclude that marijuana is not the harmless substance that many believe. Marijuana, they found, has a

> deleterious impact on cognitive development in adolescents, impairing executive function, processing speed,

---

[483] Bill Donohue, "Legalizing Marijuana Is a Death Sentence," Catholic League for Religious and Civil Rights, April 19, 2022, https://www.catholicleague.org/legalizing-marijuana-is-a-death-sentence/.

memory, attention span and concentration. The damage is measurable with an I.Q. test. Researchers who tracked subjects from childhood through age 38 found a consequential I.Q. decline over the 25-year period among adolescents who consistently used marijuana every week. In addition, studies have shown that substantial adolescent exposure to marijuana may be a predictor of opioid use disorders.[484]

They add that the brain is still developing in young people to age twenty-five. Moreover, according to one prominent physician, "One joint today is like 17 joints in the 1970s."[485]

If legalizing marijuana were inconsequential, we would know it from studying what has happened in Colorado. Between 2012, when marijuana was legalized, and 2019, marijuana-related traffic deaths increased by 151 percent, while overall state deaths increased by only 35 percent. Emergency room visits for users increased 52 percent, while marijuana-related hospitalizations increased by 148 percent.

Marijuana did not become available for recreational sales until two years after it was legalized. The *New York Times* did a review of what happened over the next five years. "Nearly twice as many Coloradans smoke pot as the rest of America."[486] The consequences have been horrific.

The *Times* reporter spoke to Andrew Monte, an emergency and medical technology physician and researcher at the University of Colorado. Some of the heavy users he treated suffered from "severe vomiting." Patients in the emergency room with marijuana-related

[484] Ibid.
[485] Ibid.
[486] Ibid.

cases were "five times as likely to have a mental-health issue as those with other cases."[487]

That's not all. Violent crime since legalization increased in Colorado by 19 percent; it increased by only 3.7 percent nationwide. Property crime increased by 8 percent compared with a national *decrease* of 13.6 percent. No wonder one study concluded that "for every dollar gained in tax revenue, Coloradans spent approximately $4.50 to mitigate the effects of legalization."[488]

Coloradans like their drugs so much that they embarked on a campaign to legalize other drugs. In 2019, lawmakers made the possession of small amounts of heroin and cocaine a misdemeanor, not a felony. The Democrat-controlled legislature even decriminalized fentanyl, one of the most dangerous drugs of all. Colorado prosecutors pleaded with lawmakers to exempt fentanyl—four grams is the equivalent of thirteen thousand deadly doses—but they refused. What happened? Opioid overdose deaths increased by 54 percent in 2020.

In 2018, King County, Washington, which encompasses Seattle, and neighboring Snohomish County, stopped charging people for small amounts of hard drugs. Meth overdoses skyrocketed, going from 18 deaths in 2008 to 197 in 2019. Heroin overdose deaths jumped from 45 to 147 during the same period. Fentanyl-related deaths climbed from 9 to 106. Seattle radio-show host Jason Rantz says decriminalization made "the problems worse." In fact, he brands it "an unmitigated disaster."[489] Calls to reverse course have been mounting.

No one can stop the demand for drugs. Human nature can be very self-destructive. But making it easier to access drugs is the worst

[487] Ibid.
[488] Ibid.
[489] Ibid.

of the bad alternatives. If further proof is needed, consider that approximately one in five adults in Portland, Oregon, is addicted to drugs. That's what happens when heroin, meth, and fentanyl are treated like chewing gum.

Crime and drug abuse have increased in the third decade of the twenty-first century largely because policies and laws promulgated by the ruling class have undermined self-discipline, personal responsibility, and perseverance. In some cases, these decisions have been the result of ignorance and stupidity. But mostly, they are the result of design. And either way, they are causing the American dream to go up in smoke for millions of Americans.

# Conclusion

It is a tribute to the patriotism of most Americans that they still believe in the goodness of the nation. It is a tribute to their commitment to the vital virtue of perseverance that they refuse to give up on the prospect of realizing the American dream. This is especially true of minorities who refuse to give up, despite the obstacles deliberately erected by the ruling class.

"The fundamental problem the Ruling Class faces, going forward," writes Ben Weingarten, a fellow at the Claremont Institute, "is that while it scapegoats, smears and suppresses the non-progressive patriots who refuse to submit to its reign, it can't distract the public from the fact its agenda is killing the economy."[490]

The exercise of the vital virtues — self-discipline, personal responsibility, and perseverance — has brought Asians, Jews, Mormons, Nigerians, and many others spectacular success. But their achievements were possible in the context of a healthy, market-based economy. The ruling class, however, now seems determined

---

[490] Ben Weingarten, "2021: The Year of the Ruling Class' Crackdown on Dissent, Opinion," *Newsweek*, January 3, 2022, https://www.newsweek.com/2021-year-ruling-class-crackdown-dissent-opinion-1664757.

to sabotage the very economic system that has allowed so many—including, in many cases, themselves—to climb to the top.

"Behold the Hewlett Foundation and Omidyar Network's $40 million gift to the paupers at Harvard and MIT to 'reimagine capitalism,'" wrote the editorial board of the *Wall Street Journal*. Hewlett and Omidyar grants are going to other elite institutions as well, all designed to "indoctrinate young people in socialism."[491] Perversely, the wealth being distributed was created by the very capitalist markets that the ruling class now undermines.

The tech giants—Facebook, Apple, Amazon, Netflix, and Google—are similarly pushing the left-wing agenda. Silicon Valley is very good at promoting "environmental, social, and governance" (ESG) investing, as well as diversity, equity, and inclusion (DEI) in hiring. But none of these ruling-class entities can be persuaded to advocate for social policies that nurture intact families, facilitate school choice, or provide for a more civil society. Those things are ignored, or disparaged, by corporate elites.

One of the reasons the members of the ruling class do not get exercised about these matters is that they have never experienced them as problems in their own lives. As we have seen, they normally come from intact families, have attended the finest schools, and live in safe neighborhoods. Moreover, they seriously misunderstand and underestimate the enormous power of what they take for granted—namely, the much-maligned bourgeois virtues.

The late Gertrude Himmelfarb warned us about denigrating virtue. The social pathologies that mar American society—from

---

[491] "Hijacking Philanthropy to 'Reimagine Capitalism,'" *Wall Street Journal*, February 23, 2022, https://www.wsj.com/articles/reimagining-capitalism-hewlett-foundation-bill-hewlett-11645566987.

out-of-wedlock births to crime—are a function of the absence of virtue. "Today, confronted with an increasingly de-moralized society," she wrote, "we may be ready for a new reformation, which will restore not so much Victorian values as a more abiding sense of moral and civic virtues."[492]

She was not pessimistic or Pollyannaish about the future, anticipating that a "religious-*cum*-moral revival will become increasingly moral rather than religious."[493] Similarly, Francis Fukuyama sees a "re-norming" of society underway, one in which the role of religion will be prominent. "We have not become so modern and secularized that we can do without religion."[494] Let us hope—and pray.

If there is one institution that has been the seedbed of the vital virtues, it is the family. Asians, Jews, Mormons, and Nigerians ascended to the top of the socioeconomic scale precisely because they come from strong, two-parent families where they were reared on the vital virtues. They are a role model for everyone.

Yet, as we have seen, elites in the corporate world and education have bombarded the nuclear family with malevolence. This is a grand act of social suicide. No one pays a bigger price for this delinquency than black and brown Americans. If progress is going to be made, the restoration of normal, two-parent families must be the number-one priority. We must also stop pretending that other variants of family are all equal. They are not.

In a survey released in 2022, 88 percent of American voters said it was important for children to be raised in a household with both their father and their mother. The ruling class knows this

---

[492] Himmelfarb, *The Demoralization of Society*, 257.
[493] Himmelfarb, *One Nation*, 143.
[494] Fukuyama, *The Great Disruption*, 279.

too. The question is: What will it take to get them to help others to live as they do?

We are not going to succeed as long as the ruling class remains fixated on other issues. In a lecture he gave at the University of Notre Dame, Supreme Court justice Clarence Thomas spoke about our "race-obsessed world." Instead of bringing people together, he said, "We just seem like we keep dividing."[495] Not only does this subvert the good society, it does nothing to help blacks seeking to advance.

Another prominent black American, John McWhorter, doubles down on what Thomas said. He says that "if the mantra is that what we need to do to solve black America's problems is 'get rid of systemic racism,' we're in trouble." He notes that such an analysis "is based on a third-grader's understanding of how a society works. More importantly, that analysis does not help black people and often hurts us."[496]

Walter Williams was a brilliant black economist who shared the same antipathy for race-obsessed solutions expressed by Thomas and McWhorter. He looked to Malcolm X, of all people, for a more mature analysis of what to do. "Malcolm X was absolutely right about our finding solutions to our own problems. The most devastating problems black people face today have absolutely nothing to do with our history of slavery and discrimination. Chief among

[495] Carley Lanich, "Justice Clarence Thomas Laments a 'Race-Obsessed World,' in Lecture at Notre Dame," Yahoo! News, September 17, 2021, www.yahoo.com/news/justice-clarence-thomas-laments-race -121156376.html.

[496] John McWhorter, "Can We Please Ditch the Term 'Systemic Racism'?," It Bears Mentioning, May 10, 2021, https://john mcwhorter.substack.com/p/can-we-please-ditch-the-term -systemic.

them is the breakdown of the black family, wherein 75 percent of blacks are born to single, often young, mothers."[497]

To punctuate Williams's observation, consider that when racism and discrimination were a ubiquitous feature in American history, the kinds of social problems we see today were largely absent. When Thomas was asked about the effect of social programs on blacks, he did not mince words: "It's a disaster. When I grew up, you had family, you didn't have drugs, you didn't have gang-banging. You could walk the street." He grew up in Savannah, Georgia, where segregation was a problem. Now, he says, "You don't have the segregation, but you've got pathologies that we didn't have before." He also said something that implicitly condemned the ruling class: "You didn't have to do that to poor people, and it's just heartbreaking."[498]

Yes, it is our well-educated and (sometimes) well-intending white elites who have delivered the most punishing blows to the poor. The welfare system they created generated dependency and completely eviscerated the vital virtues. There is a direct line between the racist and paternalistic thinking of George Fitzhugh—that blacks can't make it by themselves and must be protected by white people—and the ruling class that has for so long had low expectations for blacks. The elites have been very good at lowering the bar for blacks in school and in the workplace; they have been

---

[497] Walter Williams, "The Worst Enemy of Black People," CNSNews, January 2, 2019, https://www.cnsnews.com/commentary/walter -e-williams/walter-williams-worst-enemy-black-people.

[498] Clarence Thomas, "How Liberal Policies Have Killed Black Communities," *New York Post*, June 22, 2022, https://nypost.com/2022 /06/22/how-liberal-policies-have-killed-black-communities -clarence-thomas/.

very poor at helping them clear it. To do so would require them to respect the vital virtues.

If the ruling class were to come to its senses, it would pick up on an idea promoted by the distinguished black scholar Kenneth B. Clark. In the 1960s, Clark, who was a psychologist, called for the establishment of Cadet Corps programs in the inner city, endorsing an idea pioneered by a Harlem youth association. It was "an attempt to tap the magnetic appeal that uniforms, military organizations, martial music, and rhythms seem to have for the vast majority of Americans." He believed that "the most neglected, rejected, and 'all but abandoned' children are probably even more susceptible to this appeal than others would be because they have very little in life on which to base a sense of personal worth and a feeling of pride."[499]

Clark envisioned a program that would intrinsically promote the vital virtues. "A Cadet Corps program could be organized and operated to use the natural appeal of uniforms, rank, insignia, and other concrete symbols of status to involve young people in more serious programs such as developing reading skills, a sense of reliability, and a sense of responsibility for the welfare and performance of others."[500]

Nearly sixty years later, political scientist Scott Yenor recommends something similar. "We should consider mandatory training in military schools for boys from broken homes so that they have a better chance of becoming marriageable men."[501] Though

[499] Kenneth B. Clark, *Dark Ghetto: Dilemmas of Social Power* (New York: Harper and Row, 1965), 102.

[500] Ibid.

[501] Scott Yenor, "Sexual Counter-Revolution," *First Things*, November 2021, 33.

this proposal would strike many as too controversial, what he says makes good sense.

But if we really are going to change the thinking of the ruling class, we need to do a better job of educating the sons and daughters of elites in American society. We are raising a generation of young people who have no idea what it is like to give back or to develop a sense of responsibility to others. The sons and daughters of the middle and bottom rungs of society routinely serve in the armed forces. Perhaps we should consider a two-year program of national service so that every young person serves either in the military or in some other institutionalized setting. Other countries have programs like this. If the children of the ruling class developed a greater appreciation for the duties of citizenship, everyone in the country would benefit.

If "re-norming" society is to take hold, we will also need a more vibrant religious coalition. The fight over Proposition 8 in California united traditional Catholics, Protestants (especially Evangelicals), Orthodox Christians, Orthodox Jews, and many Mormons and Muslims in a common goal. The overturning of *Roe v. Wade* was made possible because many religious leaders kept the faith and educated the faithful about the rights of the unborn. We need more such efforts.

The time is ripe for the Catholic Church to lead the way. We must not be deterred from doing so because a tiny percentage of the clergy engaged in homosexual abuse back in the 1960s, 1970s, and 1980s.[502] Every priest who failed us did so because he *violated* the teachings of the Catholic Church. Those teachings do

---

[502] For more on this subject, see my book *The Truth about Clergy Sexual Abuse: Clarifying the Facts and the Causes* (San Francisco: Ignatius Press, 2021).

not need to be reformed—those who violated them need to be reformed—and punished. This needs to be said because many of today's social problems are the result of the compliance of too many Americans with the professed views of the ruling class. Americans should instead ignore those views and should defend the truth.

Though religious leaders should help lead the efforts for renewal, we should not depend exclusively on them. In recent years, more and more Americans have gotten involved in the affairs of their communities. From school boards to ballot-box initiates, the passive have been mobilized. For the first time in many years, the ruling class is experiencing pushback.

More than anything else, the "re-norming" of society will require that we ensure that every American can realize the American dream. That will mean a concentrated campaign to instill the vital virtues in every young person. The ruling class does not have to have the last say any longer.

# Acknowledgments

Writing this book has been fun, but it has also been exasperating. Many of the social problems that we have in America are wholly unnecessary—they are the result of totally misguided policies devised and promoted by the ruling class. Their pompous and paternalistic attitude toward the least among us is at the root of the problem.

I am grateful to Charlie McKinney, president of Sophia Institute Press, for moving expeditiously and for securing talented editors. Andrew Oliver's suggestions were spot-on, and I also appreciate the keen eye of Nora Malone.

At the Catholic League, I benefited from the advice of Bernadette Brady-Egan, the vice president, Michael McDonald, director of communications, and policy analysts Donald Lauer and Nicholas Palczewski. I also want to thank the board of directors, led by chairman Walter Knysz, for their support.

My family—Valerie, Caryn, Paul, Caitlin, and Jay—are a steady source of happiness, and this is especially true of Grant and Nina, my grandchildren. In this regard, I must also mention Maggie and Mike Mansfield, Linda and Tom Boyle, the McGetricks, and my always thirsty friends at Doc's.

# Index

# Index

# About the Author

Bill Donohue is president and CEO of the Catholic League for Religious and Civil Rights and publisher of the league's journal, *Catalyst*. He holds a PhD in sociology from New York University and is the author of several books on civil liberties, social issues, and religion.

# CRISIS Publications

Sophia Institute Press awards the privileged title "CRISIS Publications" to a select few of our books that address contemporary issues at the intersection of politics, culture, and the Church with clarity, cogency, and force and that are also destined to become all-time classics.

CRISIS Publications are *direct*, explaining their principles briefly, simply, and clearly to Catholics in the pews, on whom the future of the Church depends. The time for ambiguity or confusion is long past.

CRISIS Publications are *contemporary*, born of our own time and circumstances and intended to become significant statements in current debates, statements that serious Catholics cannot ignore, regardless of their prior views.

CRISIS Publications are *classical*, addressing themes and enunciating principles that are valid for all ages and cultures. Readers will turn to them time and again for guidance in other days and different circumstances.

CRISIS Publications are *spirited*, entering contemporary debates with gusto to clarify issues and demonstrate how those issues can be resolved in a way that enlivens souls and the Church.

We welcome engagement with our readers on current and future CRISIS Publications. Please pray that this imprint may help to resolve the crises embroiling our Church and society today.

Sophia Institute Press® is a registered trademark of Sophia Institute. Sophia Institute is a tax-exempt institution as defined by the Internal Revenue Code, Section 501(c)(3). Tax I.D. 22-2548708.